WELCOME TO *CHARACTER DESIGN QUARTERLY 29*

Artists we feature in *CDQ* often work across many different disciplines, from storyboarding and concept art, to animation, and book illustration. Ben Eblen, the artist behind this issue's stunning cover design, may be the first to show us how he has taken his character-design skills into the world of sculpting! As well as discussing the business side of creating content online, Ben speaks to us about his new-found love of sculpting, and how he brought his passion into the cover design.

Elsewhere in this issue Erica Hodne tackles our Classic Character feature, taking an exhaustive look at the character of Robin Hood and creating a fantastic new take on the legendary outlaw. Iz Ptica transforms the three-word prompt 'nature, party, tiny' into an enchanting moonlit scene, with a character inspired by the beautiful patterns of moth's wings. We also chat to two artists returning to *CDQ*, John Loren and Kate Pellerin, about their varied careers and the influences behind their unique artstyles.

There are plenty more tutorials to discover and our usual gallery of fantastic art, so turn the page and start being inspired!

SAM DRAPER
EDITOR

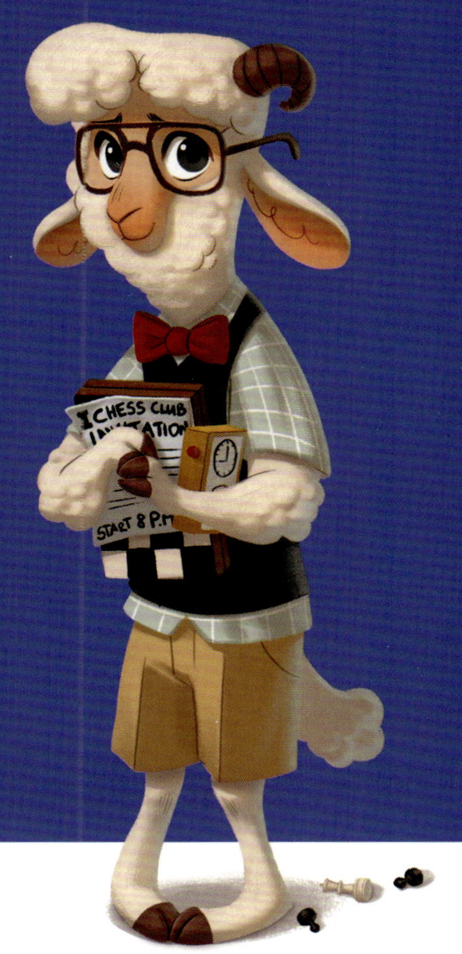

Image © Sarah-Lisa Hleb

66 76 84 88

ARTIST
CATCH-UP

Kate Pellerin (aka Poopikat) returns to *CDQ* to discuss her art style and managing her time

THE
GALLERY

Featuring a selection of art by Kenny Leoncito, Dan Sprogis, and Haiyang Sun

YOU ARE WHAT
YOU WEAR

Laura Dimitriu shows us how costumes are an intergral part of character design

ROBIN HOOD
REBORN

Another classic character is reimagined in this in-depth tutorial by Erica Hodne

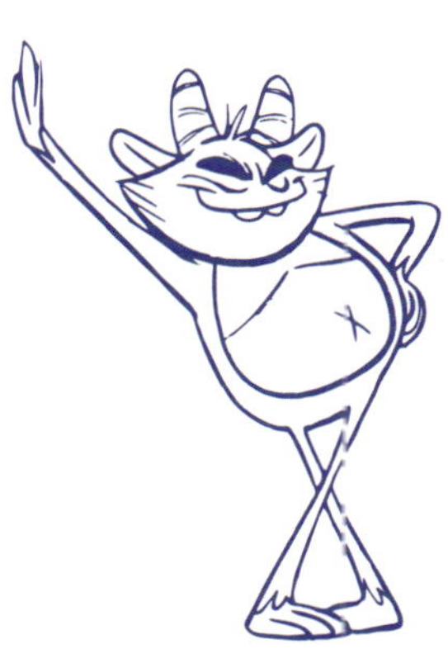
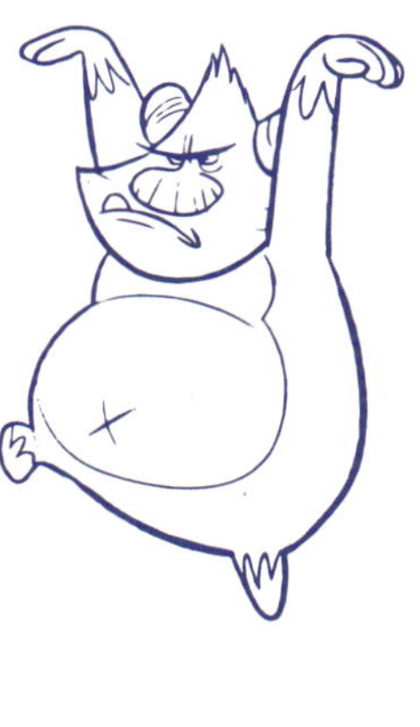

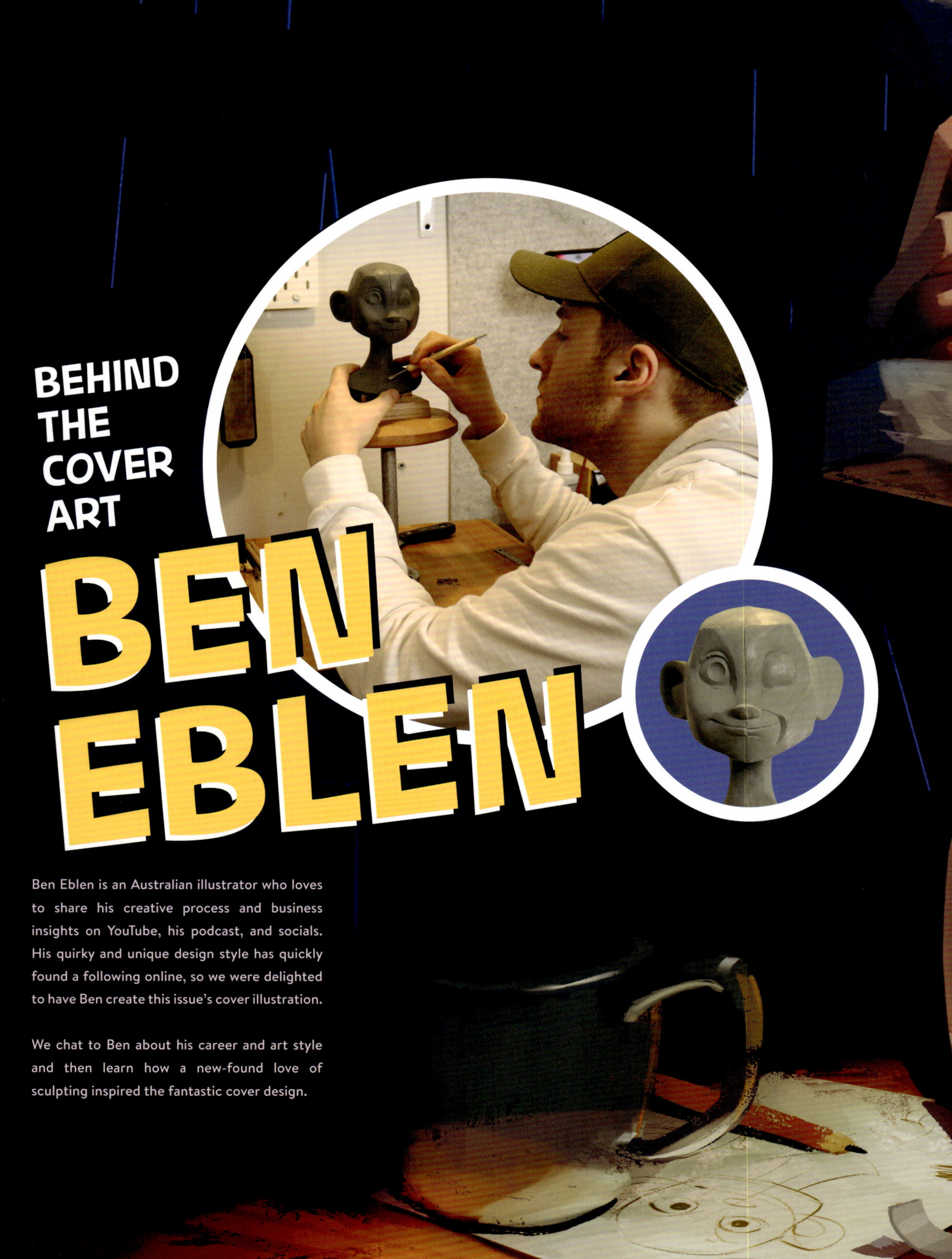

BEN EBLEN

Ben Eblen is an Australian illustrator who loves to share his creative process and business insights on YouTube, his podcast, and socials. His quirky and unique design style has quickly found a following online, so we were delighted to have Ben create this issue's cover illustration.

We chat to Ben about his career and art style and then learn how a new-found love of sculpting inspired the fantastic cover design.

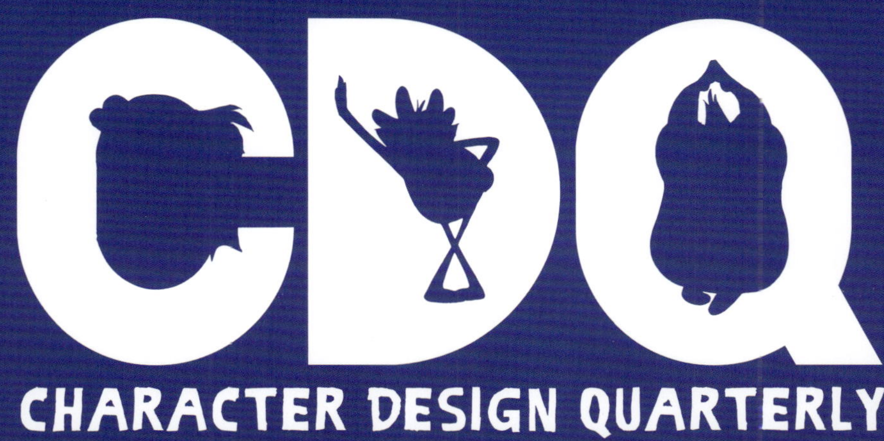

CDQ
CHARACTER DESIGN QUARTERLY

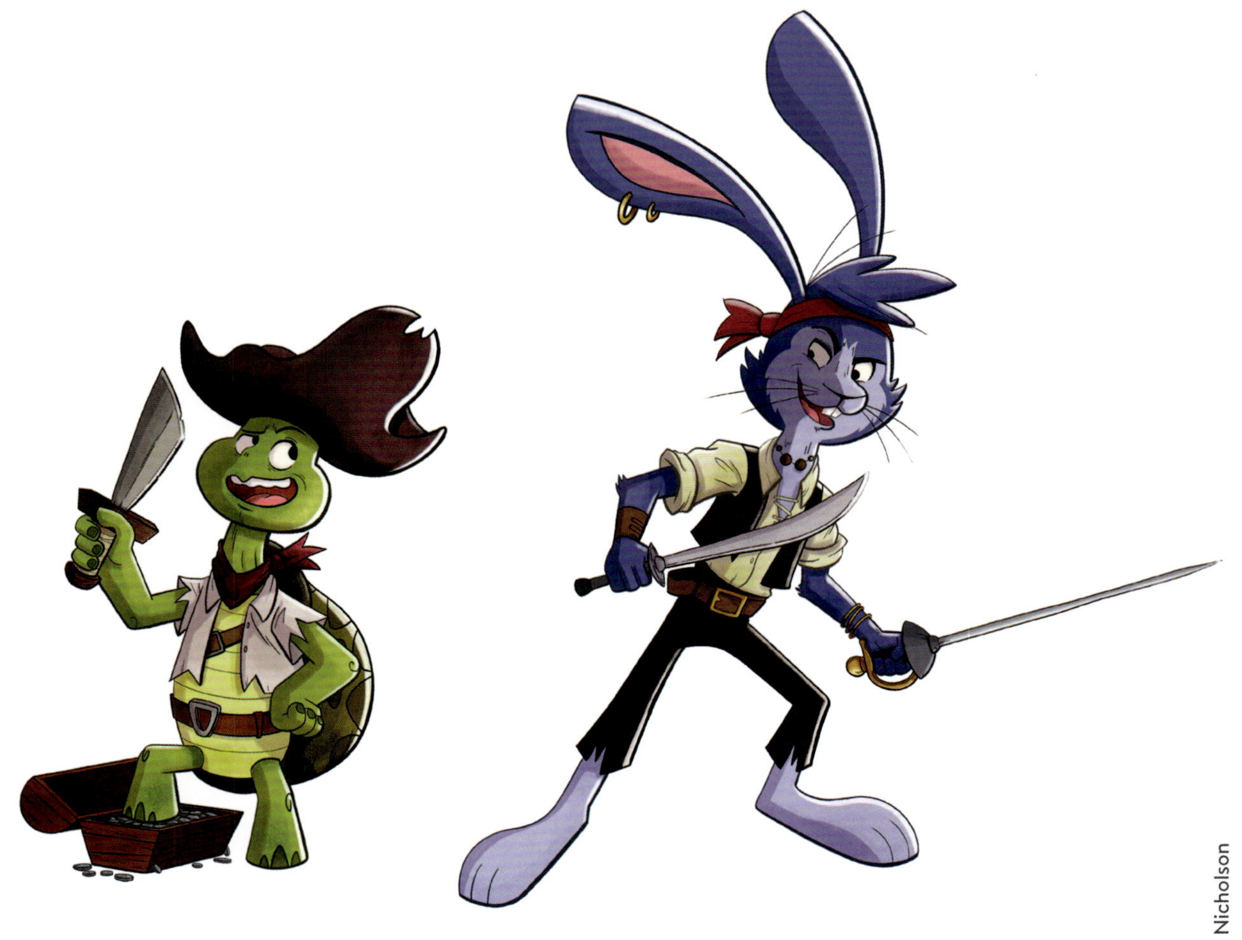

CONTENTS

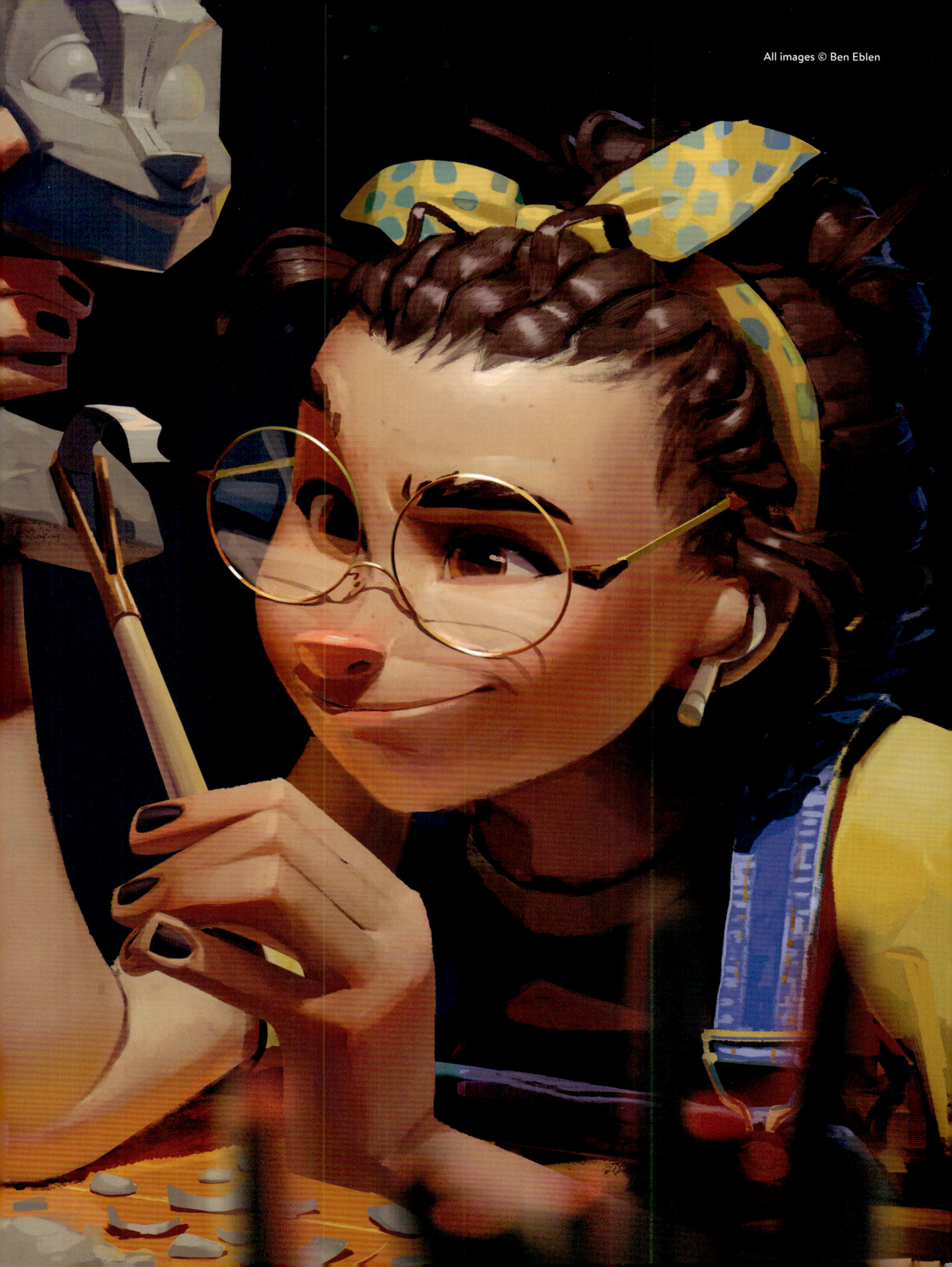
All images © Ben Eblen

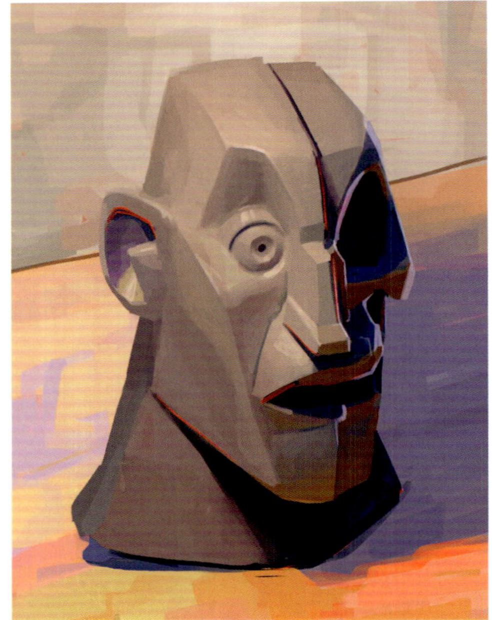

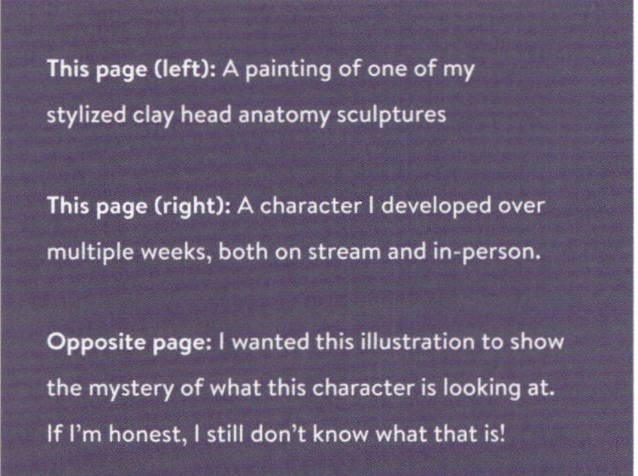

This page (left): A painting of one of my stylized clay head anatomy sculptures

This page (right): A character I developed over multiple weeks, both on stream and in-person.

Opposite page: I wanted this illustration to show the mystery of what this character is looking at. If I'm honest, I still don't know what that is!

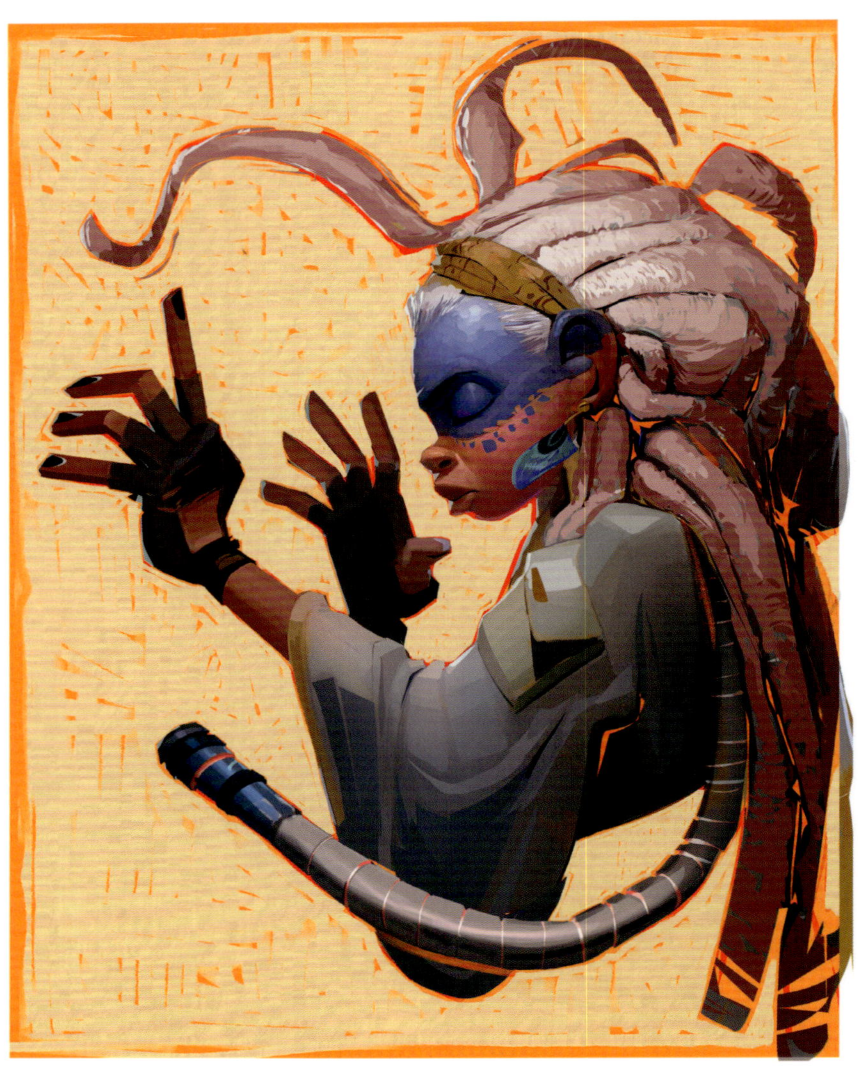

'WHEN I CREATE A CHARACTER, I TRY TO MAKE THEM BELIEVABLE AND RELATABLE'

Hi Ben, welcome back to *CDQ*! Can you tell our readers a little about yourself?

Thanks so much for having me back! I'm an Australian illustrator, developer, podcast host, and chaser of 'aha' moments, and I love sharing my process and findings online. I've been drawing and painting on and off for most of my life, but in 2021 I began sharing my art, process, and thoughts online, and began to amass a bit of a following. This has opened up many different career opportunities for me. I also have a new-found passion for sharing my process – not only my art, but my journey navigating both the creative and business side of content creation.

What do you consider the key features of good character design?

Because I've had no real formal training, I don't have a textbook answer for this! When I create a character, I try to make them believable and relatable. I also look to add something unique that makes them stand out, whether that be a situation that they find themselves in or something about their personality.

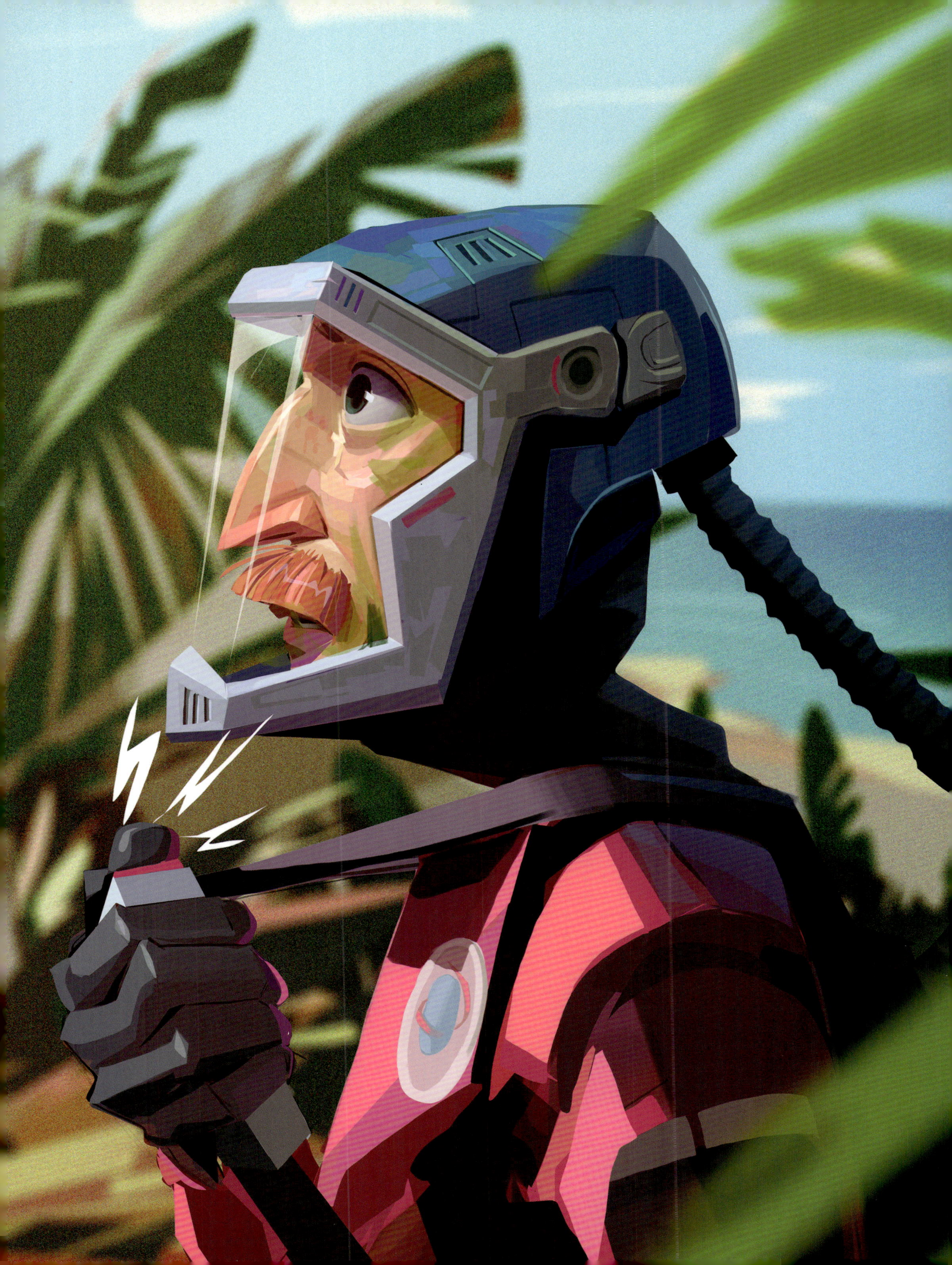

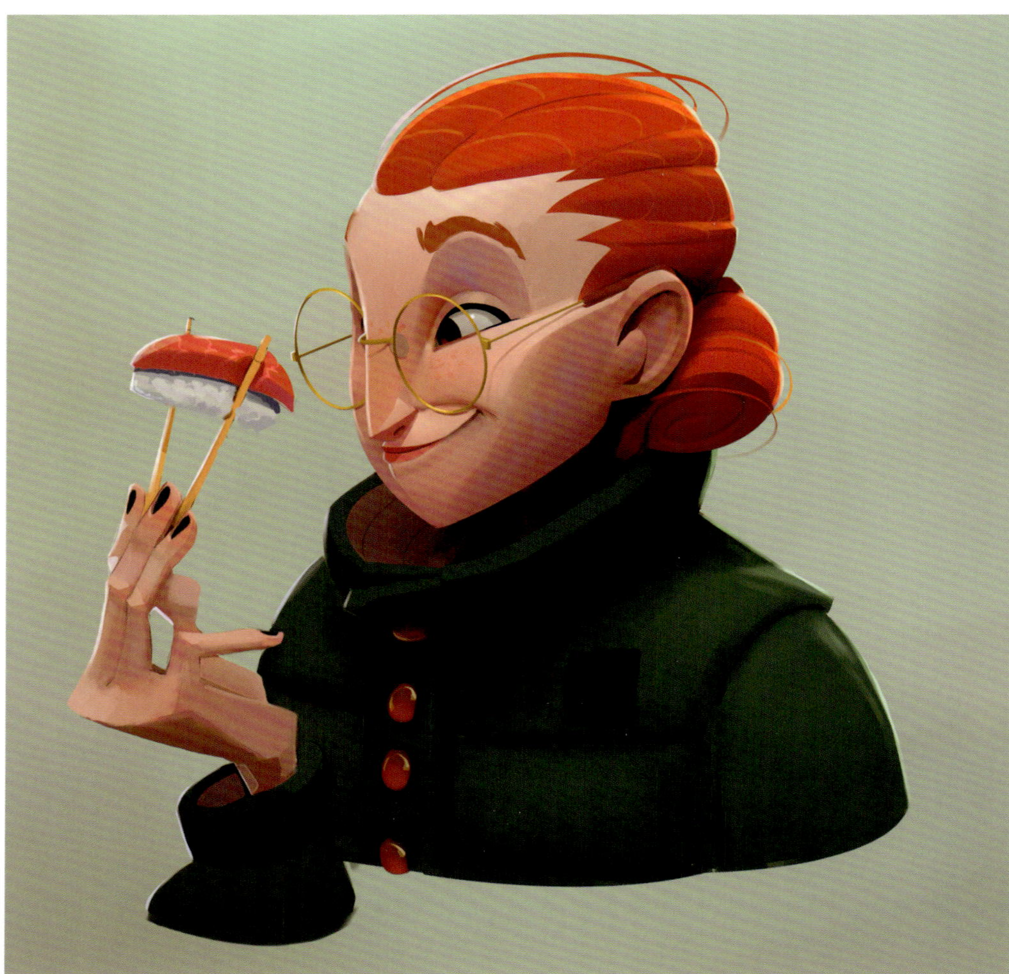

How have your character-design skills transferred across to sculpting? Have you had to relearn how you think about modelling at all?

I've only recently begun to get into traditional sculpting and I was really surprised at how many principles of 2D drawing translate over into the 3D space. I've had experience in the past with digital sculpting and those skills carry over into the real world a lot as well. One of the most useful tips that has helped me a lot when experimenting with traditional sculpting is the idea of working from larger to smaller shapes. Just like there's a tendency for me to get stuck into the details too early in an illustration, the same thing is true for sculpting. If I fall into that trap, it almost always ends up with me having to scrap it to start again.

Who are the biggest influences on your art style?

There's too many to count and the list is always changing! Currently, the biggest influences on my line work are Jin Kim, Shiyoon Kim, TB Choi, and Glen Keane. And when it comes to rendering, Sam Neilson, Max

Grecke, Loish, and Dice Tsutsumi are really inspiring me at the moment. All of these artists have phenomenal shape language and character designs as well.

Have you got any upcoming projects we should know about?

I've recently started posting to YouTube, which has been a blast, and I'll be investing a lot more time into these videos moving forward. I've got a course in the works and I'll also be starting up another side of the business where I'll be selling my sculptures and prints, starting with 'Plane Jane' as shown in my cover illustration. I'm super excited to get started as I've only really dealt with digital products up to this point – moving into the physical product space will be a challenge that I'm really looking forward to tackling.

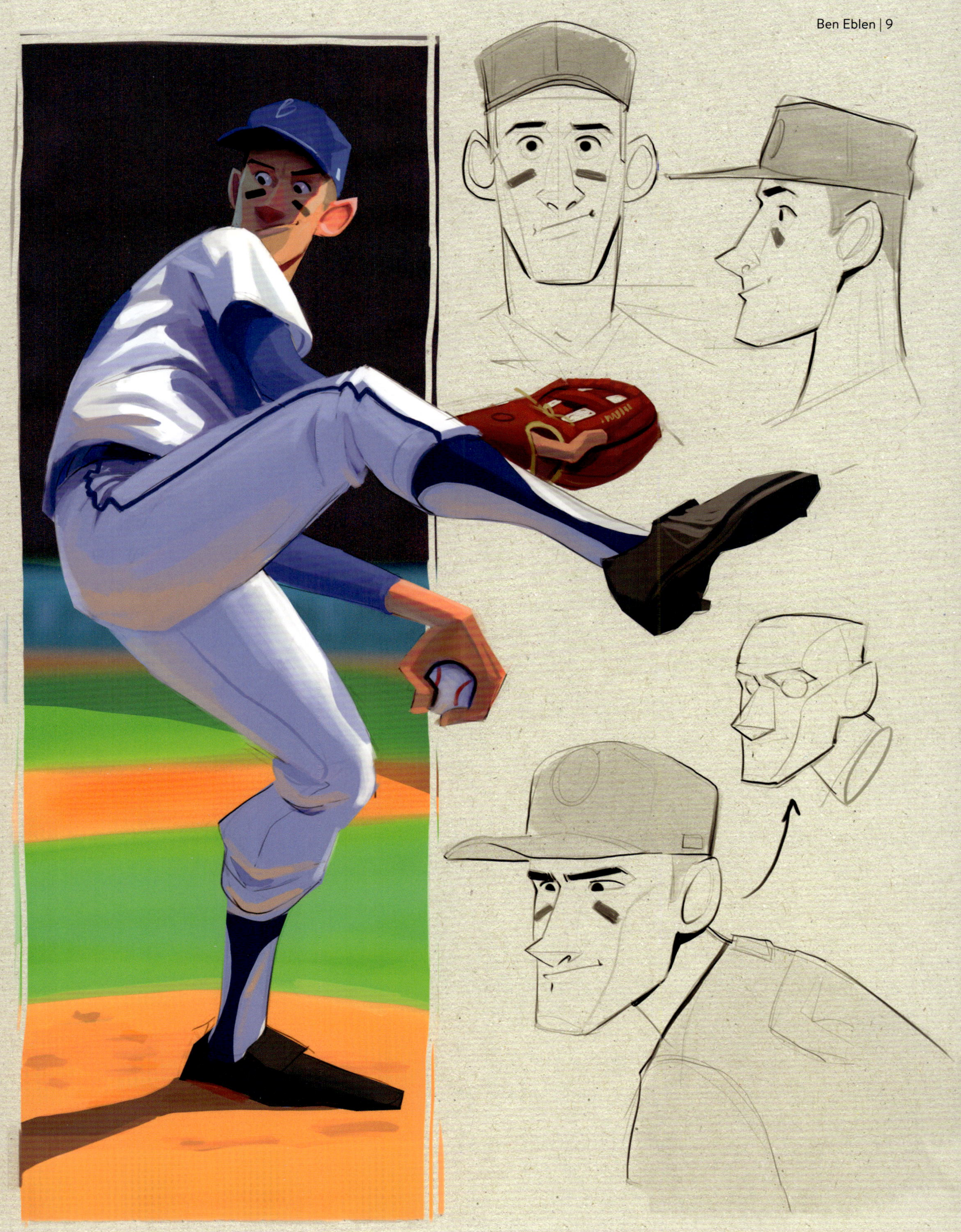

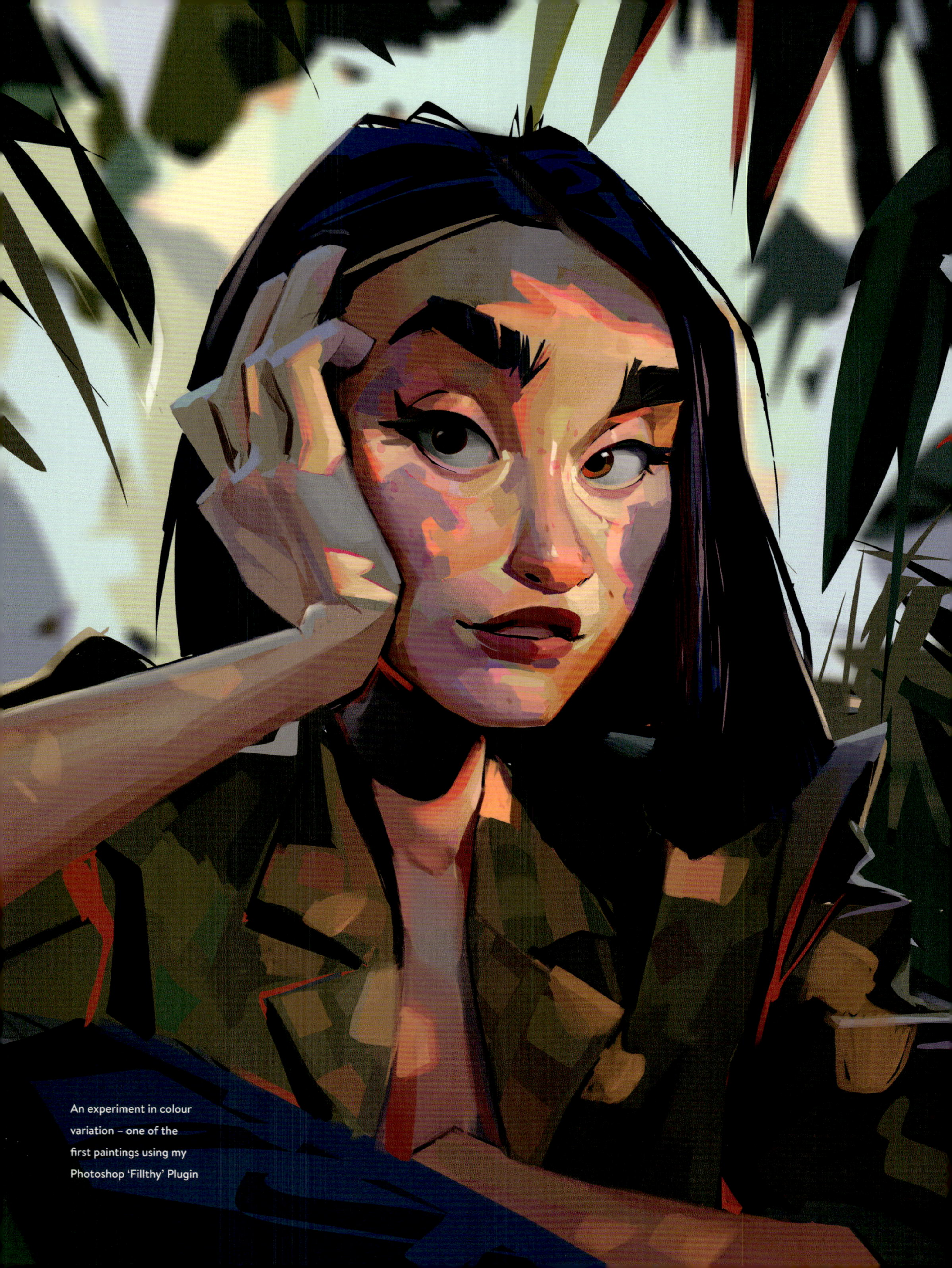

An experiment in colour variation – one of the first paintings using my Photoshop 'Fillthy' Plugin

BEN SHARES SOME OF HIS TOP TIPS ON THE BUSINESS SIDE OF CONTENT CREATION AND HOW TO TURN YOUR HOBBY INTO A CAREER

- Ask yourself why you want to grow your audience – understanding this will help give you clarity on what type of content you should post

---

- When one post doesn't perform as well as your others, it can feel like a kick in the guts. Don't panic and don't let a bad post influence your content – the numbers can be fickle

---

- Rather than worrying about the 'algorithm', try to think about people instead! I find it easier to adjust what I'm doing when I consider why a post isn't connecting with people, instead of thinking 'Oh, the algorithm hates me'

- Study other content that resonates with you. Ask yourself: why did I stop and take notice? Why do I like this person? Just as you study other artists, you should be studying other content creators, as well

---

- I strongly believe that content creation is a skill that can be learned. Yes, luck comes into it, too, but less than you might think

- Share the process of what you're working on. It doesn't have to be a tutorial, but at least for me, I often find behind-the-scenes content more interesting than seeing the final piece

---

- Likes are nice, but do they actually help to expand your business? Saves and comments can be better indicators of a successful, valuable post

---

- Promoting yourself and your product can feel weird when you first start out, but it's absolutely essential. I like to create value in my videos up front before I put a CTA (call to action) or promotion so I feel like I've 'earned' it

---

- Make sure you enjoy what you're doing. By developing a love for creating content (videos, tutorials, and so on) just as much as drawing, I've found it much easier to keep producing consistently high-quality output

---

- When it comes time to try and sell a product, the number one thing to remember is to listen to your audience!

SCULPTING THE COVER

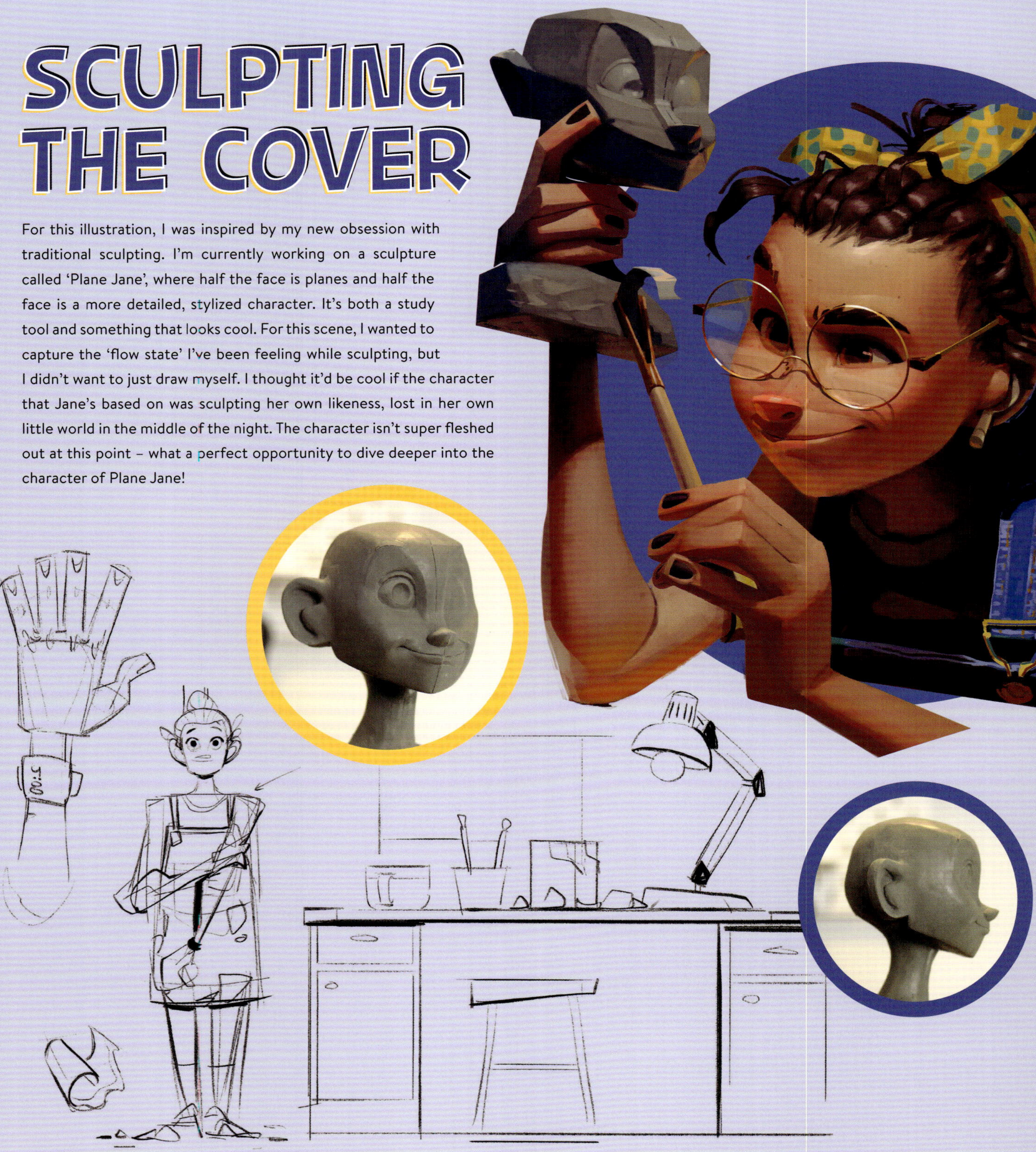

For this illustration, I was inspired by my new obsession with traditional sculpting. I'm currently working on a sculpture called 'Plane Jane', where half the face is planes and half the face is a more detailed, stylized character. It's both a study tool and something that looks cool. For this scene, I wanted to capture the 'flow state' I've been feeling while sculpting, but I didn't want to just draw myself. I thought it'd be cool if the character that Jane's based on was sculpting her own likeness, lost in her own little world in the middle of the night. The character isn't super fleshed out at this point – what a perfect opportunity to dive deeper into the character of Plane Jane!

THE INITIAL IDEA

I start with a basic idea of what I want the scene to be, but I'm still going to need to work out who the character is and what their environment is going to be like. I haven't finished the Plane Jane sculpt completely, so this character exploration may inform the final sculpt as well.

I start by loosely sketching out what I think Jane would look like. I know I want her to be friendly, artsy, and a little bit dishevelled. Drawing some sketches of the environment and her workstation will give me a bunch of good ideas to move forward with.

IN THE ZONE

As I start to understand more about Jane's kind, considerate, artsy personality, I find myself drawn to 'friendly' shapes. In its simplest form, her head is a rounded, upside-down pentagon from the front, with big, round ears. I want her eyes to be large and kind, again using simple rounded shapes.

When it comes to the pose, I want to show how focused she is, slowly scraping away the clay with her sculpting tool. For those of you that have sculpted before, you'll know how satisfying and somewhat meditative the process can be.

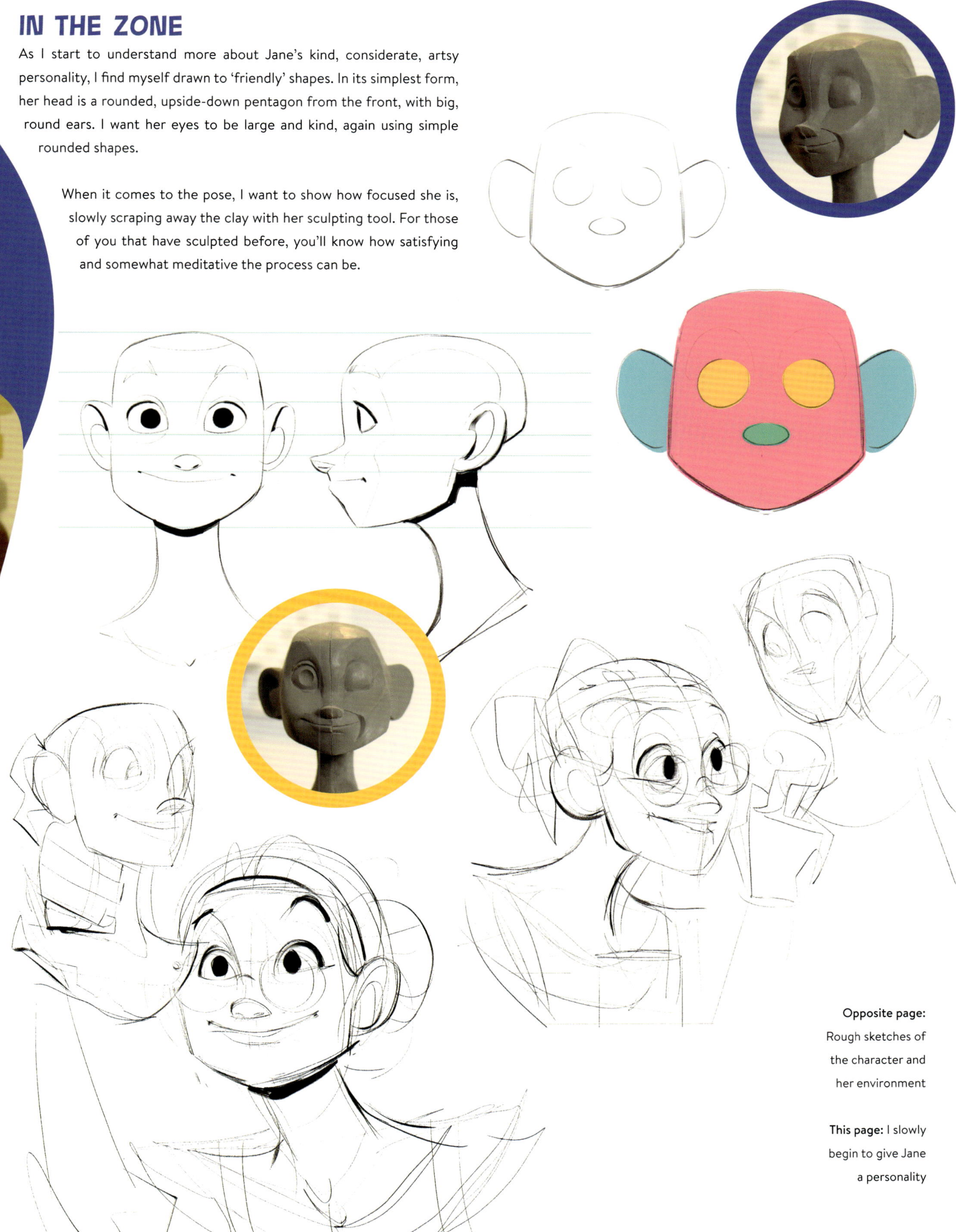

COMPOSITION AND LIGHTING

I know that I'm making this piece for the magazine's cover, so I need to ensure there's balance in the image, taking into account the *CDQ* logo that will be in the top right. I want it to be clear that my character is burning the midnight oil and 'in the zone'. If I use the desk lamp to illuminate just her and the sculpt, that will reduce all the other detail into the background, putting the focus on Jane and what she's doing. I can also play with the warmth of the desk lamp and the cools of the rest of the dark room for some nice contrast as well. Testing this value structure in black and white will help me to double check the image for clarity.

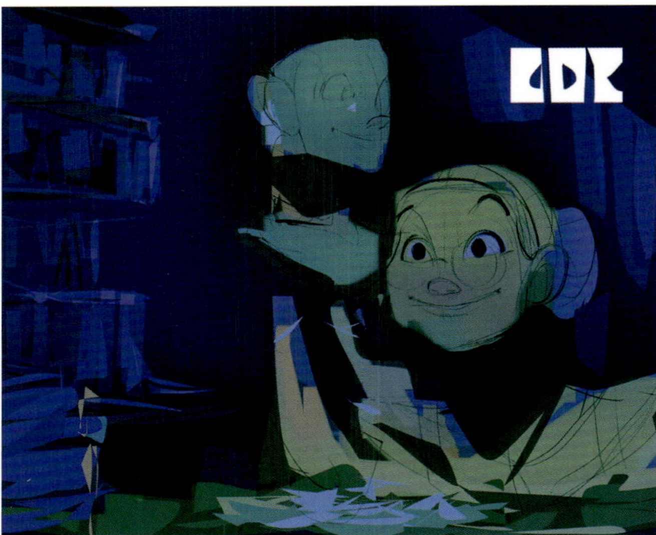
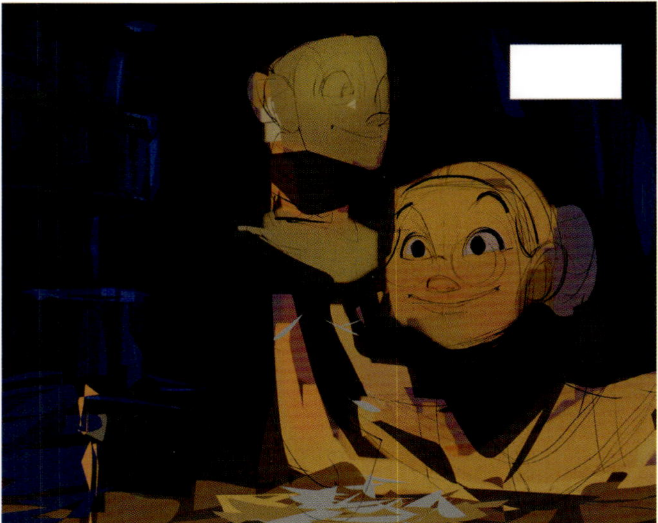
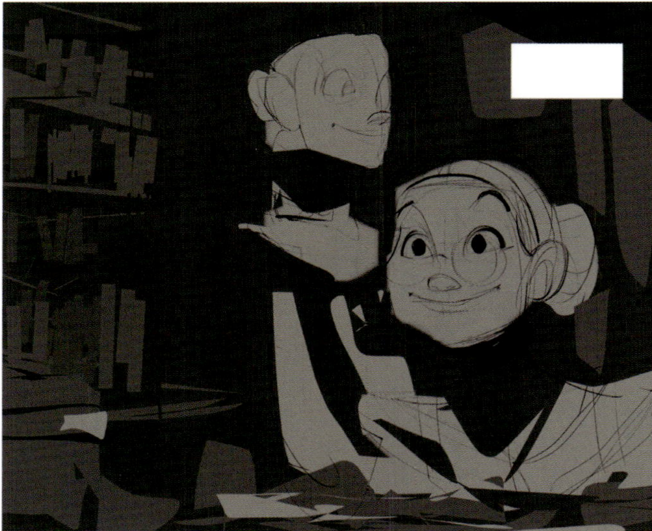
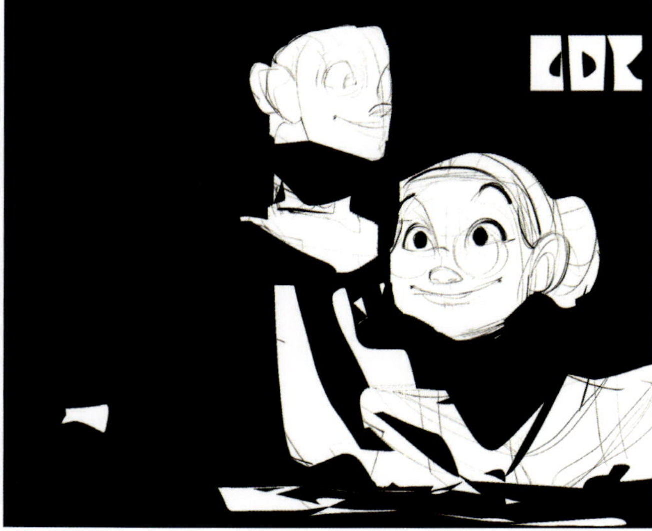

'STARTING WITH SIMPLE SHAPES MAKES IT EASIER TO PLAN OUT THE LIGHTING FOR THE SCENE'

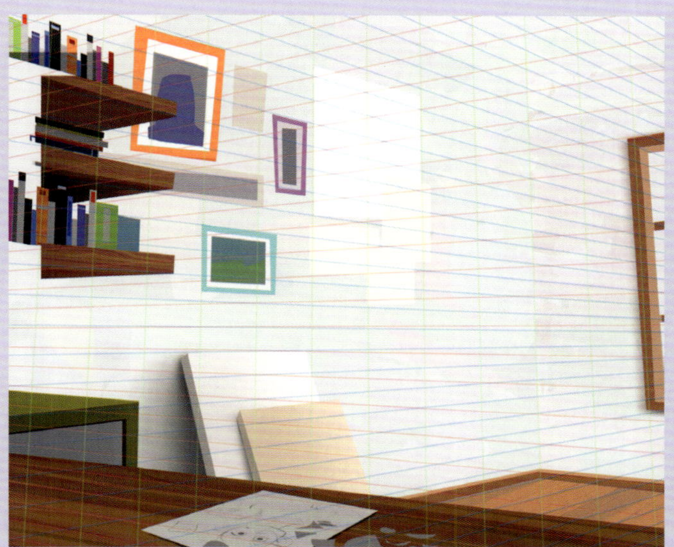
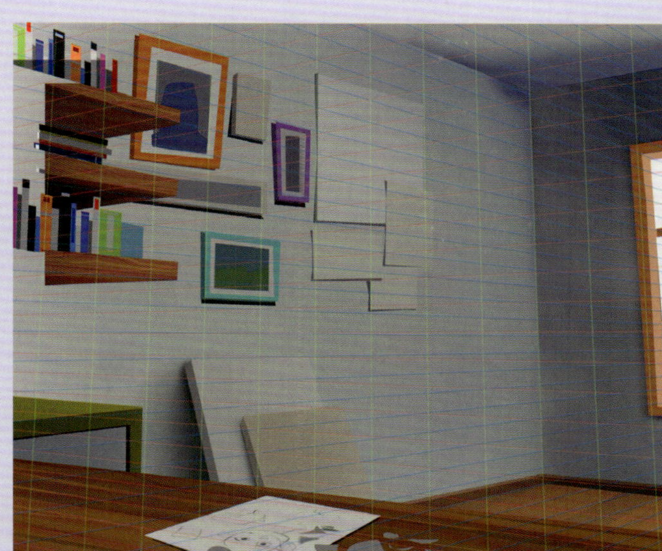

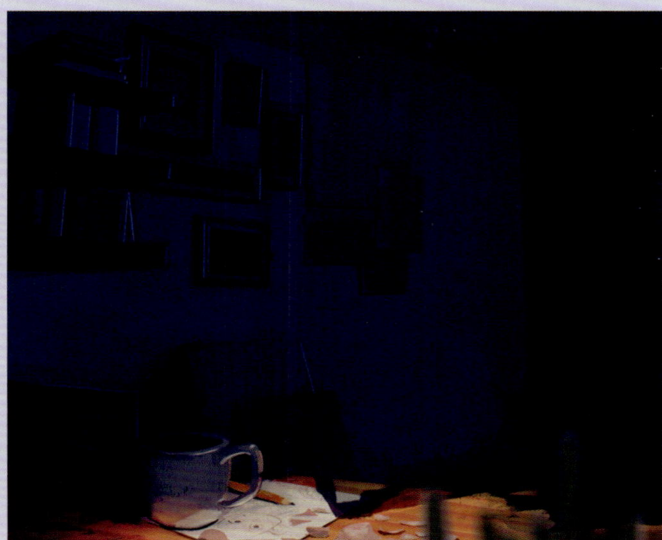

BACKGROUND INVESTIGATION

Next, I want to take some time to think about how Jane's studio looks. It has to show a bit of personality, but at the same time it shouldn't overpower the main focal point of the illustration. I use grids to make sure my perspective is on point, then I start adding simple shapes for each element in the room, like her bookshelf, pictures, and canvases leaning against the wall. I add a little more personality by adding a sketch she made of the sculpt to the table, reinforcing the 'story' of the scene.

Starting with simple shapes makes it easier to plan out the lighting that I want for the scene. I start with a diffused neutral lighting set up (meaning a bunch of soft shadows) coming from the window and then I use Layer Modes to adjust the lighting set up. I add moonlight from the window, subtly filling the room, and the glow from the off-camera desk lamp, illuminating the table.

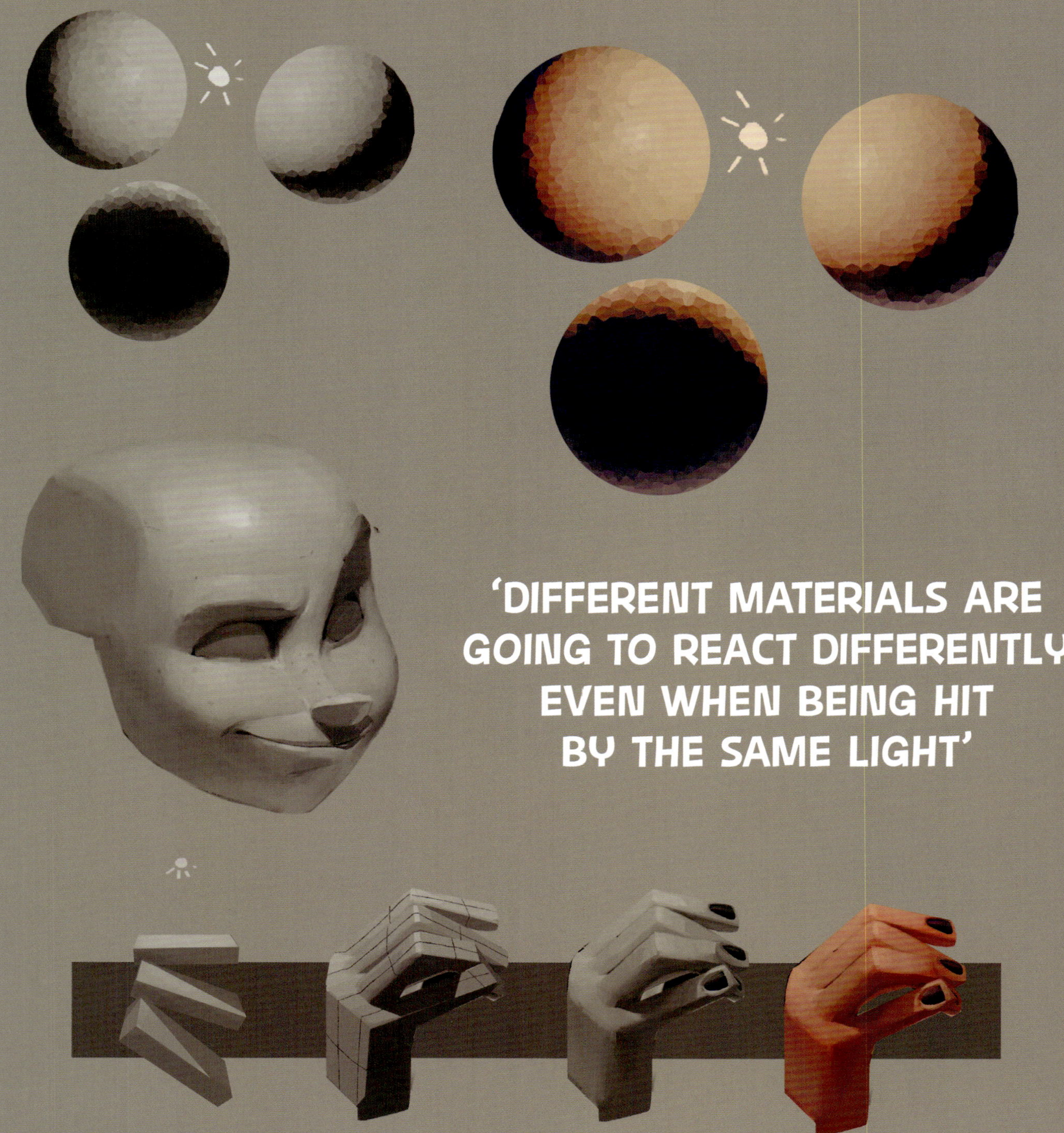

'DIFFERENT MATERIALS ARE GOING TO REACT DIFFERENTLY EVEN WHEN BEING HIT BY THE SAME LIGHT'

STRUCTURE AND MATERIAL

When painting light and shadow, I think about the structure of the drawing I'm painting, specifically the 'planes' – without this, I'd be completely lost. Sometimes I'll feel like I'm not getting anywhere with rendering after hours and hours of noodling, only to realize my understanding of the forms and light sources is off.

Different materials are going to react differently even when being hit by the same light, so we should take care to understand the properties of these materials. Sometimes, I'll paint spheres to help me get to grips with complex lighting and use them as reference as I go. This is particularly helpful when multiple lights are in play, like key lights, diffuse lights, bounce light, rim light, and so on.

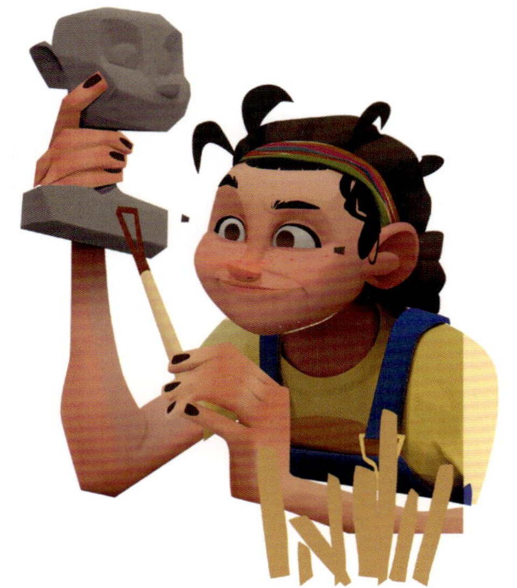

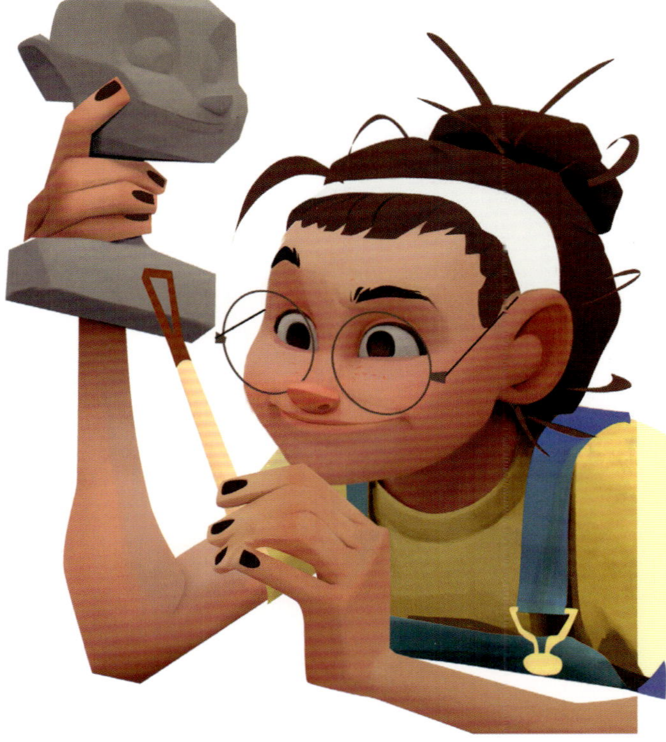

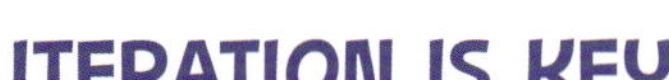

ITERATION IS KEY

Where I start, even with a line drawing, is very rarely where I end up when I finish painting. I continue to iterate even if I've sunk a bunch of hours into a single area, like Jane's face. Sometimes, what looks good on the sketch can get lost or become unclear when I start to paint in the lights.

I also need to think about the tone and what I'm trying to express with this character. I want to capture her focused determination to show how into the sculpting session she is. Sometimes, I'll take a photo reference of myself to see if I can find a way to exaggerate a pose or expression further.

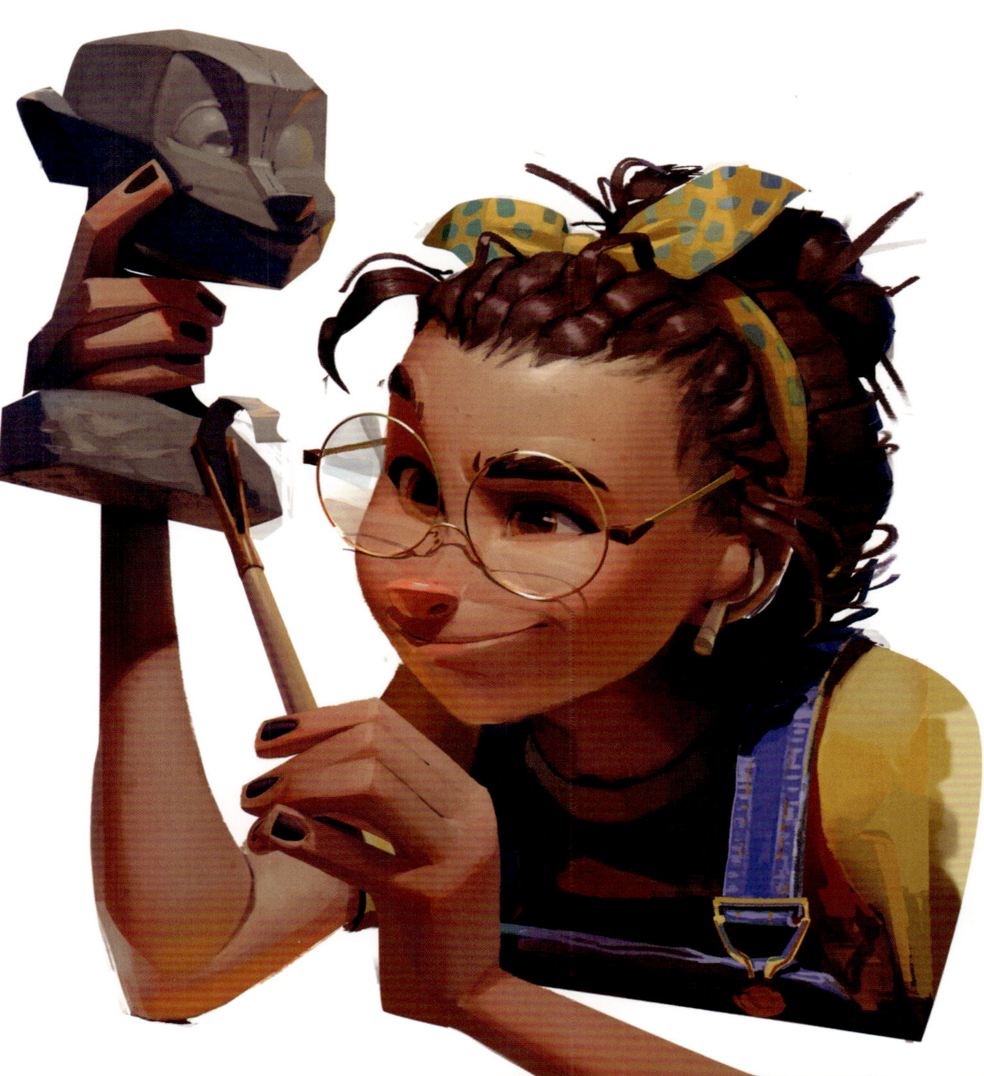

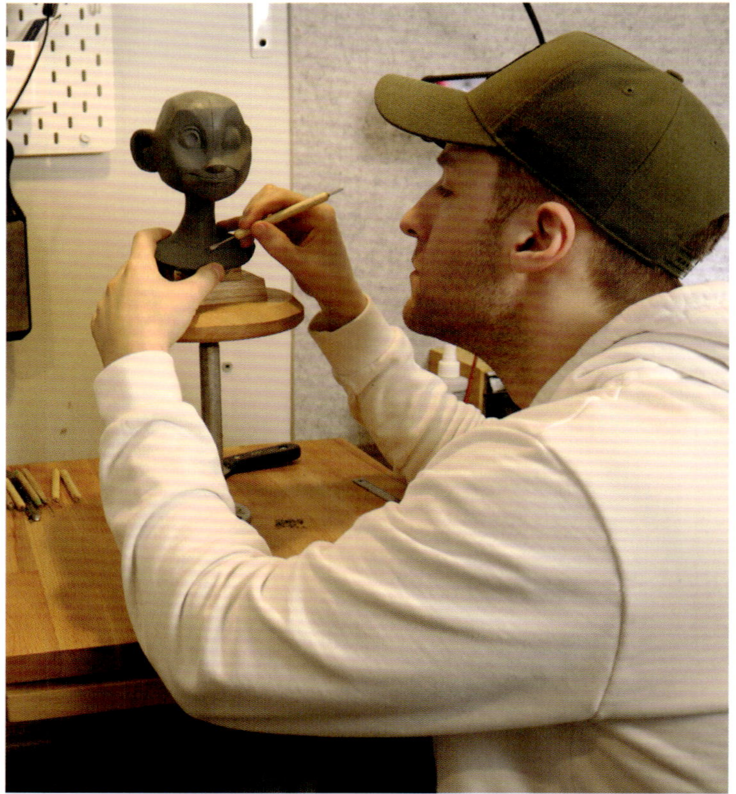

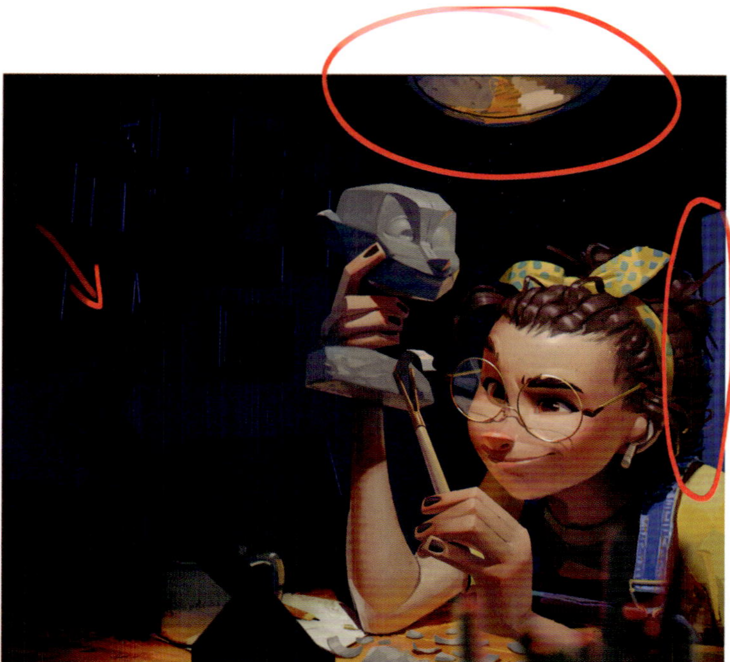

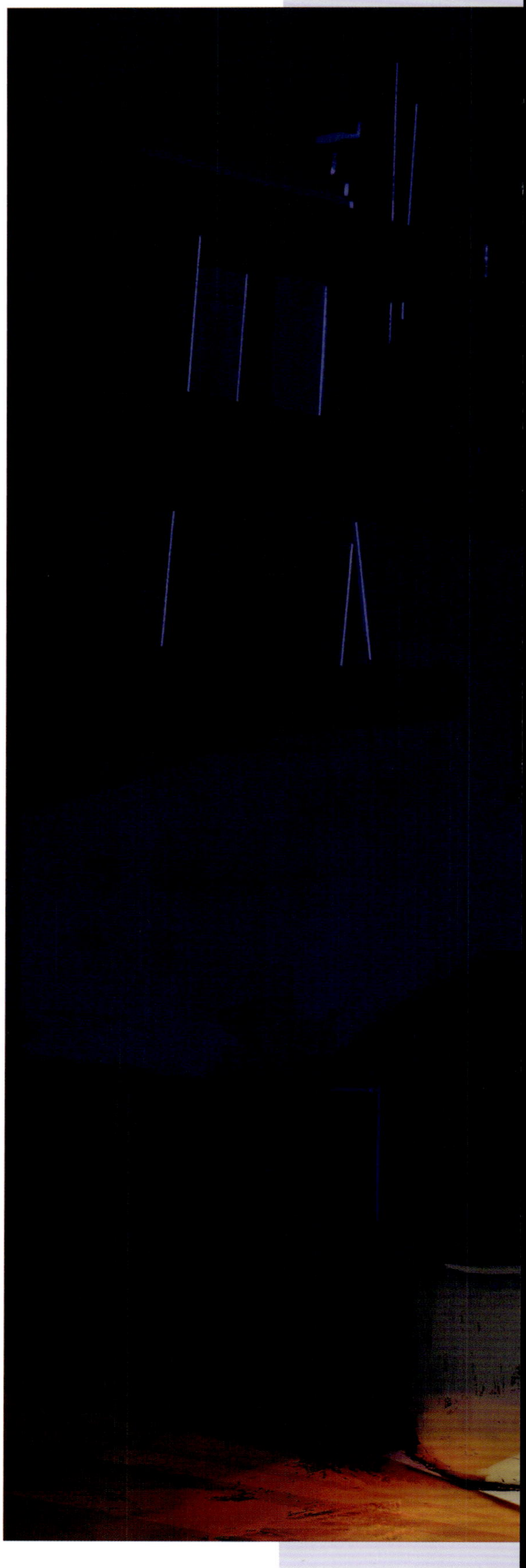

KEEPING THE FOCUS

I initially wanted to show the window light and the desk lamp, but the scene quickly started to feel cluttered, claustrophobic, and distracting. I want the focus to be on Jane and the sculpt and still have some room for the eye to rest.

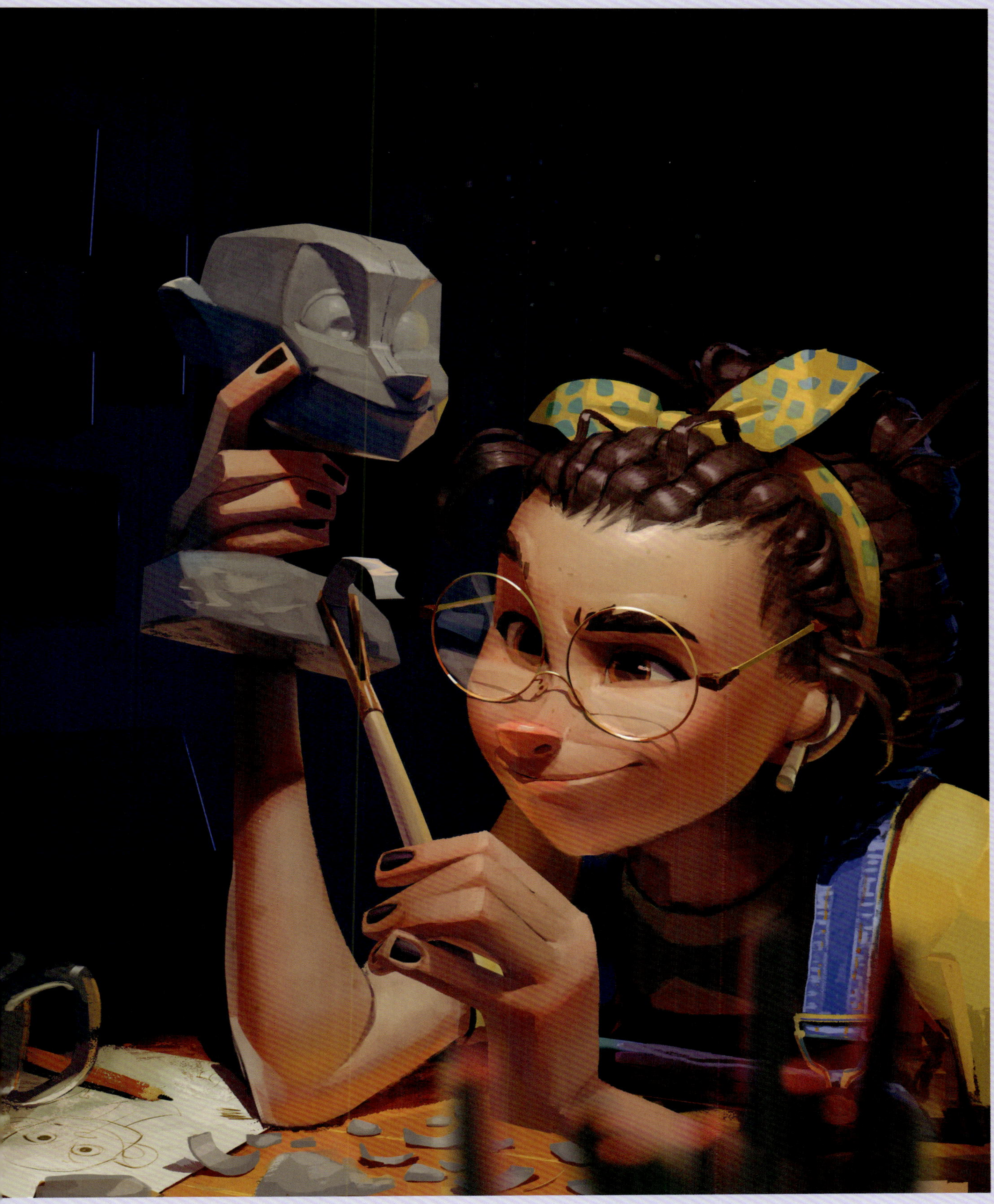

THE SHEEP'S GAMBIT

SARAH-LISA HLEB

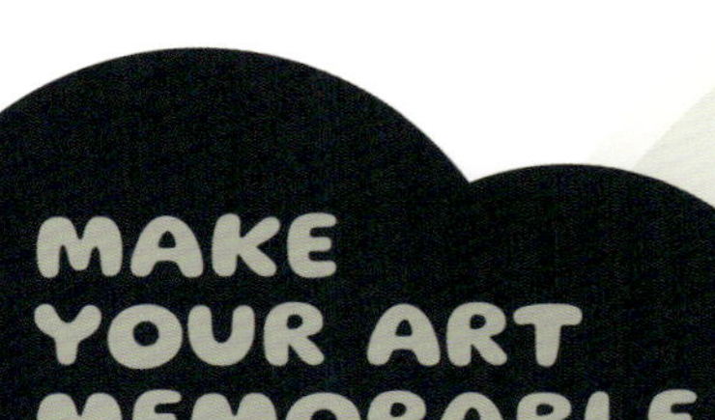

The creative process often takes you on an unexpected journey. You think you have an idea, and suddenly, while you're in the middle of the project, you end up somewhere else entirely. For this article, the assignment was to design a 'shy sheep' character. At first, my idea was a 1980s inspired sheep girl, but the character turned out very differently! Sometimes your original idea doesn't work, but just keep working on it and trust the process – the result will usually be better than your original plan.

OPENING MOVES

I start by browsing Pinterest for inspiration and study the animal I want to draw. A sheep's puffy wool kind of reminds me of 1980s hairstyles, so I go in that direction.

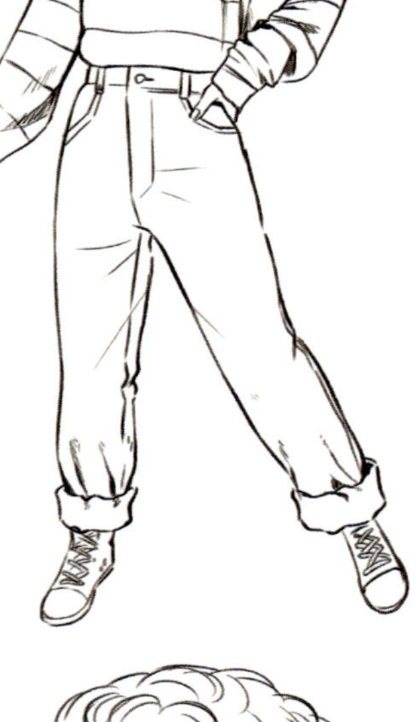

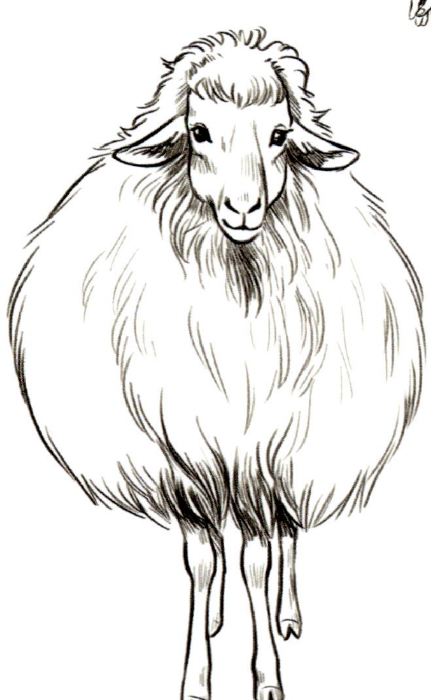

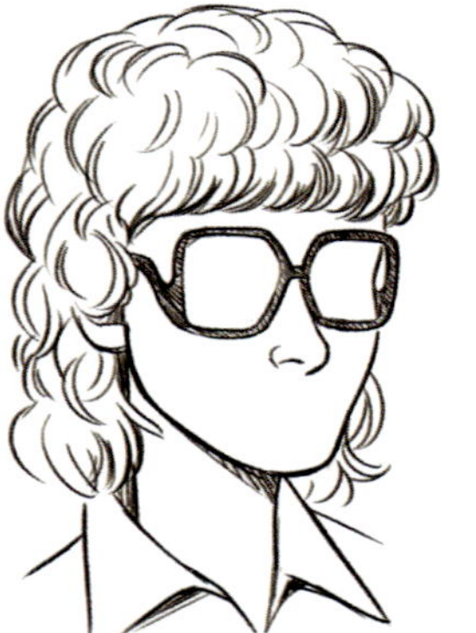

MAKE YOUR ART MEMORABLE

We all see a lot of beautiful pictures, but the ones that really stick in our minds evoke a feeling or tell a story. Try to incorporate either of these into your characters to make people remember them.

COUNTING SHEEP

At this stage, I sketch very loosely, trying to find interesting shapes and implementing what I've found through my research and studies. The sheep girl is cute but boring, so I decide to go with a little weird guy instead. What if he's a chess player?

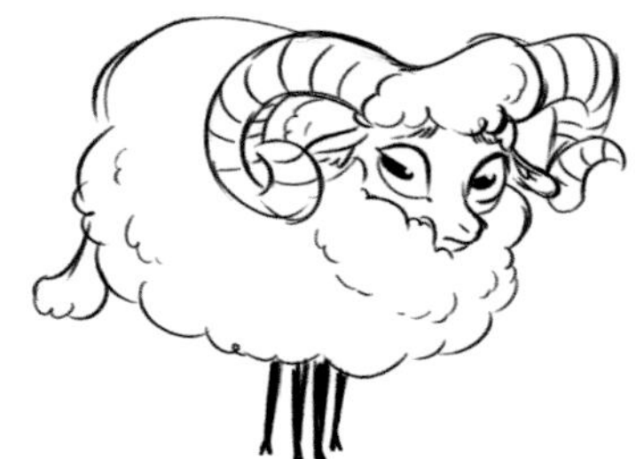
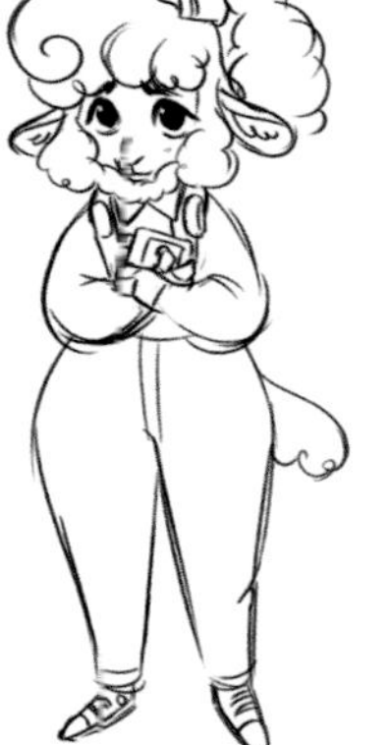
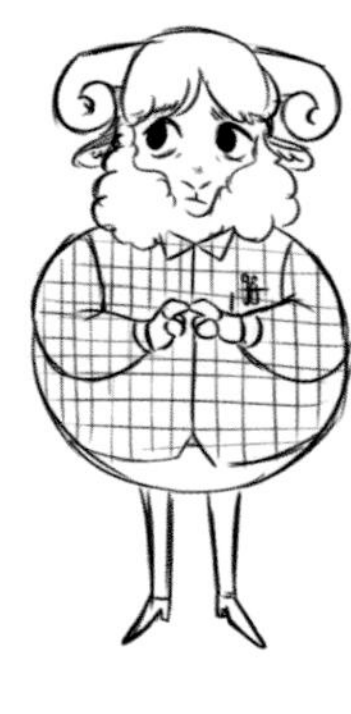
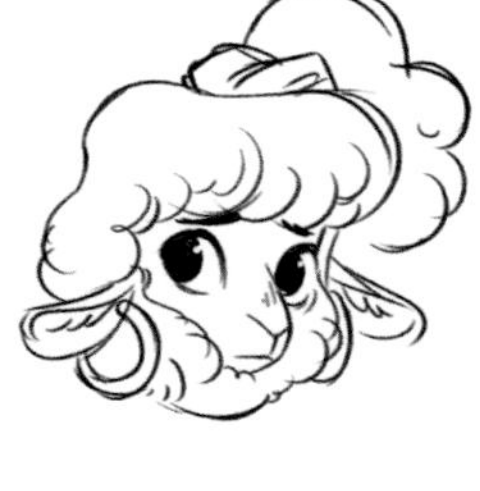
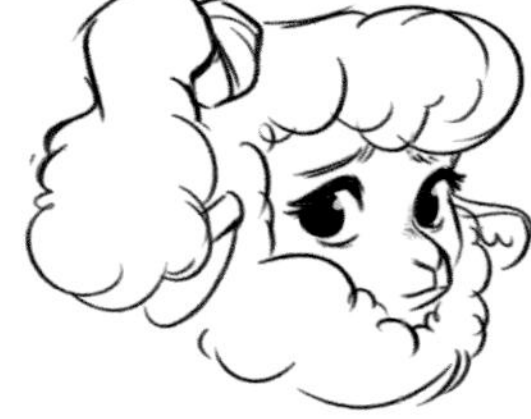
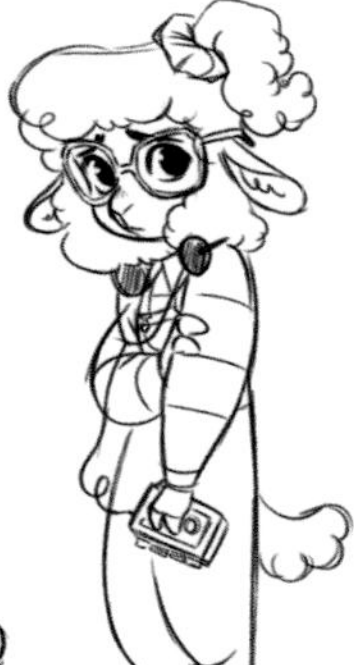
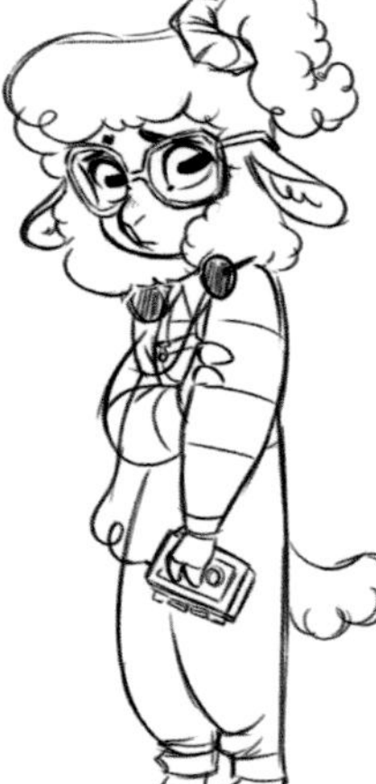
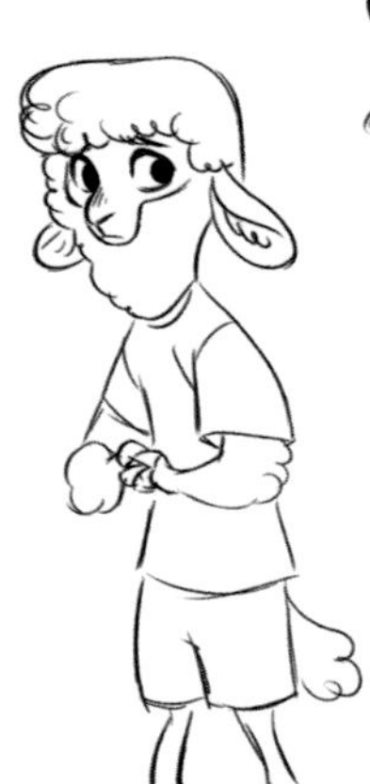
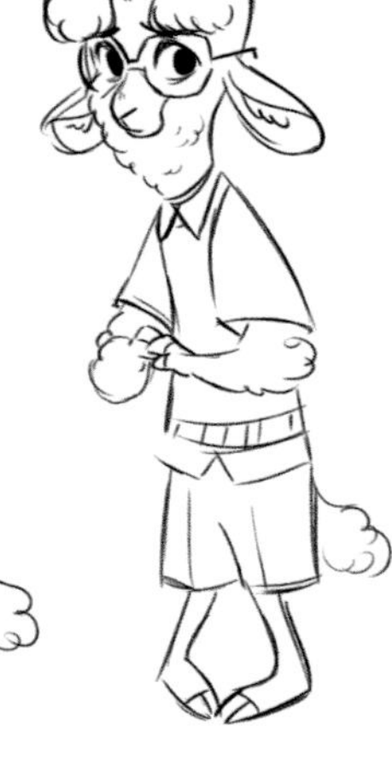
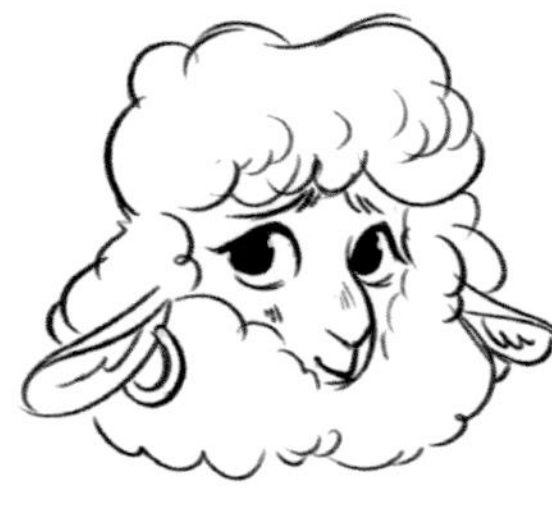
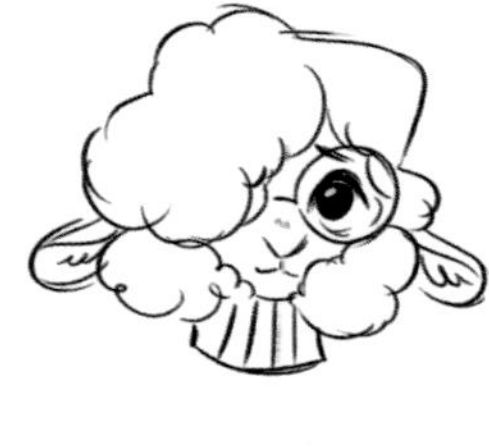
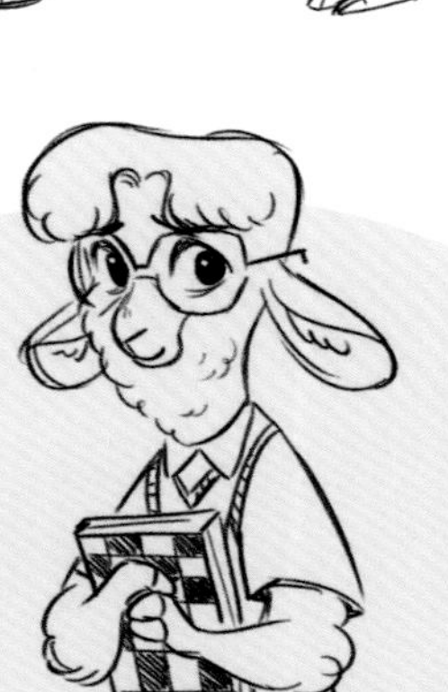
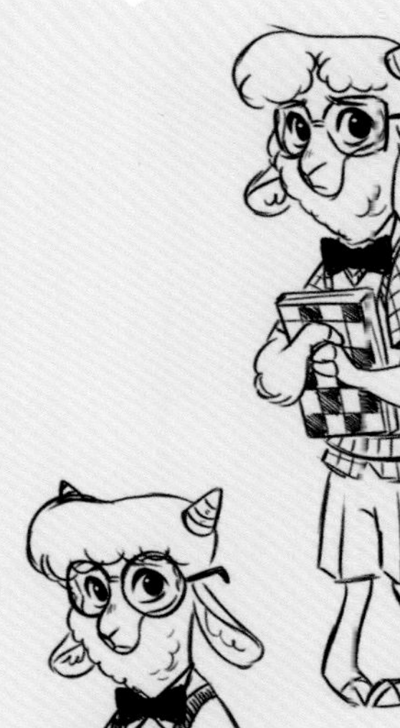
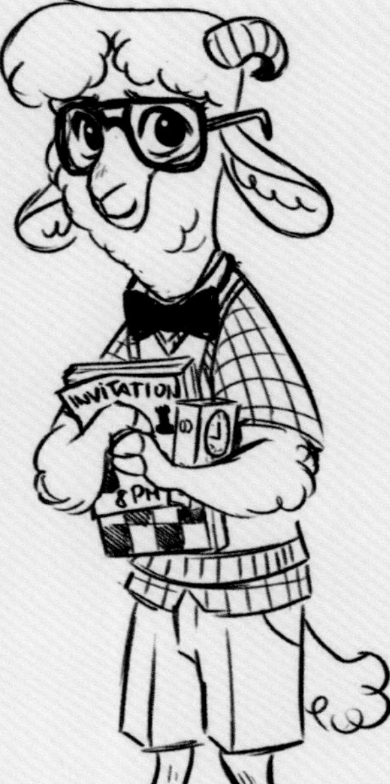
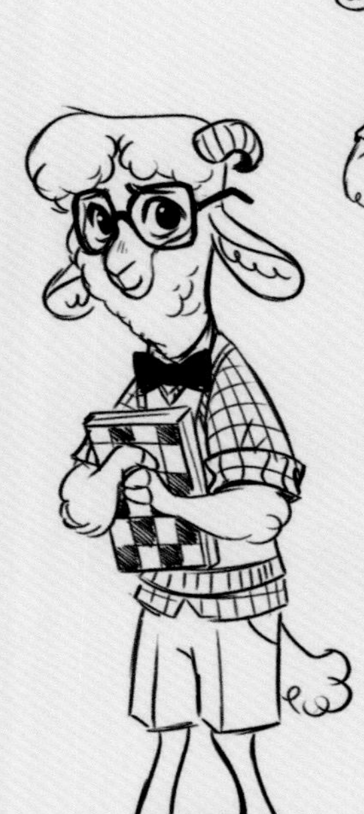
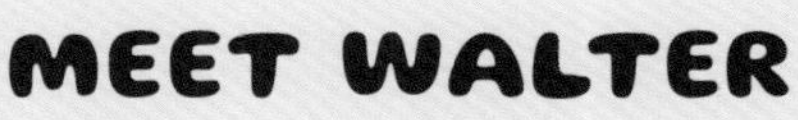

MEET WALTER

Now I've chosen my character, a narrative starts to form. It's Walter the sheep's first day at chess club. I try out different outfits, making him look a bit nerdy, and include the sort of props that he would bring to the club.

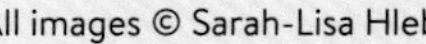

CLASSIC COLOURS

I return to my initial idea of a character from the 1980s and choose colours from pictures of that era to give him a vintage look. Since he's shy, he probably wouldn't wear anything too flashy, so as not to draw attention to himself.

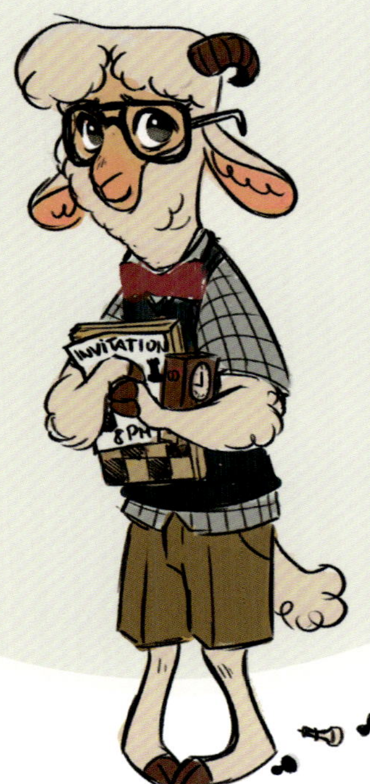
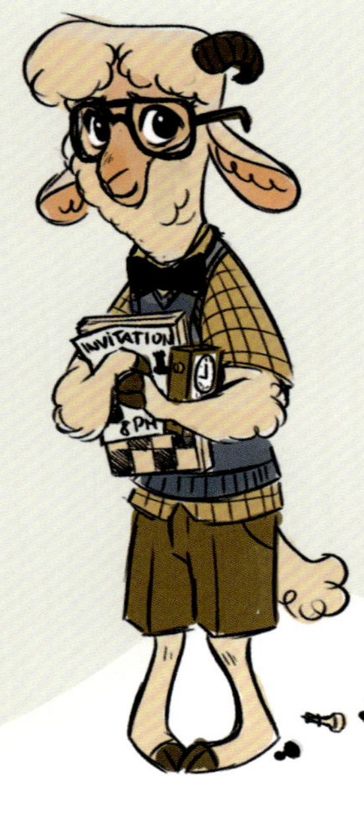
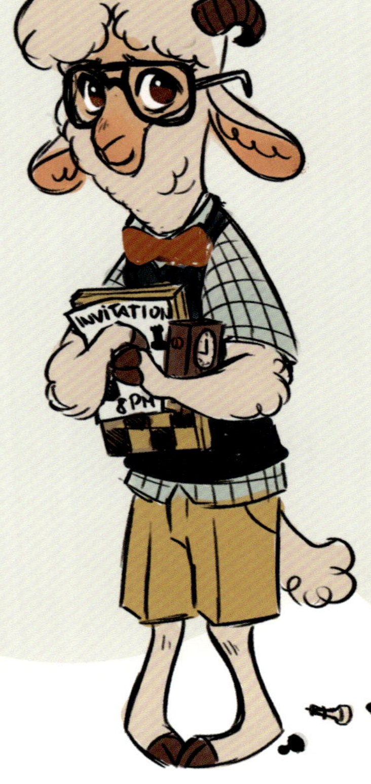
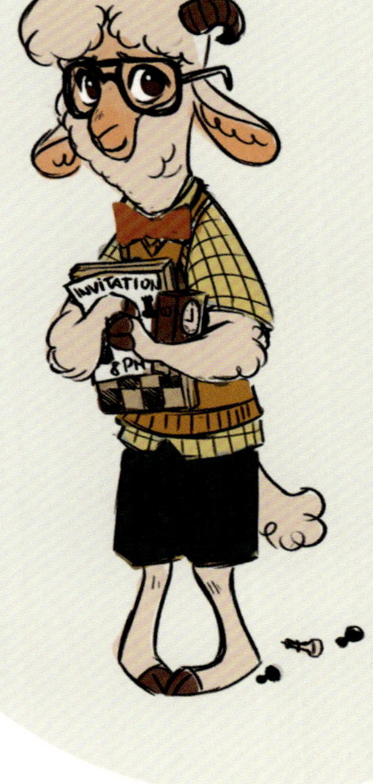

THE SHY SHEEP

A shy character might fear judgement or rejection and so guard their emotions closely. I want to clearly show how my character is feeling without exaggerating the expression too much.

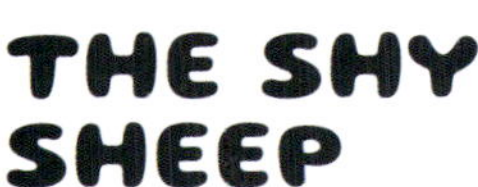
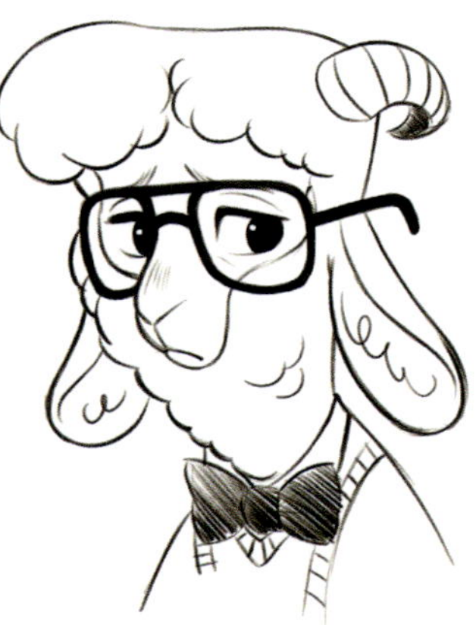
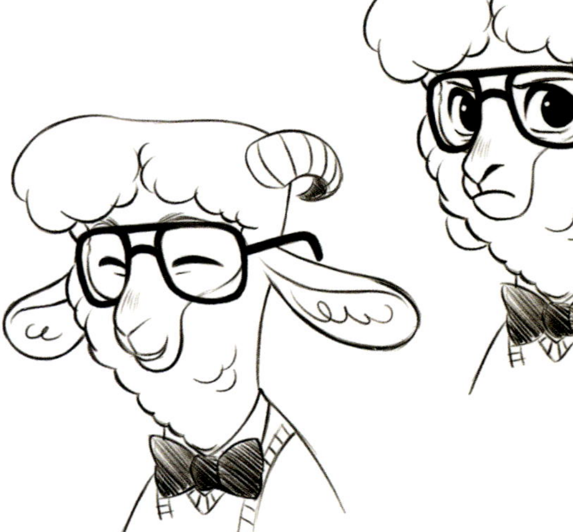
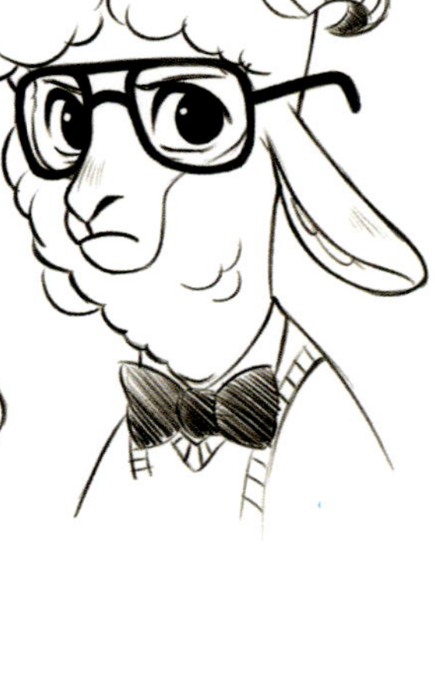

ANIMAL BEHAVIOUR

When drawing an animal character, try to include typical animal behaviour, such as drooping ears when they are sad or turned back ears when they are angry.

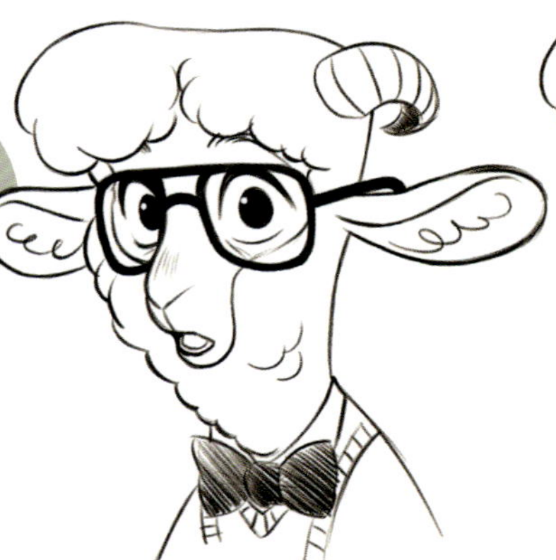
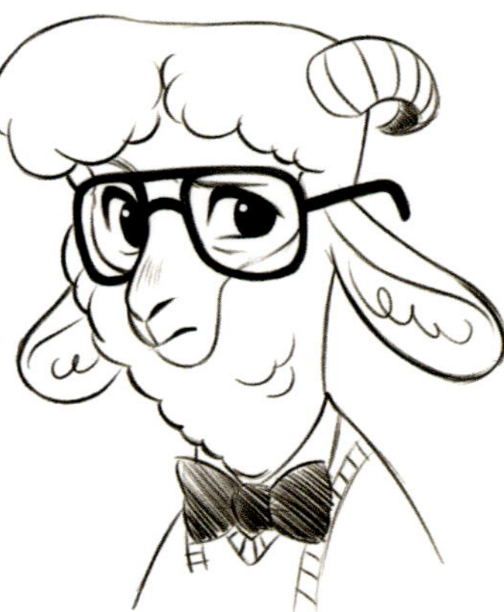

'I WANT TO SHOW EMOTION WITHOUT EXAGGERATING THE EXPRESSION TOO MUCH'

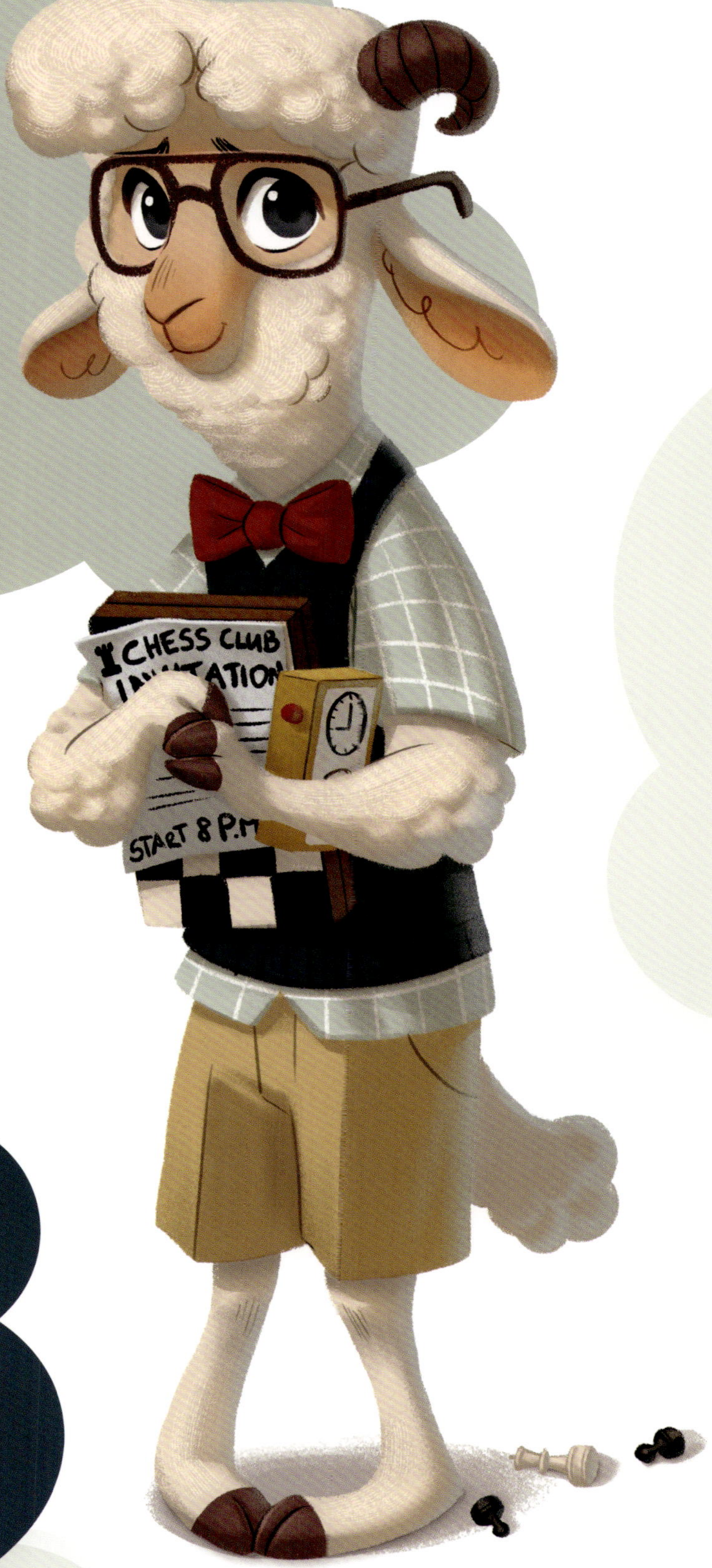

CHECKMATE

To bring out his soft and fluffy wool, I decide to render the finished drawing. For the colours, I choose a triadic colour scheme: red, blue, and yellow. These colours have that retro look I'm after and provide enough contrast throughout the design. Good luck on your first day, Walter, you can do it!

ASK FOR FEEDBACK

If you have artist friends, ask them for feedback! You never know what valuable or crazy ideas they may have to enhance your design. And if you don't know any artists, there are many feedback communities online, or you can even ask a friend or family member with whom you feel comfortable sharing your art. You'll be surprised how many useful ideas an 'art outsider' might have.

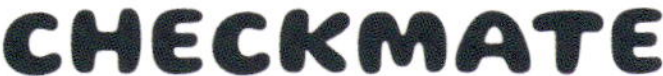

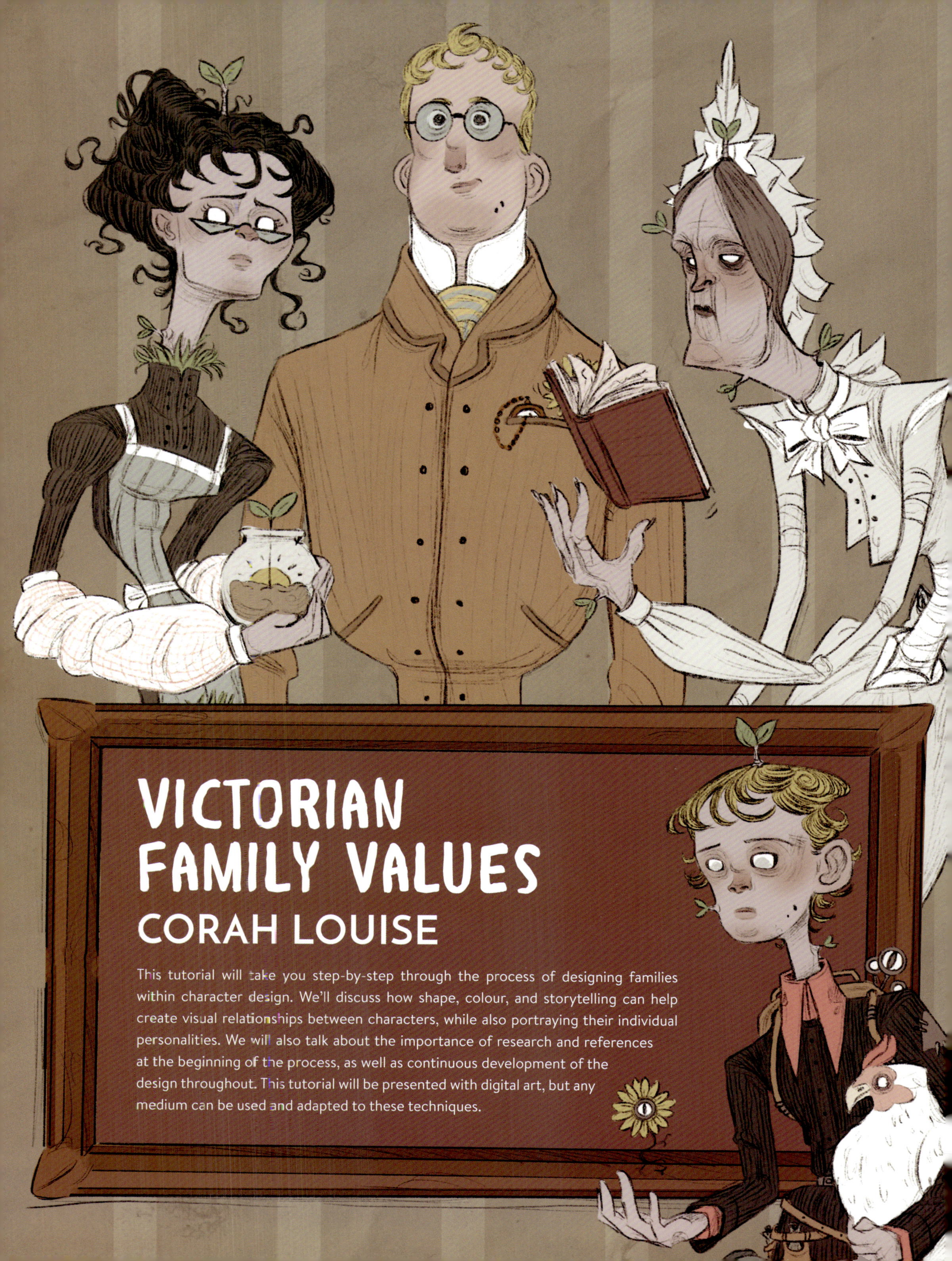

VICTORIAN FAMILY VALUES

CORAH LOUISE

This tutorial will take you step-by-step through the process of designing families within character design. We'll discuss how shape, colour, and storytelling can help create visual relationships between characters, while also portraying their individual personalities. We will also talk about the importance of research and references at the beginning of the process, as well as continuous development of the design throughout. This tutorial will be presented with digital art, but any medium can be used and adapted to these techniques.

LET'S GET STARTED

Begin the process by creating two lists. Firstly, write down the ways in which characters could be linked visually as a family. This could be through physical traits like height or facial features, or shown in similar fashion choices, poses, or expressions. In the second list, write down the ways a character could break away from familial traits, such as through their own interests or current trends.. This will ensure your characters have individuality alongside the consistency of the familial traits. Refer back to these two lists throughout the design process.

CREATING A MIND MAP

Now you are in the right mindset and thinking of family, note down all the ideas you have for them: their story, the era they live in, their jobs, and so on. I imagine a Victorian gothic family, with some magical elements mixed in. The ideas don't need to be detailed yet. This process allows you to visualize the basics of your ideas and begin building upon them, or it will help you break down a brief and all the elements you need to hit. Let your thoughts wander and be loose with your writing, as this will help keep the creative ideas flowing.

This page (top): First doodles to get the mind flowing

This page (bottom): Write down all of your original ideas for your family of characters

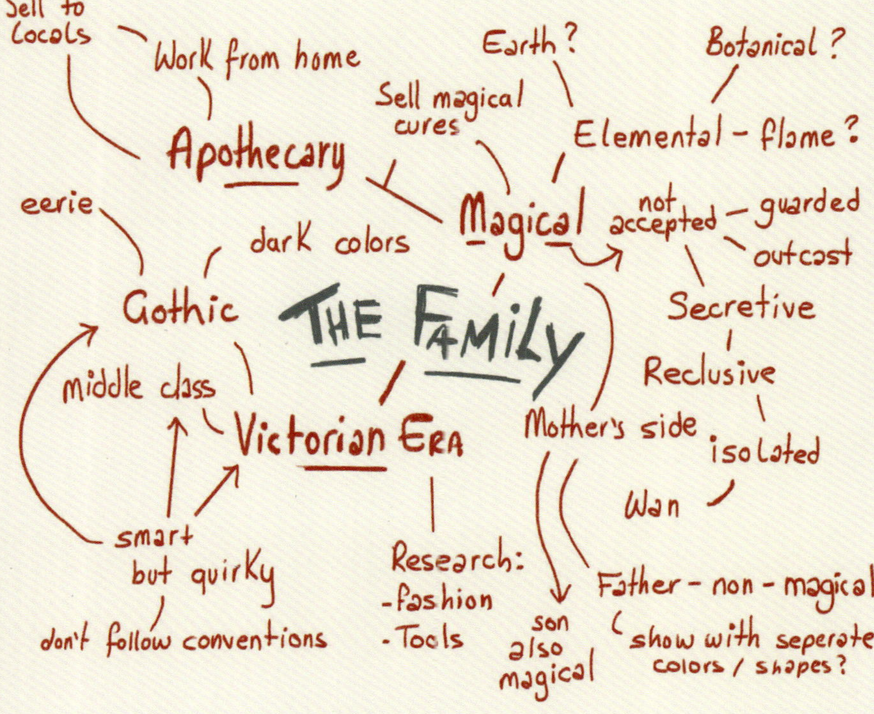

SKETCHING FACES

Gather portrait references that you feel are relevant to your imagined family. This could be images of people from the same era as the family, characters that are similar in personality, or visual references which will teach you something about the possibilities of your design. Roughly sketch these references to begin warming up and building your library of ideas. Take notice of details that will be helpful in your design, such as personality, shapes, and style.

This page: I sketch a series of faces based on the references I have discovered

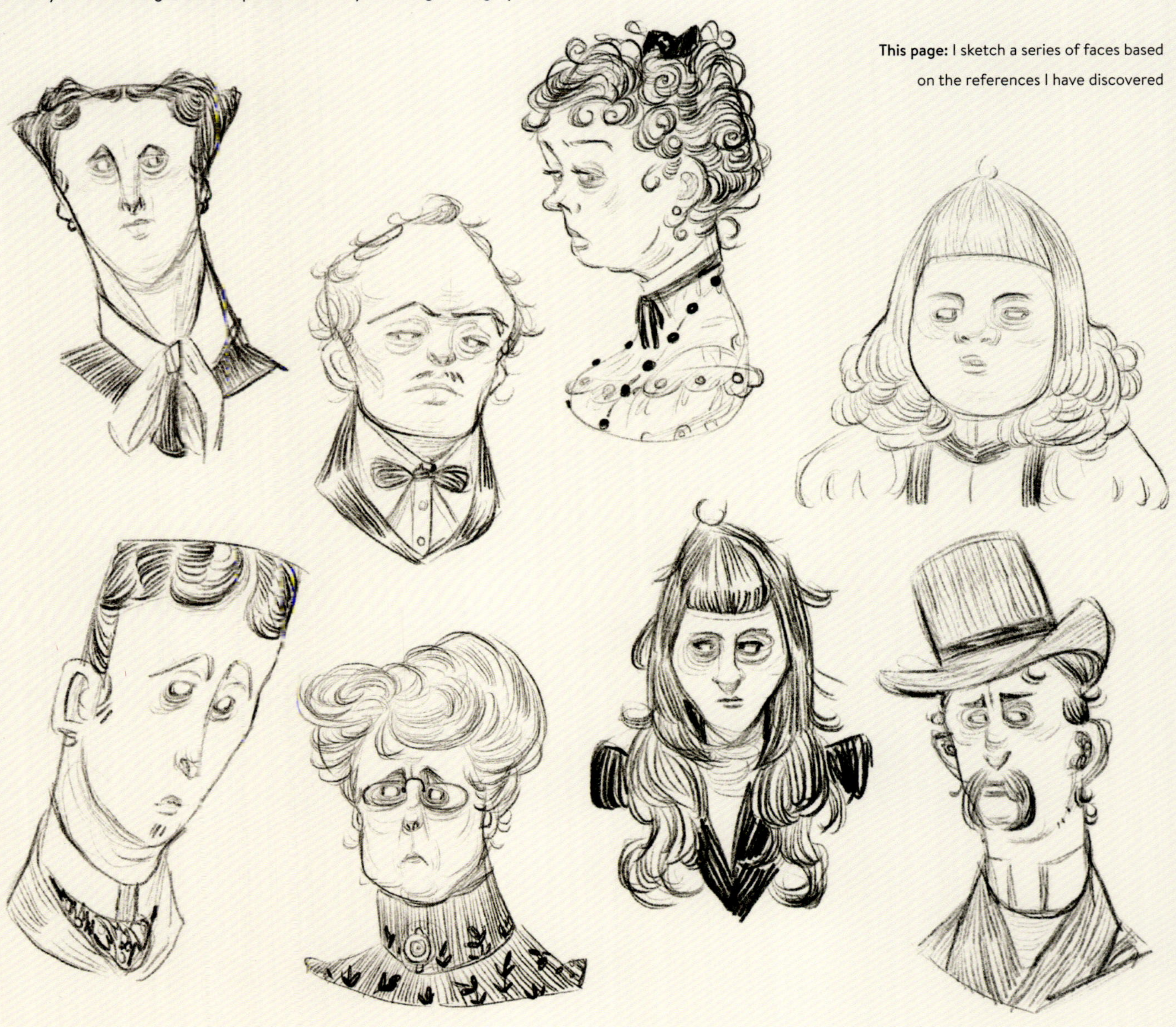

STEP OUTSIDE

When you first begin researching and collecting references for your characters, try to think outside of your own medium. Look for inspiration in film, television, photography, magazines, nature, sculpture, comics, patterns – the list is endless! Inspiration can be found anywhere and pulling from references beyond art will help you create unique and original characters. If you're struggling to begin, sketching actors or film characters that give off a similar vibe is a great place to start.

FASHION FIRST

Continue warming up by taking your research a step further with full bodies and fashion. Remember to keep these sketches loose and rough as we still aren't designing our final characters just yet. Research images from the era your characters live in – perhaps a fashion trend, job, or school uniform. All these can influence the way someone presents themselves, particularly through fashion. People may also be influenced by older members of the family or perhaps want to be the exact opposite and use fashion to portray that. I look at Victorian fashion and sketch out some preliminary ideas.

EXTENDED FAMILIES

The final step before we begin drawing our family is to gain a deeper understanding of everyone's story and how they relate to one another. You already have a mind map portraying a basic idea of the family – now take each member and get to know them by writing a list of their traits. I write notes for the four members of my magical family, delving deeper into their individual stories. The more detail you can add, the better – think about your characters' names, age, profession, interests, likes, dislikes, and more. In this family, we have mother Fairy, father Dorsey, their son Lucian, and Fairy's mother (Lucian's Nana), Drucilla.

This page (top): I look at references of Victorian fashion for my family of characters

This page (bottom): Build upon the family and characters by expanding story and detail

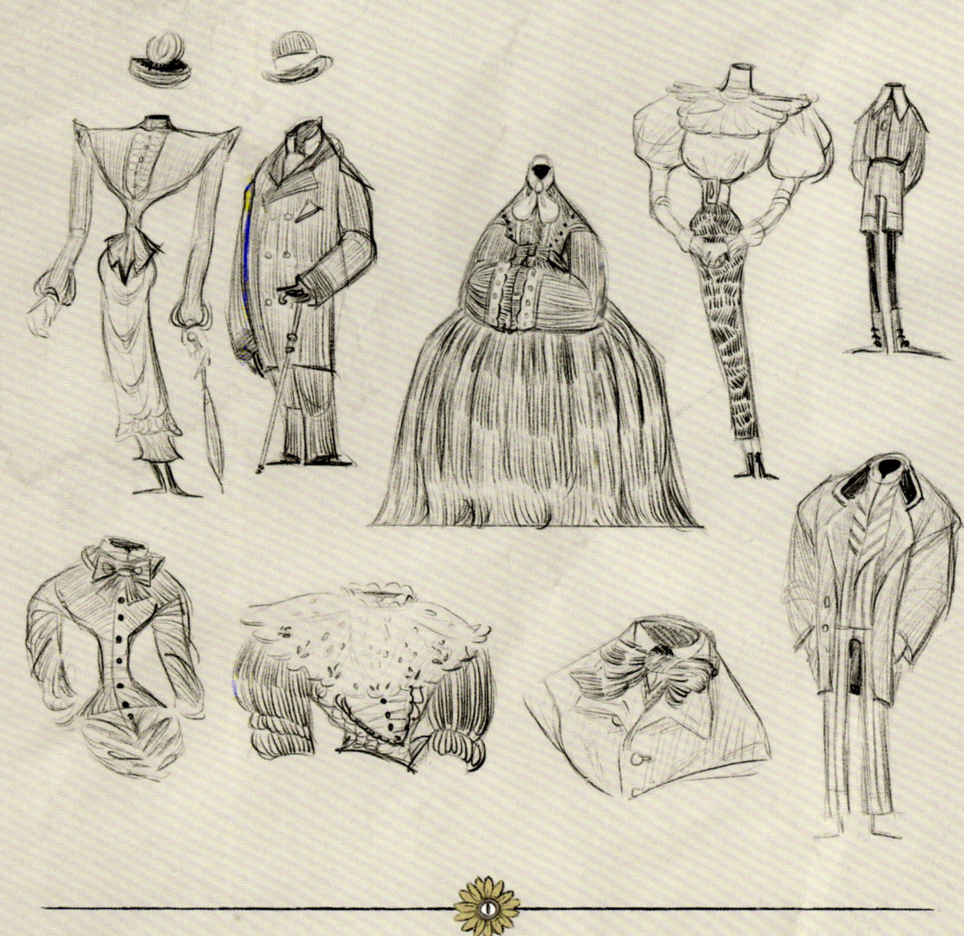

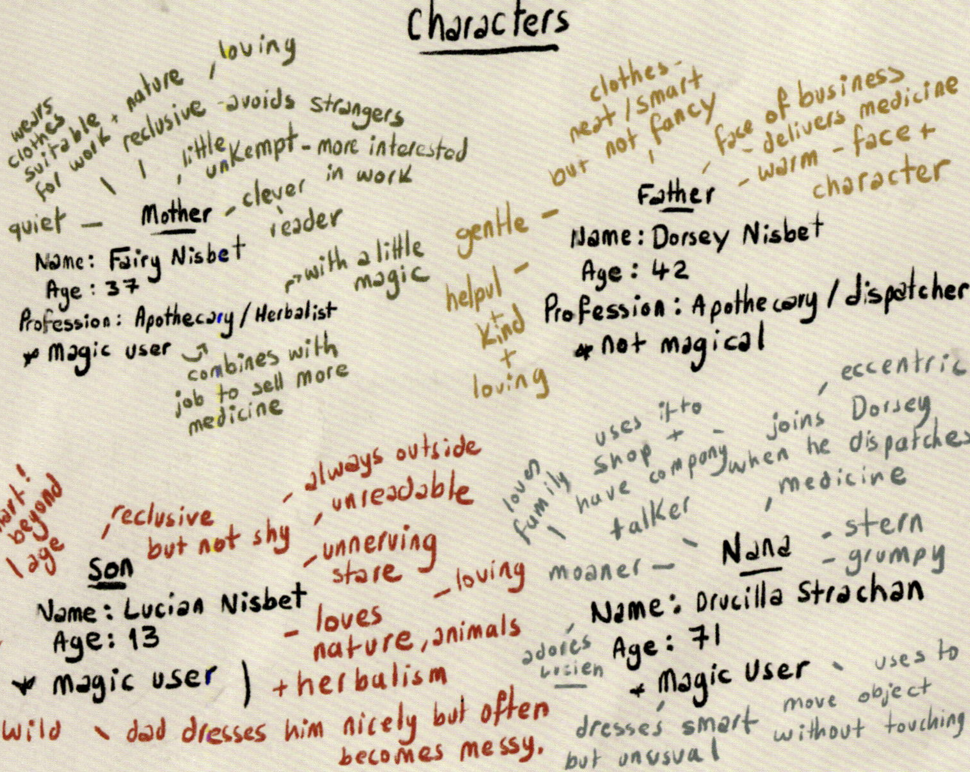

SHAPING THE NARRATIVE

Now you know who you want your family members to be, begin thinking of the shapes that will form them. All art is made from shapes that can have underlying connotations which are useful for designers to portray the personality to the audience. Triangular, sharp shapes can mean aggression or intelligence, squares convey a closed-off or reliable personality, and round shapes suggest friendliness. Use two shapes at most for each member of your family. My family's intellect is their strongest trait, so I choose triangles for three of their designs, along with circles and squares. Think about how personality and genes may be passed down through generations and visualize this by repeating shapes. For instance, Lucian, the child of my family, inherits a circle shape from his father and a triangle from his mother.

FORMING FACES

Form a first draft of your character's faces using the shapes you selected for them. Keep it loose and remember that this is just a guide. You don't need to stick completely within the shapes or keep them even – they can be elongated, stretched, and shortened to fit the design. These shapes can be used to create the big areas like the head but also smaller details like the nose or mouth too. Keep it loose – not every aspect of your character has to match your chosen shape, just let them convey the general idea.

This page (top): Select the shapes that will best suit your character's personality and family

This page (bottom): Build a first draft of their faces using the shapes like building blocks

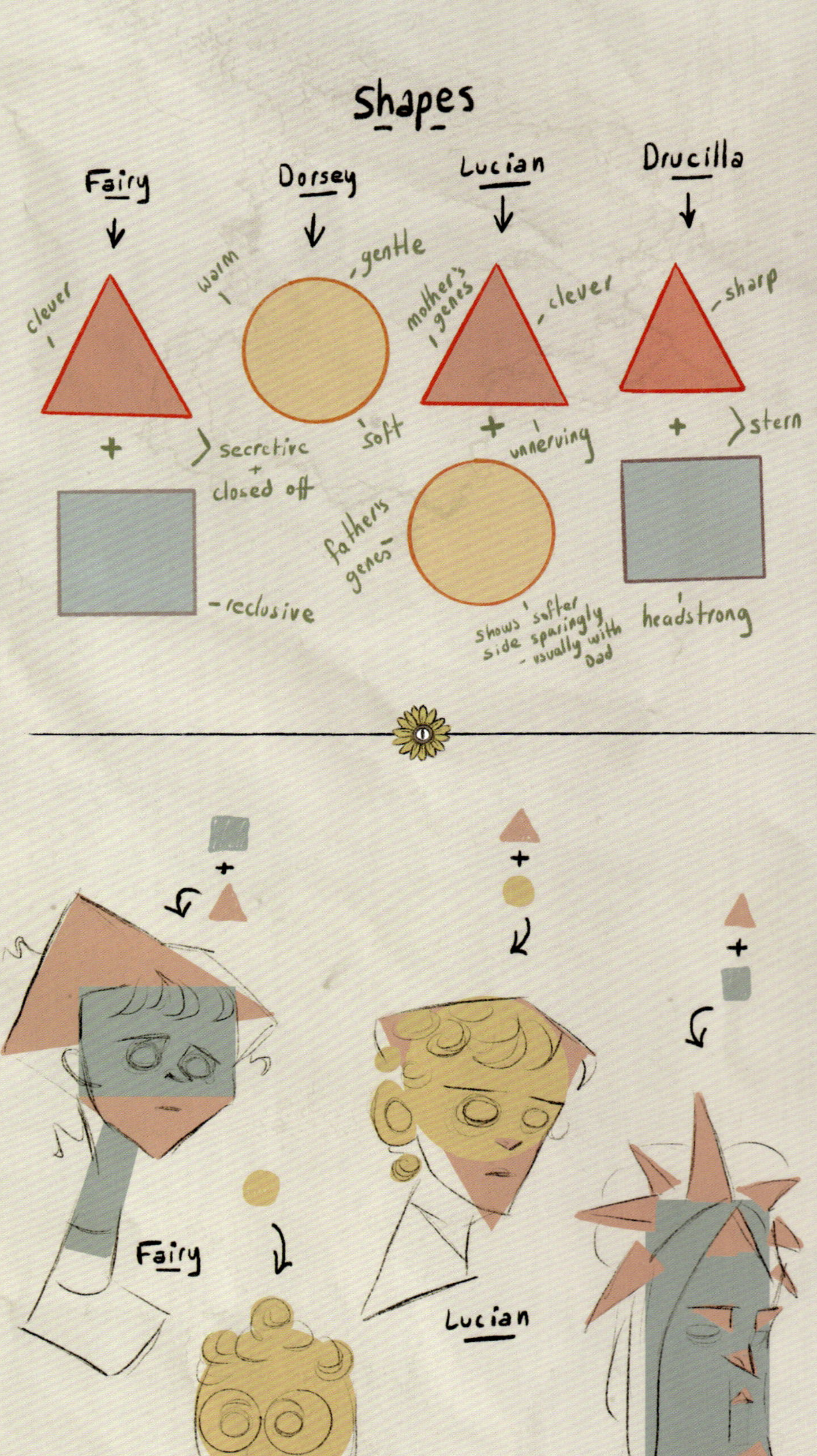

BUILDING BODIES

Next, use the same shapes to start thinking of the body. When forming the whole character, think of poses that portray each personality alongside the shapes. Poses should be unique and tell a story, but using repeating details, patterns, and shapes between the characters will cement them as a family. For my characters with two dominant shapes, I use one for the overall head shape, and the other for the body. If creating digitally, shapes can be used as an under layer to your sketch, or if working traditionally, try drawing the shapes in a light-coloured pencil and sketching with black over the top.

FAMILY RESEMBLANCE

Let's return to our shape-based face sketches and begin building up the characters in detail. Lower the opacity of the shapes layer and draw over your sketch with a new layer (or you could use tracing paper if working traditionally). Refine your ideas and bring them to life. The shapes will give you a sturdy base to explore the design without losing their core vibe. Think about facial features and how, if genetically related, they may influence each other. I draw Drucilla, Fairy, and Lucian with deep-set eyes and strong chin lines to show their lineage.

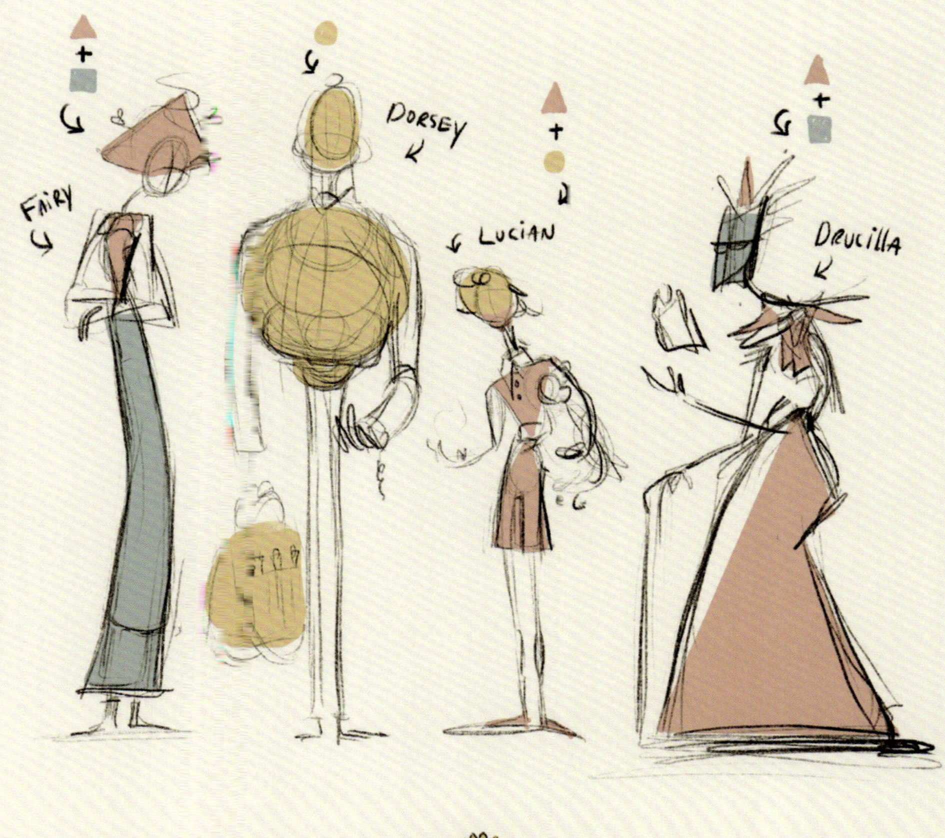

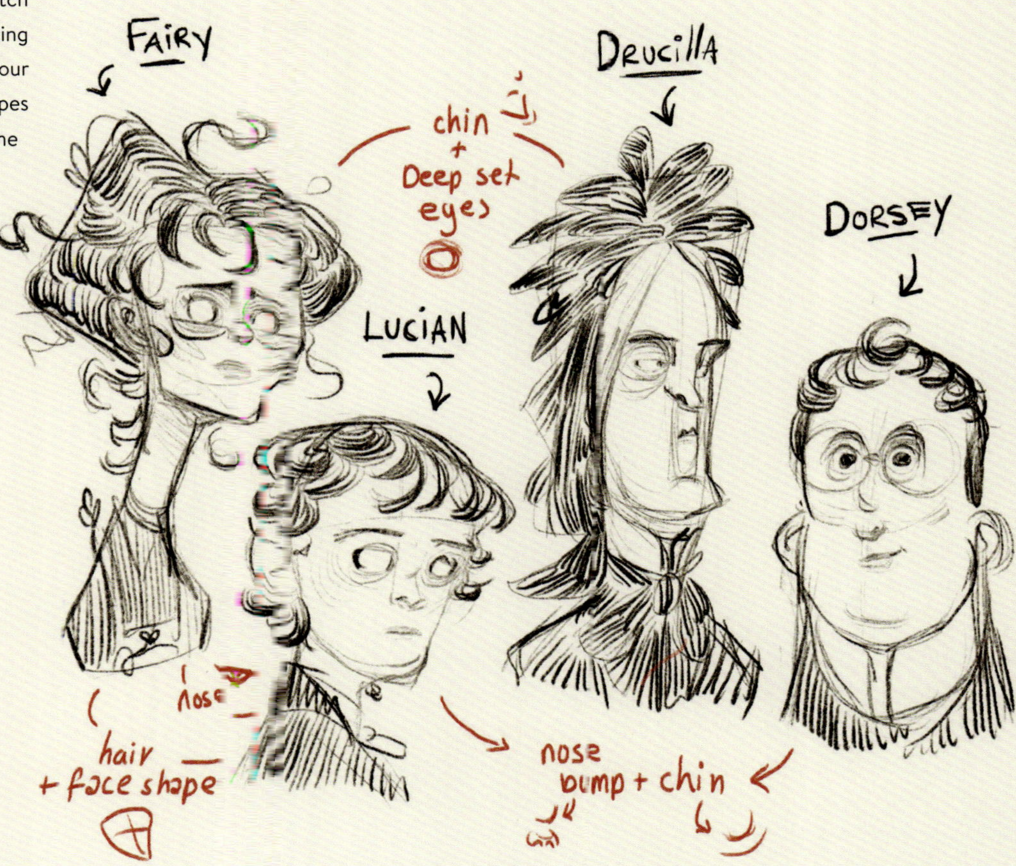

This page (top): I build the character's bodies using shapes

This page (bottom): Refine the design with a second draft, using the previous basic shapes as a guideline

THE SILHOUETTE TECHNIQUE

Test the effectiveness of your body shapes by filling your characters with just one colour ⊃ create their silhouette. Now, take a look at their outline – do they still look as though they are in their intended pose? Are they still recognizable? Do they look unique and can you read their personality from their pose? An effective silhouette will convey all of this.

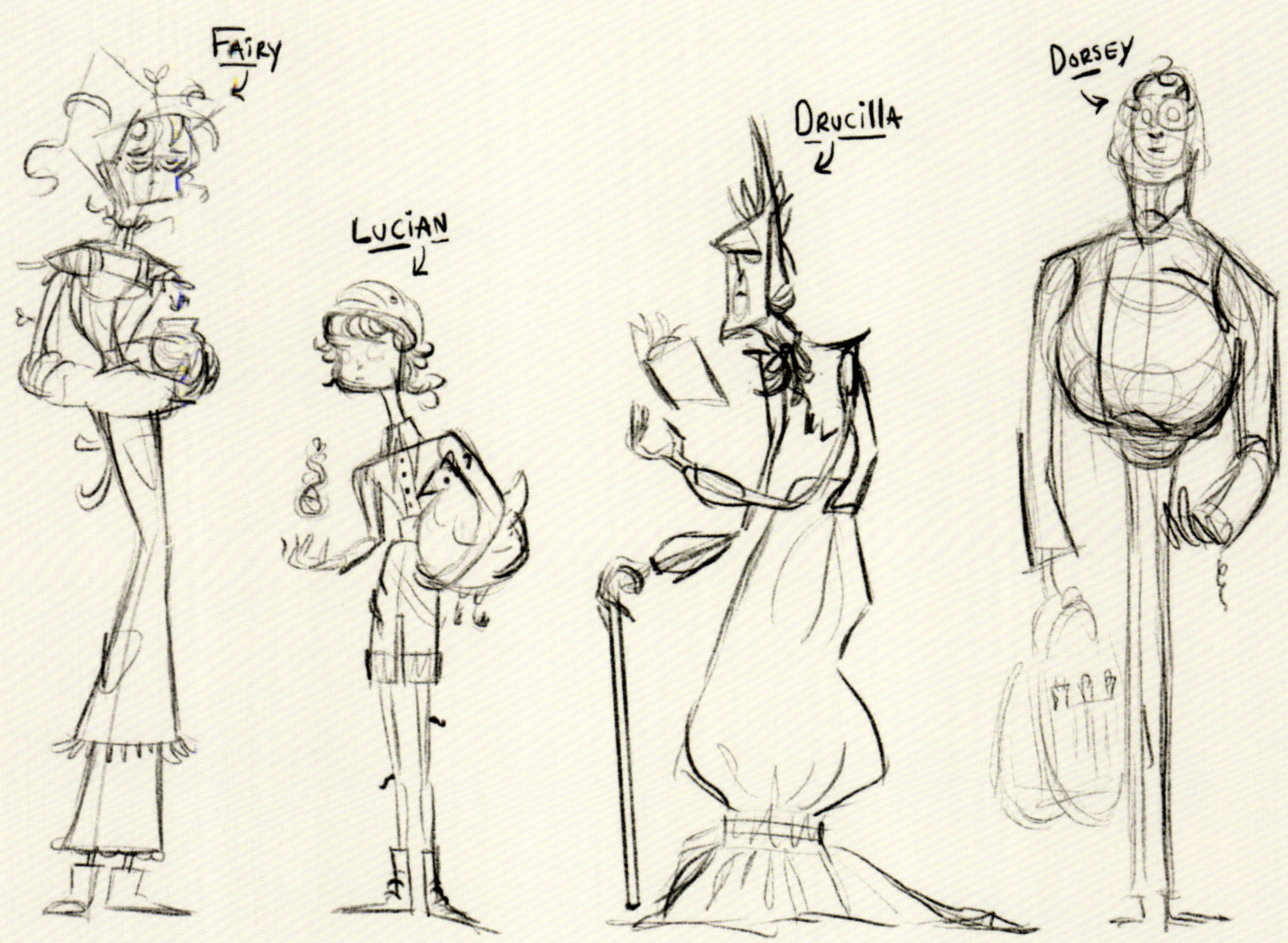

REFINING THE DESIGN

As we did with the faces, now we refine the rest of the characters' bodies. We don't need the designs to be too detailed just yet, we are adding layers of story gradually, developing the design and character slowly. Try to reach a point where you can see each personality, the basic shape of their body, and an idea of their clothes and overall style. Begin to show similarities in fashion taste between family members. I draw similar dress shapes for Fairy and her mother, Drucilla, but a very different design for Lucian, to show he wants to express his personality as separate to the rest of his family.

ALL IN THE DETAILS

Details tell the true story of your character: their back story, interests, and relationships. Smaller pieces of information can mean more to an audience than larger ones – their subtlety feels more personal and it's exciting when you spot something less obvious about a design. These details give us an insight into the character's life beyond the main plot, which makes them feel more rounded and real. I write down all the little things that make my family who they are, brainstorming ideas for props I can add to the final designs.

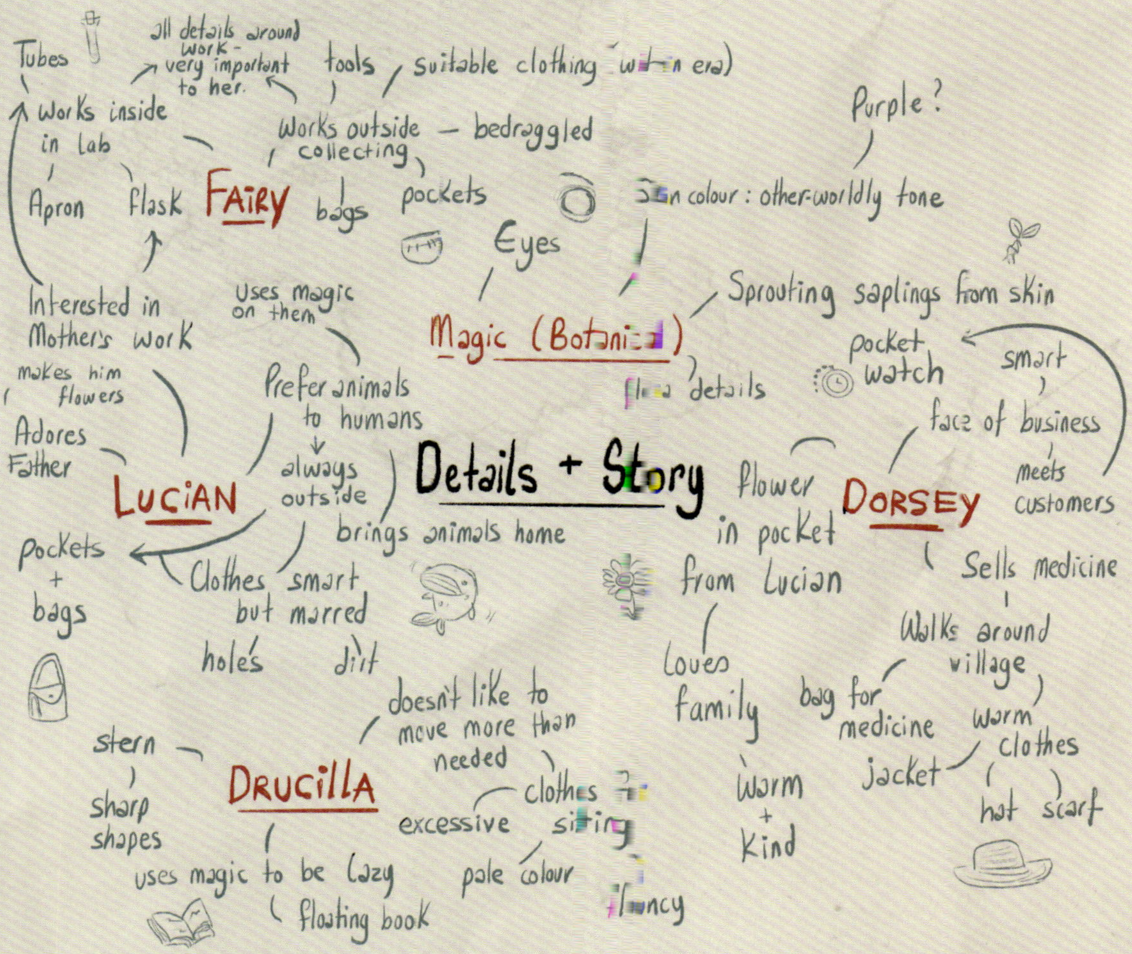

Details + Story

FAIRY
- Tubes
- all details around work – very important to her.
- tools
- suitable clothing (within era)
- Works inside in lab
- Works outside – bedraggled
- collecting
- Apron
- flask
- bags
- pockets
- Skin colour: other-worldly tone
- Eyes
- Purple?

Magic (Botanical)
- Sprouting saplings from skin
- flora details

LUCIAN
- Interested in Mother's work
- Uses magic on them
- makes him flowers
- Adores Father
- Prefer animals to humans
- always outside
- brings animals home
- Pockets + bags
- Clothes smart but marred
- holes
- dirt

DORSEY
- pocket watch
- smart
- face of business
- meets customers
- flower in pocket from Lucian
- Loves family
- Sells medicine
- Walks around village
- bag for medicine
- jacket
- warm clothes
- warm + kind
- hot scarf

DRUCILLA
- stern
- sharp shapes
- doesn't like to move more than needed
- clothes
- excessive sizing
- uses magic to be lazy
- pale colour
- fancy
- floating book

BRINGING THE STORY TO LIFE

Using your mind map as a reference, begin adding details to each design. Think about little things you wear or carry around with you that tell your story. Design is everything – jewellery with bold colours and abstract shapes will be worn by a very different character than a fine gold necklace. Make sure these details match your character's personality well and use them to tell the stories between characters, too. For instance, the buttons on the coats match between my family members to subtly show a link between them.

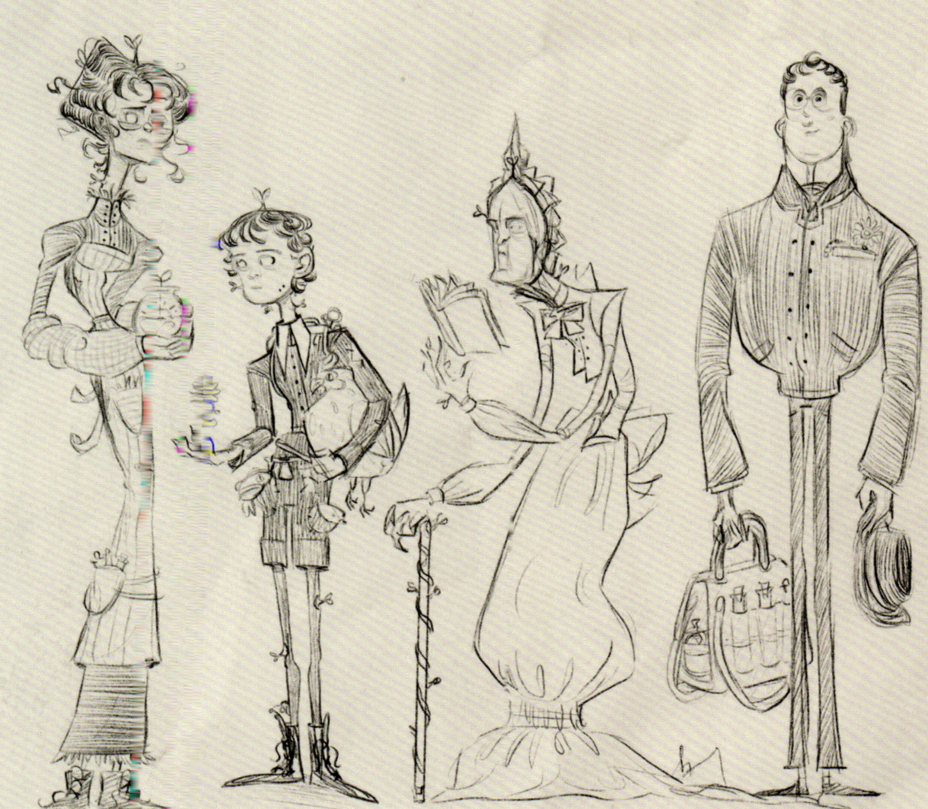

COLOURING CONNOTATIONS

Colours, just like shapes, have connotations which can be used to enhance your design and portray character. For each of your characters, select a couple of main colours which you think represent them well. Warm colours like yellows and oranges will emanate kindness and joy, red means anger or danger, blue implies sadness and peace, and so on. Try sticking to no more than two colours per character and try repeating a few throughout the family. Lucian takes his primary colours from his parents to show their familial connection.

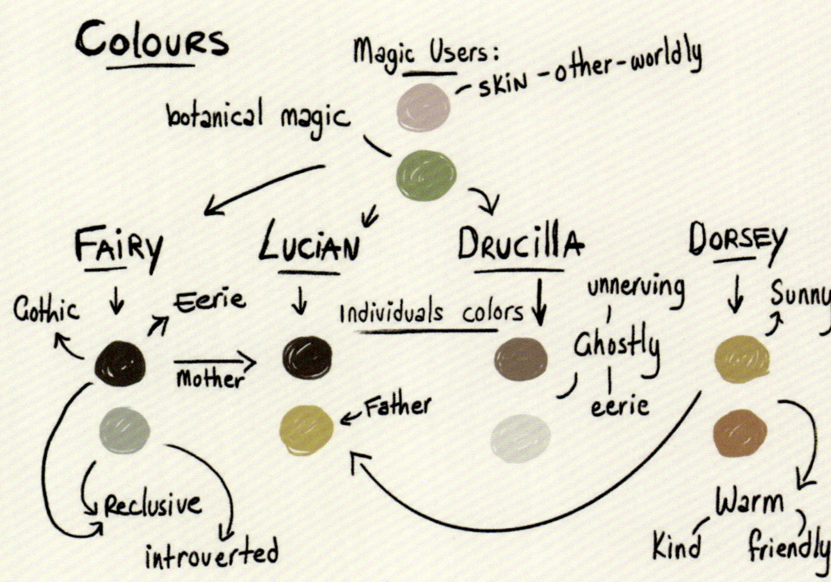

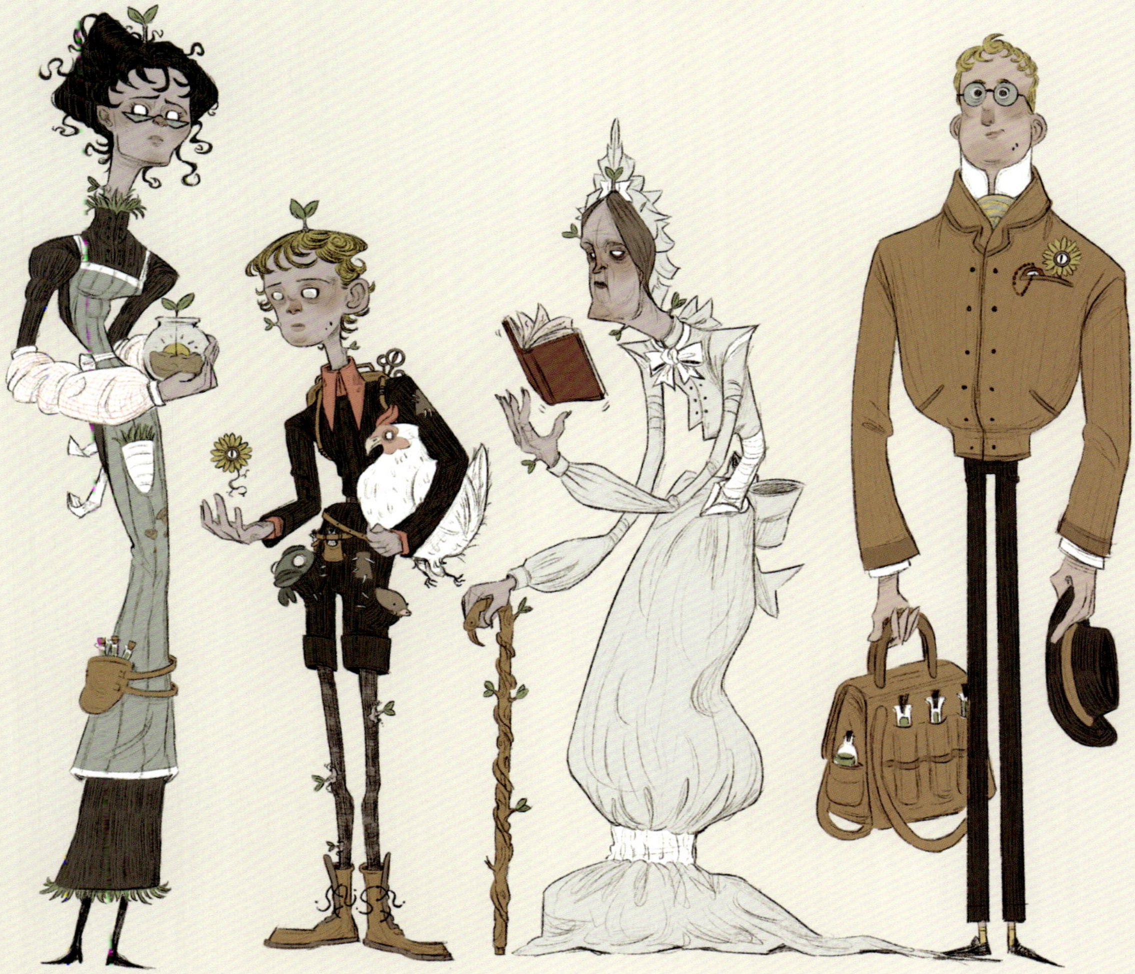

BRINGING IT ALL TOGETHER

Now, take all that you've learned about your characters along the way and combine it to bring them to life as fully formed designs. Stand them side by side to see how they work together – are they telling the story you wanted to tell? Do the characters feel cohesive, expressive, and unique in story, shape, pose, expression, and silhouette? This is a good time to go back and make changes if the characters don't look quite like the family you hoped they would.

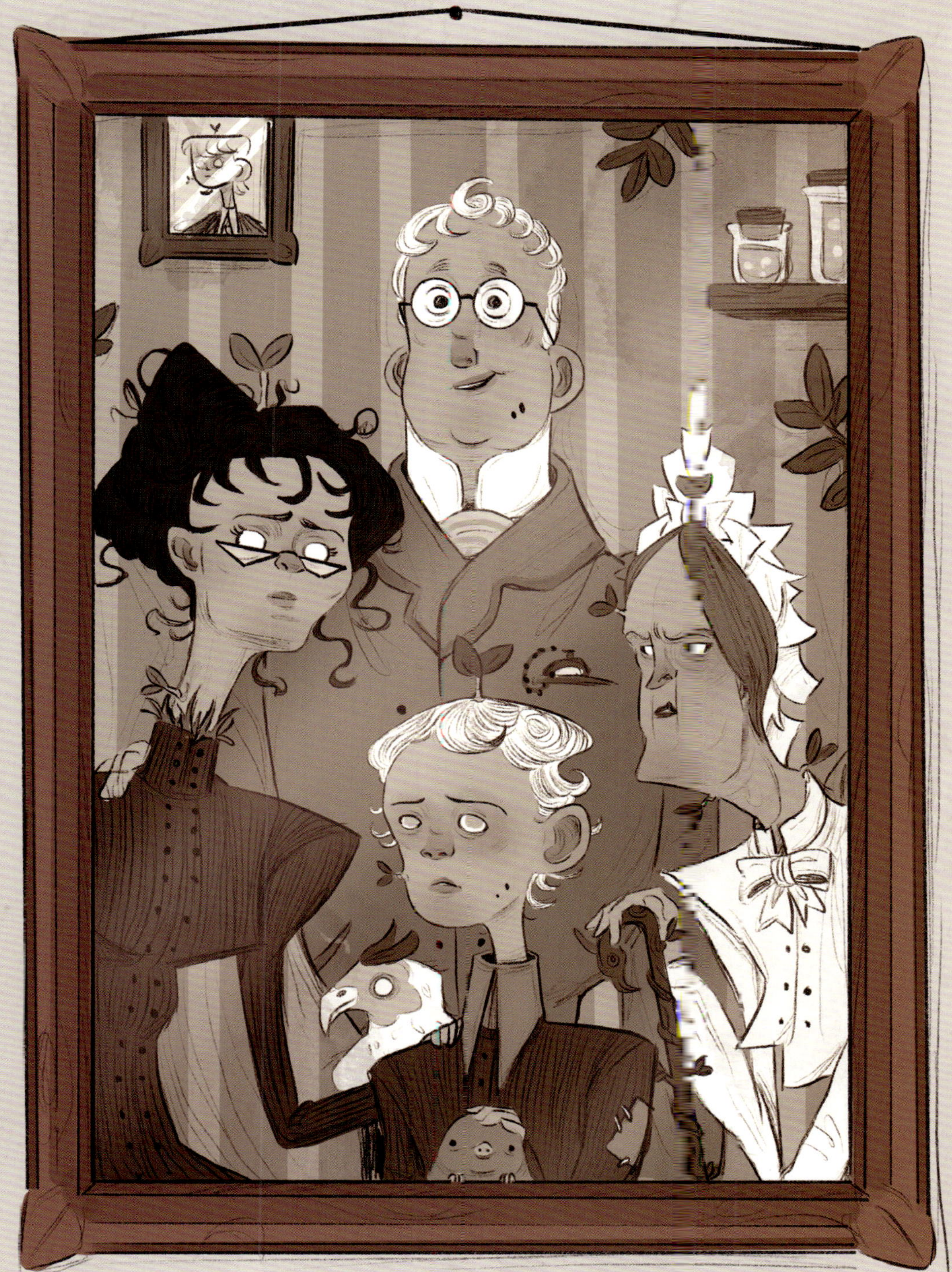

THE FAMILY PORTRAIT

Drawing your characters interacting with each other in interesting scenarios is not only fun, but a good test of how well the designs fit together. A family portrait is a nice way to create a condensed image that shows individual personalities alongside the family unit. Bringing my Victorian family together in a tight space allows me to show how they interact with one another, who smiles (and who doesn't), the dynamics between each family member, and also so much about their individual characters. Show your new family off to the world!

Final images © Corah Louise

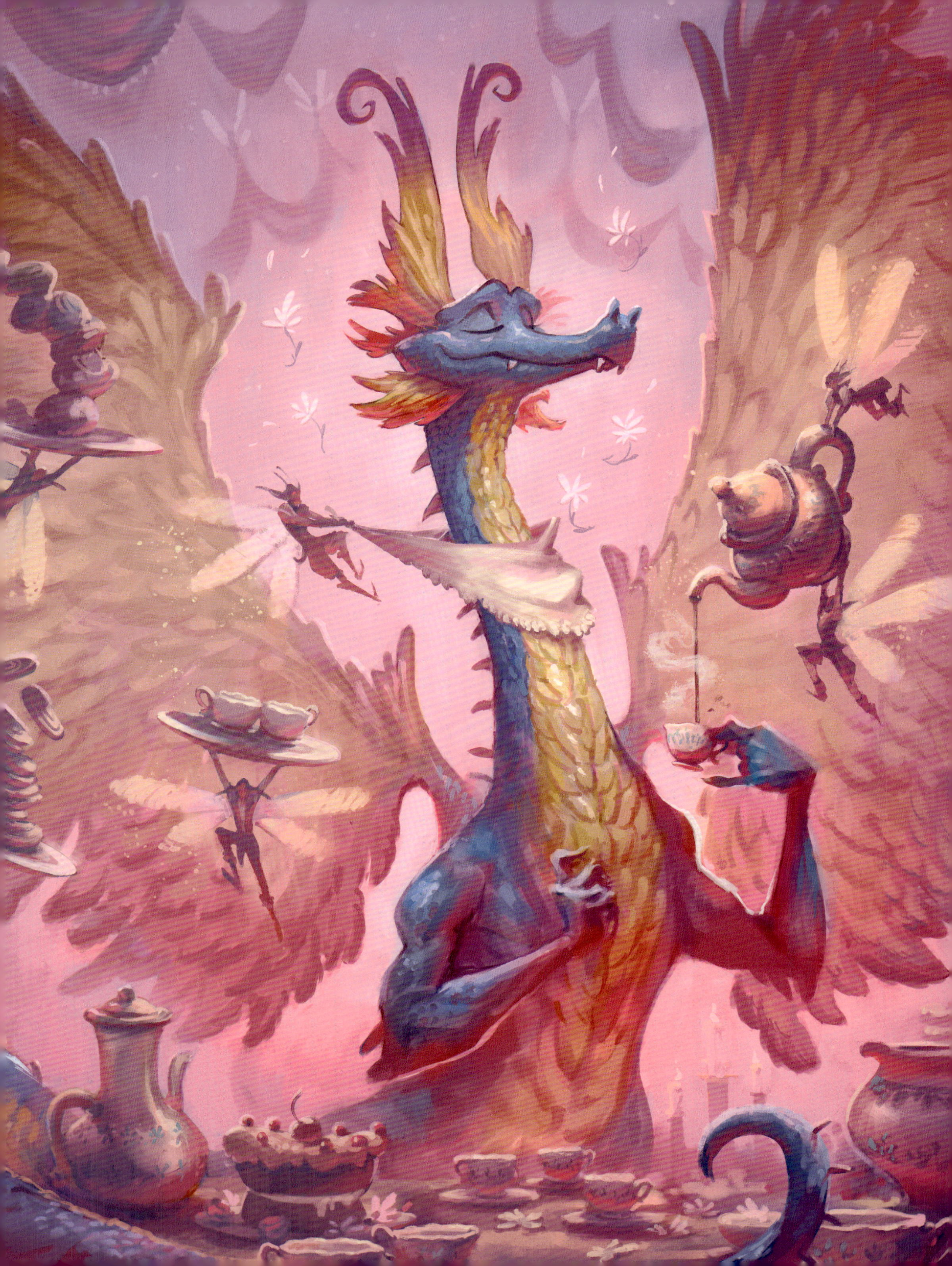

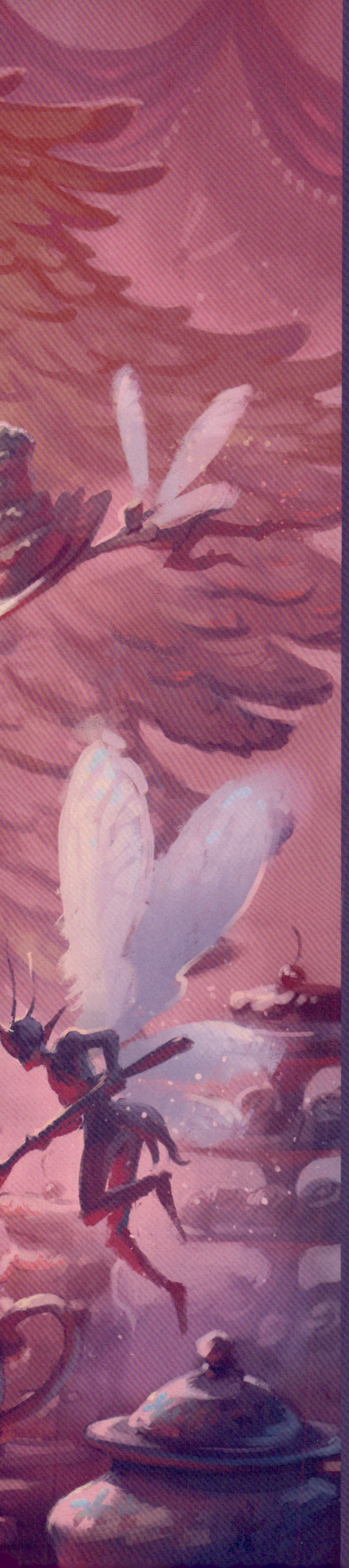

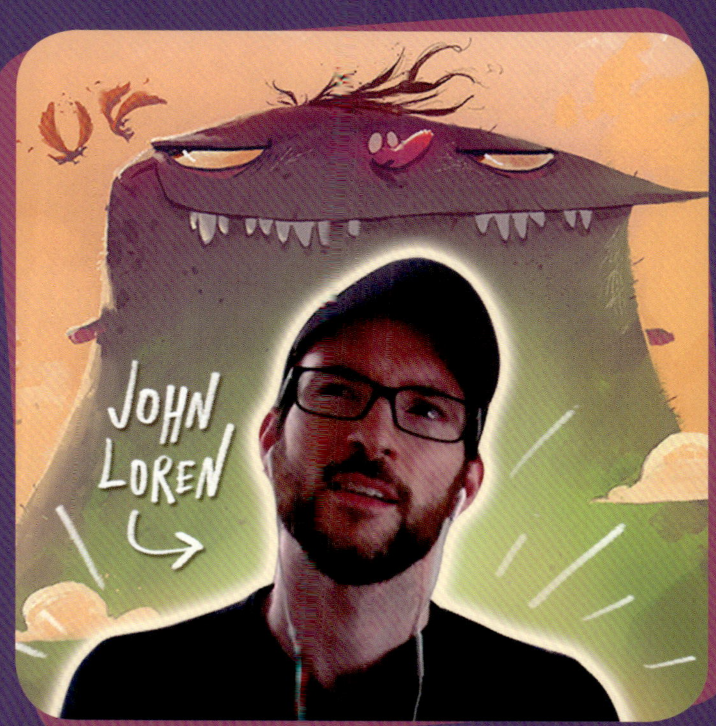

JOHN LOREN

John Loren is a freelance artist and author whose work has featured in countless video-game, animation, and illustration projects, most recently in Disney's *Lorcana*. We spoke to John about his route into the industry, working on children's books, and how to create fresh takes on beloved existing characters.

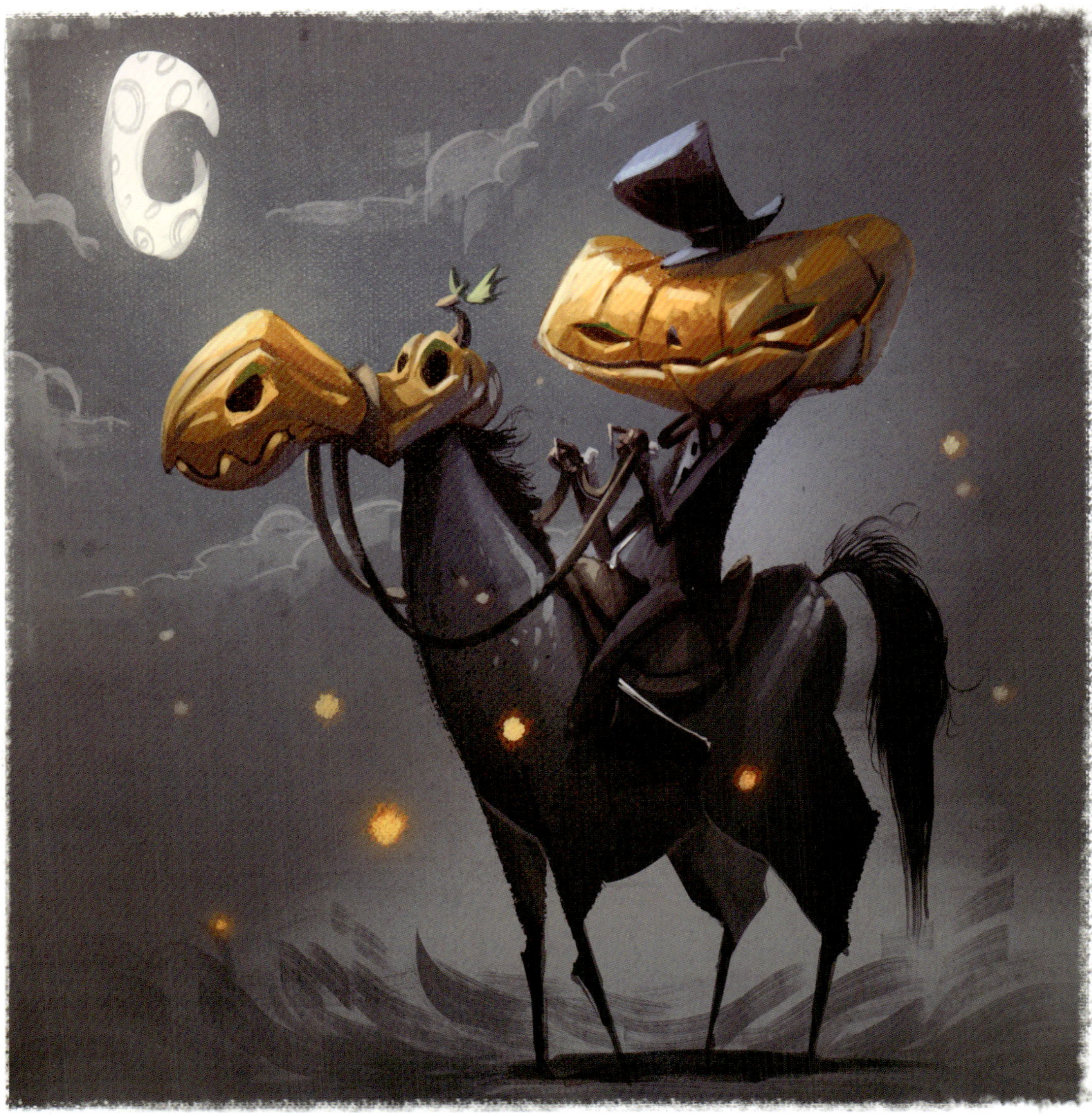

Hi John, thanks for talking to *CDQ!* Could you start by giving our readers an overview of your career so far?

I started my career as an animator, doing a mix of 2D, 3D, storyboarding, and compositing. I worked on video games, web games, animated shorts – anything that needed artists. About ten years ago, after a stretch of studio layoffs and closures, I decided to make the switch to freelance illustration and concept art. These days, I'm still a freelance artist, mostly for video games and trading-card games, and an author-illustrator of picture books. I think I'd still be quite happy as an animator if I'd stayed in that lane – I love animating! But I got too wrapped up with figuring out

How did you get started in the industry?

Initially I was working as an animator in assistant and apprentice positions at video-game and animation companies around Boston. I had a pretty generalist skill set that could fit into a lot of different media, so I was able to find consistent work. This exposed me to fantastic artists whose process and philosophies I was able to study. I became increasingly fascinated with digital painting, and I practised painting constantly before and after my day jobs. After a few years, I was starting to land freelance gigs with my 2D portfolio, and making painting my sole focus became feasible.

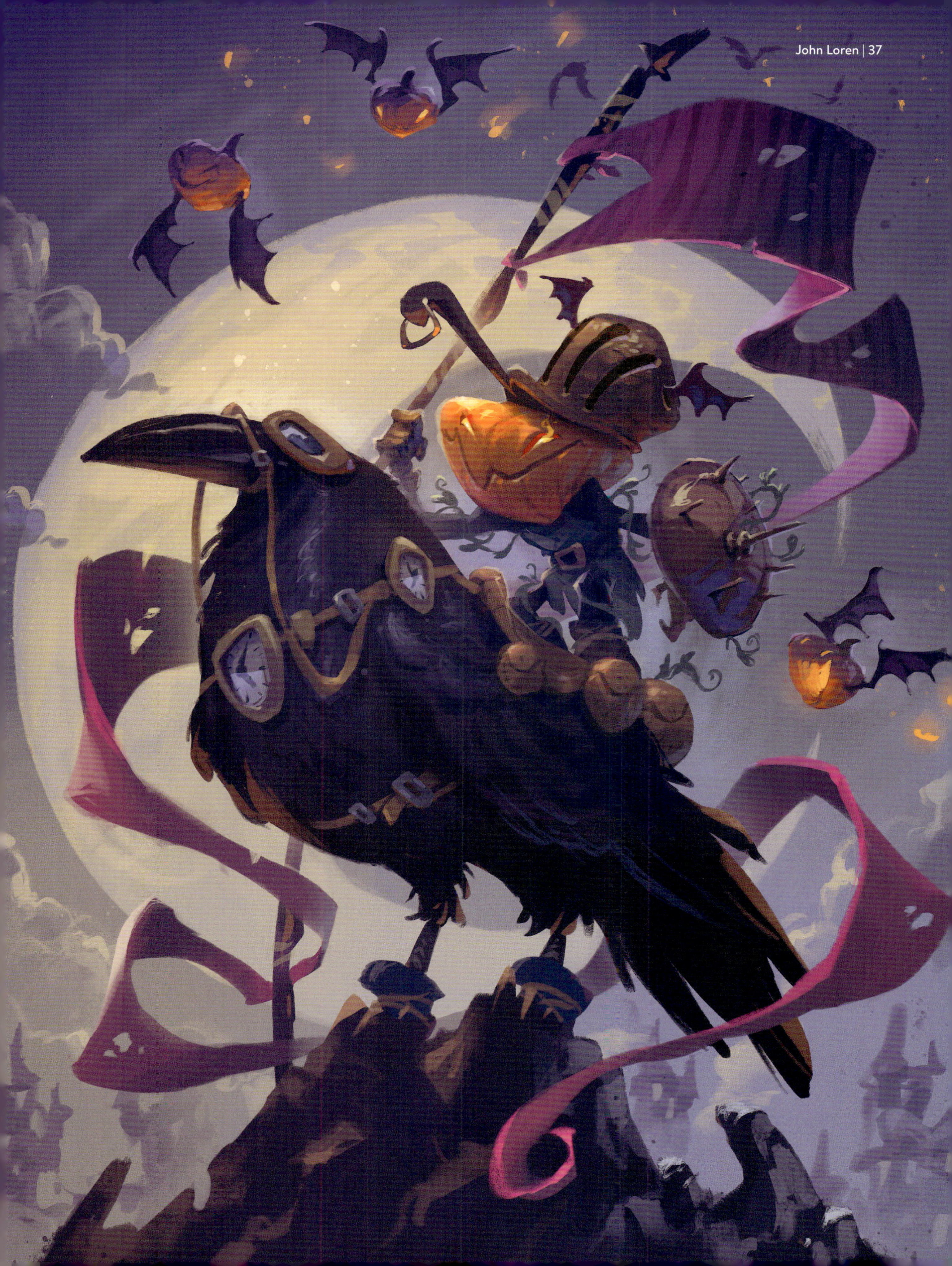

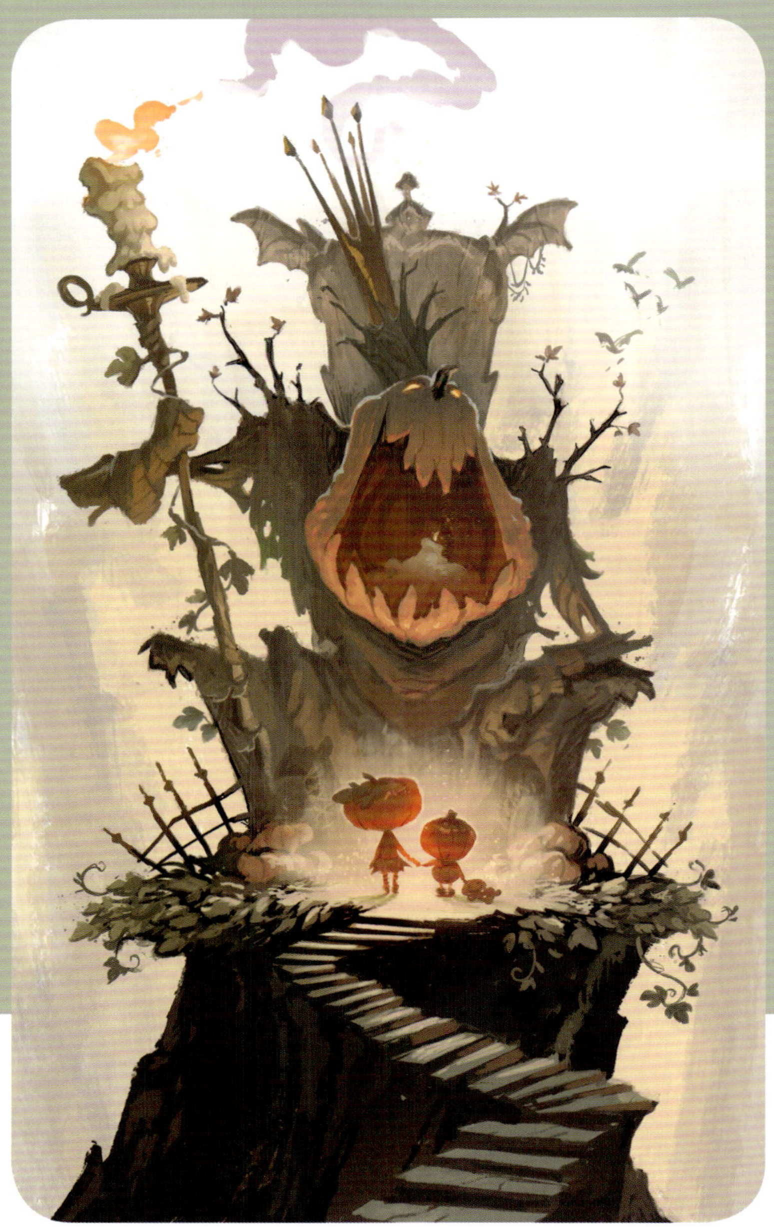

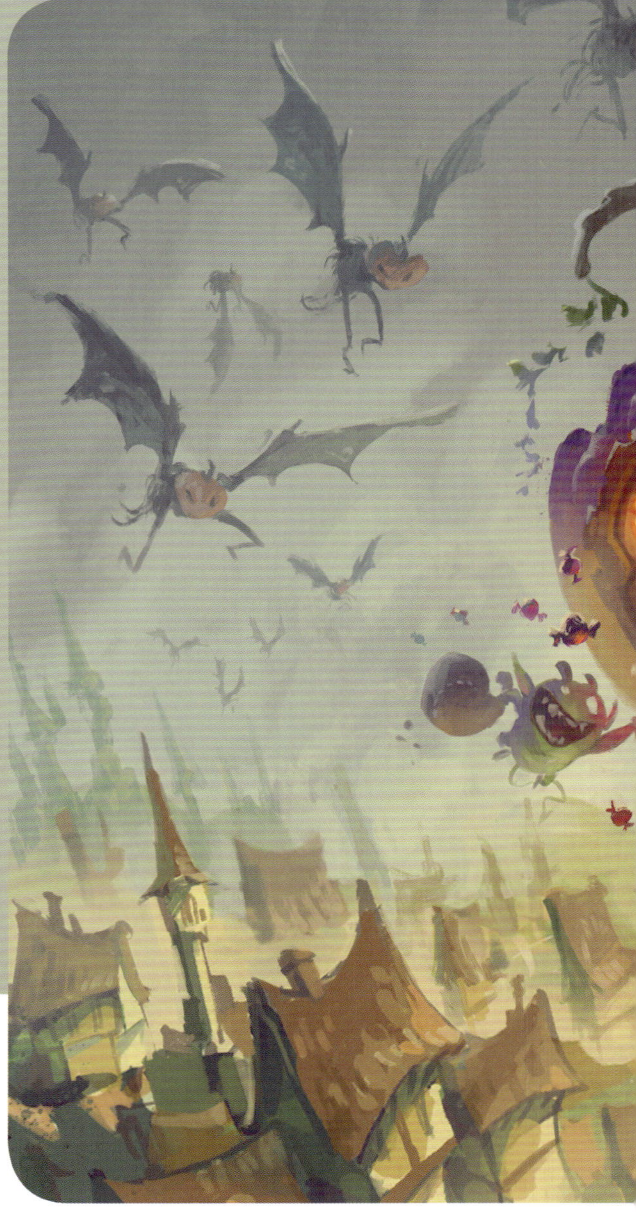

'I MOSTLY WANTED TO BE A NEWSPAPER COMIC-STRIP ARTIST'

Did you always want to be an artist?

Absolutely – as a kid, I mostly wanted to be a newspaper comic-strip artist. My parents had these big shelves of comics that I read and copied endlessly, and they supported my dream at every turn. They bought me art supplies and books on drawing and the business of being an artist. I was really fortunate to never experience scepticism. Eventually, I made my professional start in animation because it seemed like a fun, character-focused, and semi-reliable way to earn a living by drawing. Making my way back to a big comics project is still a goal of mine, but it's been a very circuitous route!

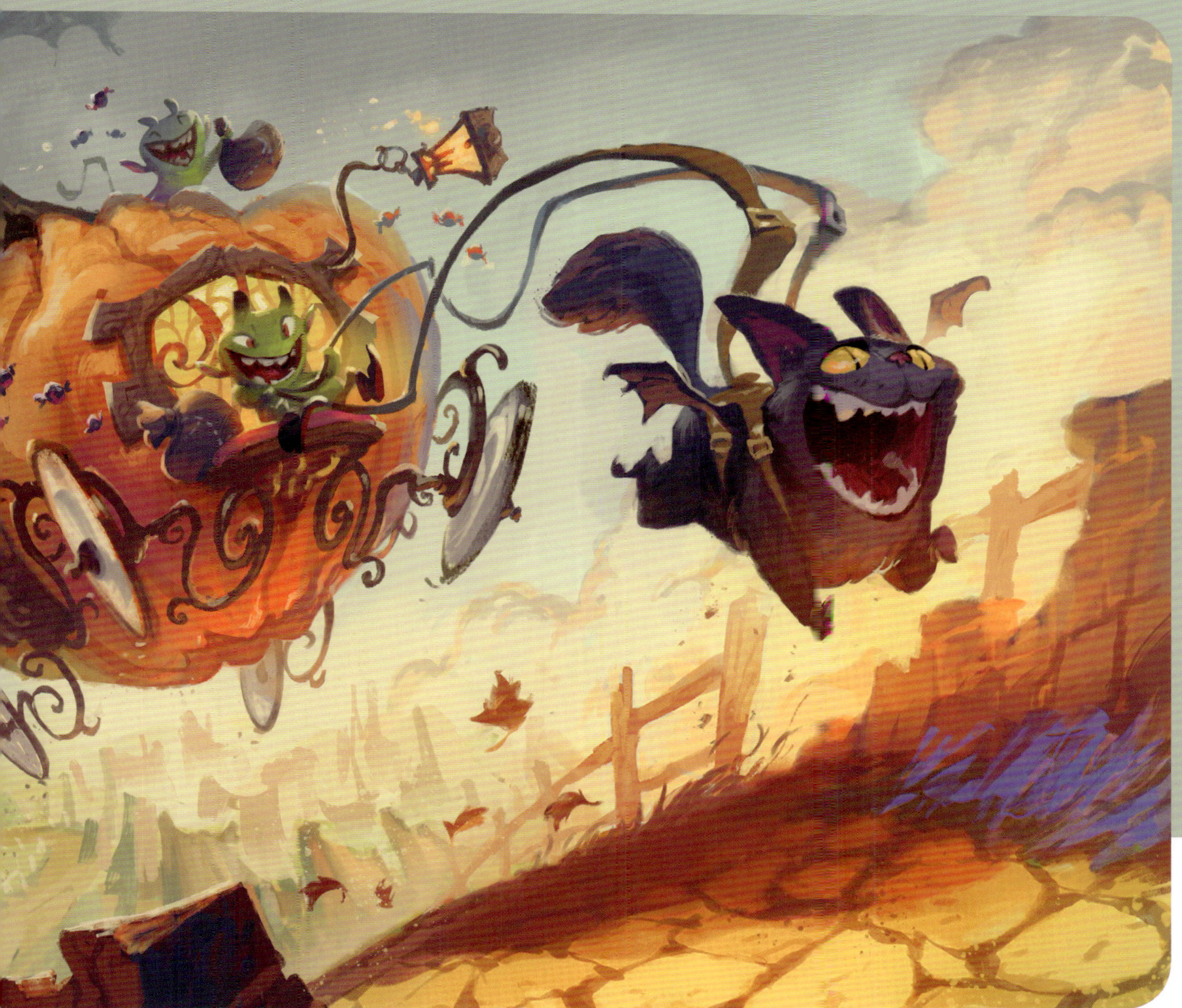

You've worked a lot with some extremely well-known IP. How do you go about finding an original take on iconic characters?

When I'm working with someone else's character, I try not to study the reference material too closely while I'm coming up with the gesture and initial sketch. I don't want to tighten up and lose any fun energy to the process of replicating what I'm seeing too closely. Then, once I have the action or the mood captured, I'll go back to studying the reference and adjust to make sure my proportions are on-model. Often, it's a matter of really nailing the iconic features, as we're used to seeing characters stretch and bend to fit the mood of the moment. The same goes for colour – as long as you honor those familiar local colour relationships, you can get really creative and produce an effective rendition that fits the moment, while still feeling true to the original.

Opposite page:
Halloween 2018

This page:
Halloween 2019

You've also written several books for children. How do you design characters differently when you have a young audience in mind?

Good question! When working on a book, I'm really concerned about communicating the humour and the action of the moment, so I often end up designing around the emotion of the character and the situation on the page. It's a much less filtered or cautious process, and sometimes it's just about finding the take that makes me laugh. All that said, I did the design work on my last book about five years ago (publication is a long process!) and even in that time I think my design approach has evolved.

There's such a great nostalgic quality to a lot of your fantasy art, for example your work for *Land of Eem*. Who are the influences and inspirations behind your art?

When it comes to fantasy art, Tony DiTerlizzi's work in the *Dungeons & Dragons Monstrous Manual* hooked me some time around 1993 – it was so whimsical, I adored it. The comic-book artists Skottie Young and Enrique Fernandez were two other huge influences that I discovered early in my career – they're just fearless with their shapes. The biggest direct influence on my work has to be my friend Nicholas Kole, because I've been able to observe his decision-making process first-hand on projects we've done together. We don't share many immediately visible shape or rendering choices, but I definitely attribute my compositional judgement to him.

These pages: I painted this scene for the *Land of Eem* RPG campaign settings book.

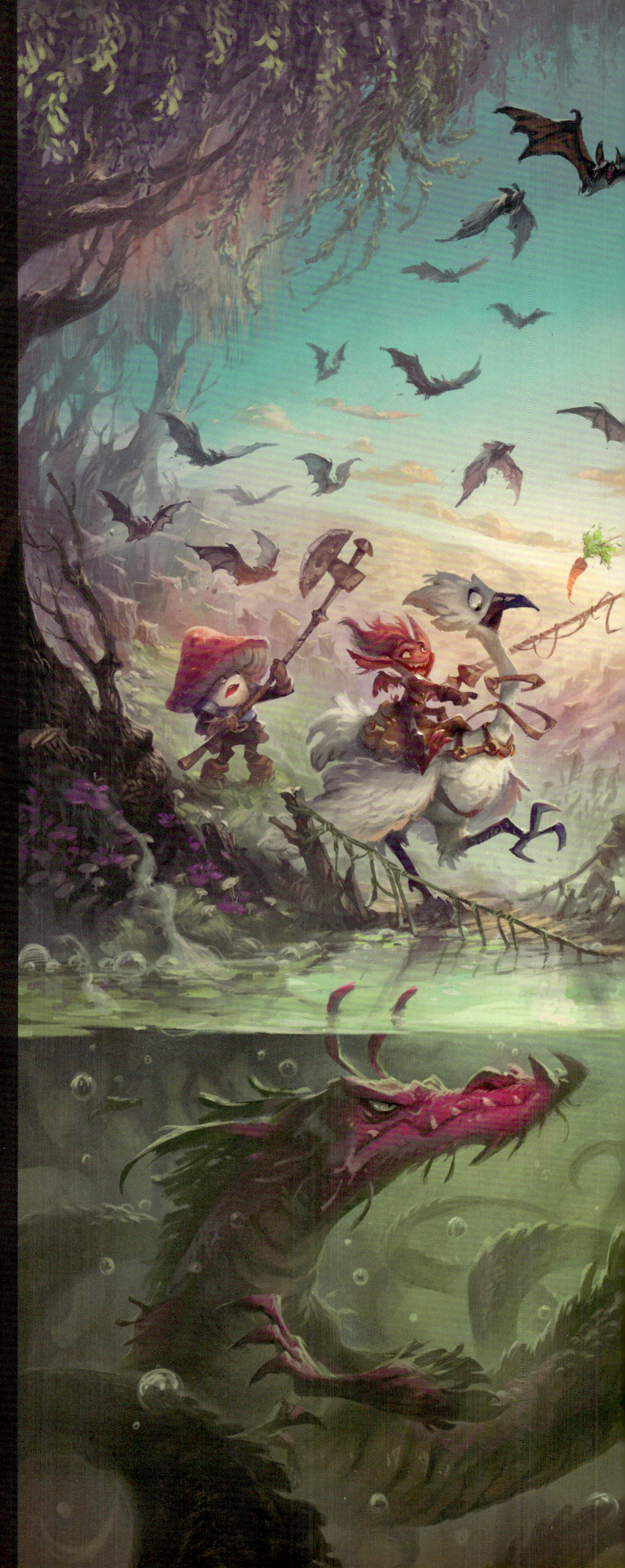

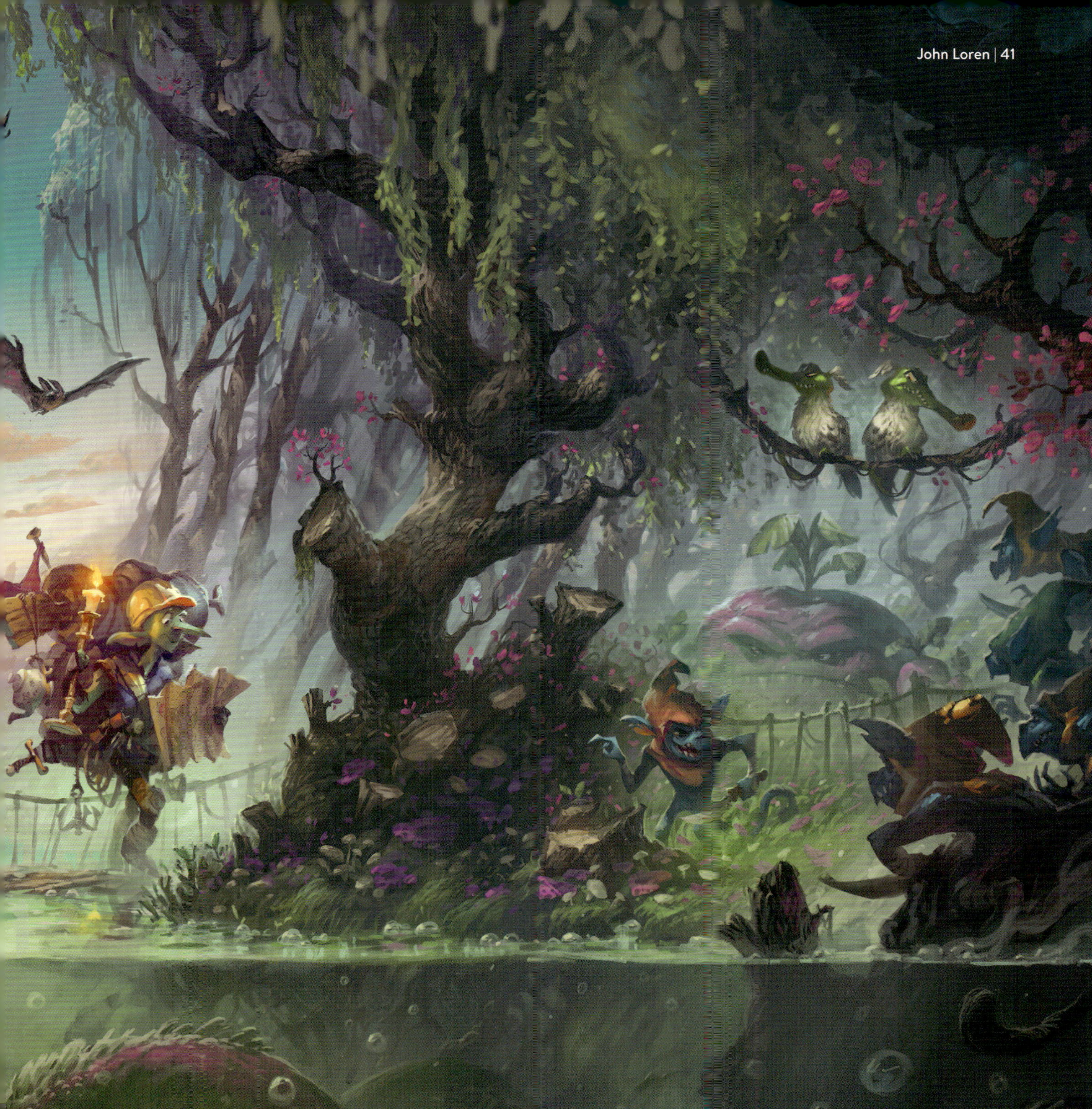
Land of Eem

This page (middle):
This was my first picture book, published in 2020. The story of a kid whose costume is ruined by cold-weather gear was partly inspired by many chilly Halloweens in Maine

This page (bottom):
This was my second picture book, published in 2021. Following in the footsteps of Jekyll & Hyde, Hugo transforms himself into a gargantuan bean-monster, to disastrous effect.

Opposite page:
An adventuring party, created just for fun!

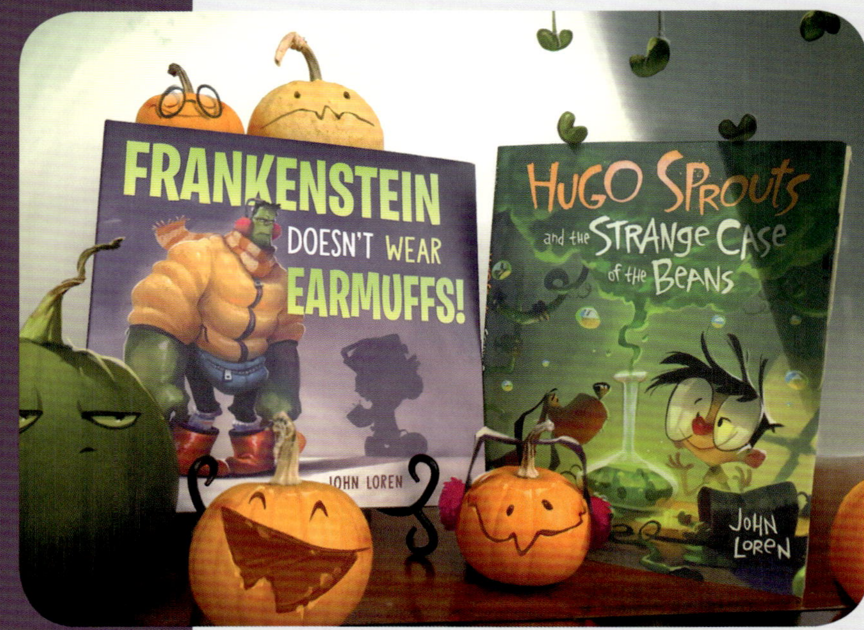

Frankenstein Doesn't Wear Earmuffs and *Hugo Sprouts and the Strange Case of the Beans* appear courtesy of HarperCollins

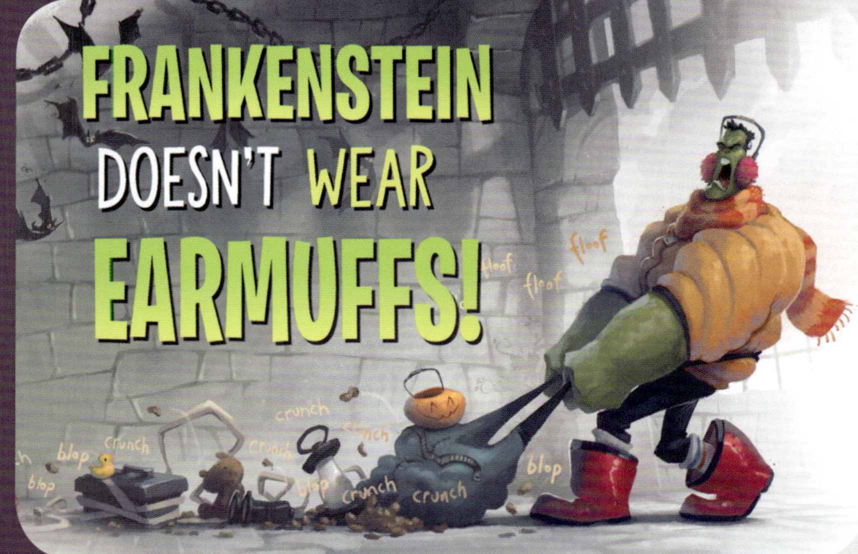

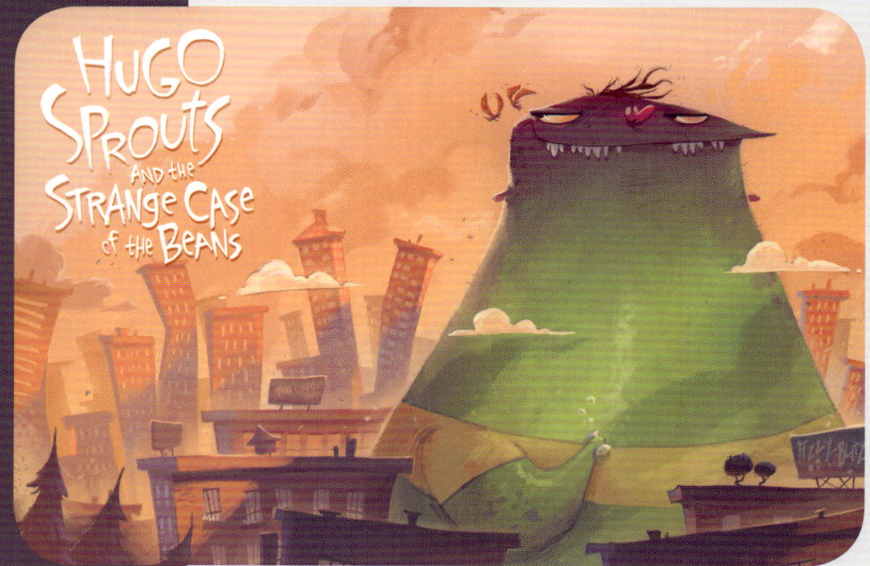

What would you say are the major differences between working in video games versus your work for books?

The biggest difference is probably the client mindset. On a video game there's a lot of interpretation of feedback and searching for solutions to problems and requests that have been posed by the client. They're the one in charge of the goal. But when you're illustrating a story you've written, you've posed the questions yourself, and then you have to find your own way to answer them. The editor and publishing art team are helping you get there, but it's not their job to set a target. If as an artist you're used to responding to small assignments, I think it can take some practice to step back and assess the impact of the whole project at once. That's something I've really tried to work on.

What's the number one piece of advice you'd give to artists just starting out in character design?

There's too many to choose – so here's everything! Be prepared for some rejection, everyone goes through it especially when starting out. A career is a long road to travel and you can make incredible progress in just a few years if you stay committed to learning, even when you already consider yourself a professional. Don't think about innate talent, just focus on the joy of drawing and the challenges of problem solving that are in front of you. Lean into the story clues, the gesture, and the scenarios your characters might live out in your imagination. They're all fuel for a cohesive and compelling final result.

Thanks for your time, John. Finally, what are you currently working on?

You can see my newest stuff coming up in the *Lorcana* trading-card game, and in my next book – when I've finally finished it!

PIRATIN' PALS

PAUL JOSEPH NICHOLSON

In this tutorial, we're going to cover how you can express personality in your character designs and breathe life into them. I've taken the concept of the hare and tortoise, as these two animals can represent two very different character archetypes and are a fun way for a character designer to explore personality in their designs. I'll begin with showing you how to build your character's temperament by brainstorming possible character traits, before moving on to look at how we can use their poses, expressions, and clothing designs to showcase their personality.

GET WRITING

A good start is to write down a list of personality traits. Try asking interesting questions of your characters – this is a great way to unlock surprising quirks, which will help convey more depth and personality to the audience.

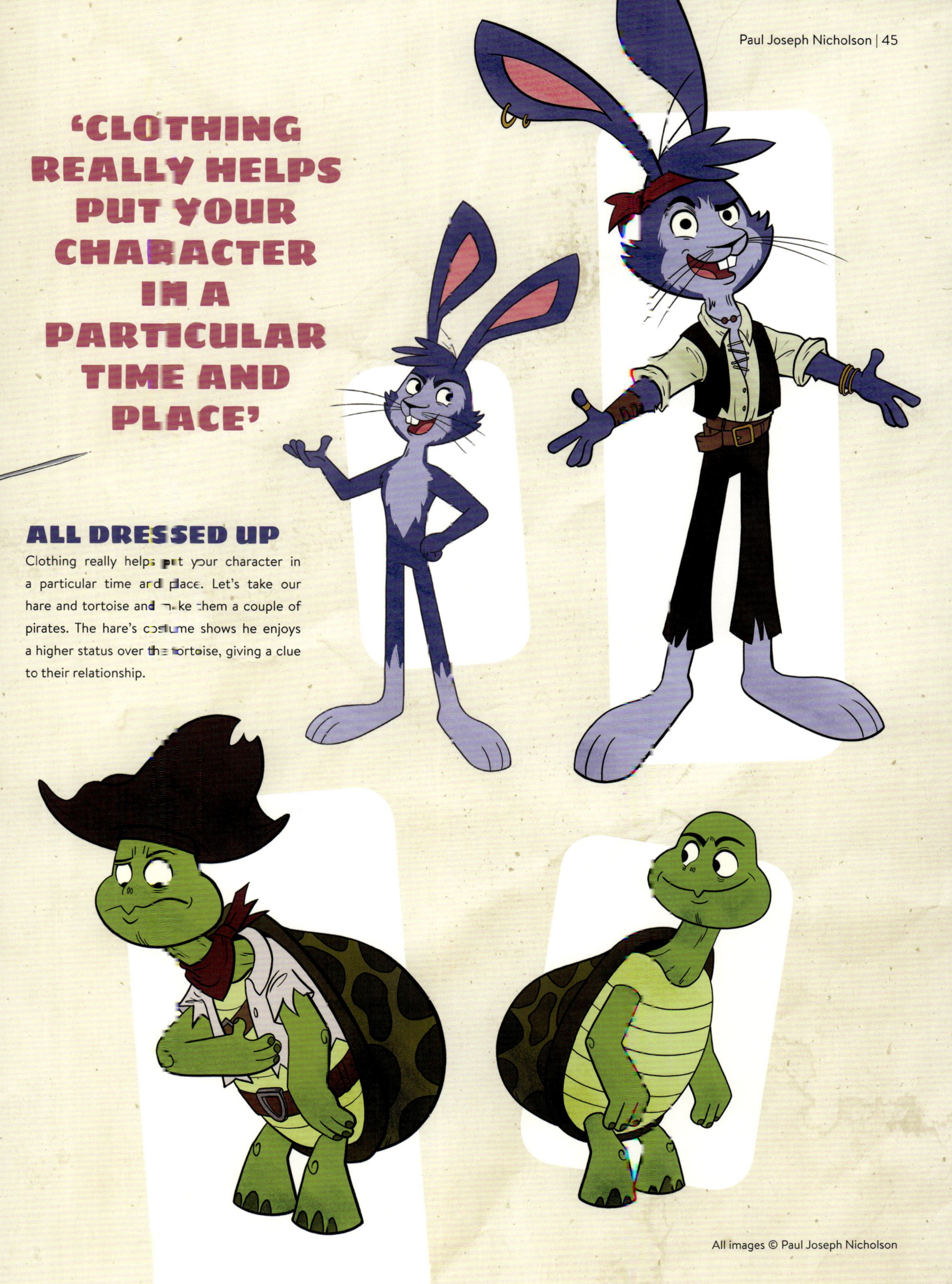

'CLOTHING REALLY HELPS PUT YOUR CHARACTER IN A PARTICULAR TIME AND PLACE'

ALL DRESSED UP

Clothing really helps put your character in a particular time and place. Let's take our hare and tortoise and make them a couple of pirates. The hare's costume shows he enjoys a higher status over the tortoise, giving a clue to their relationship.

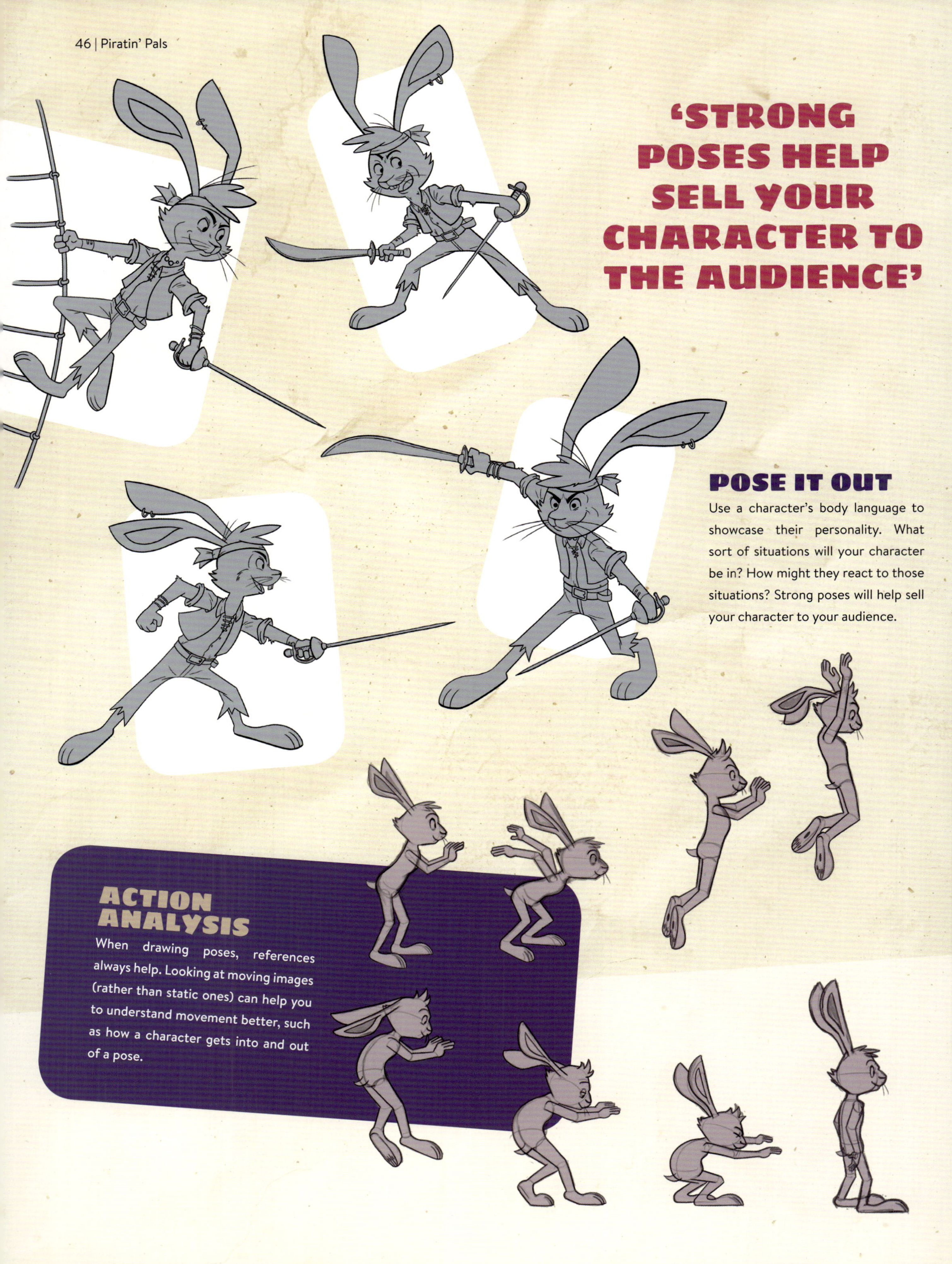

'STRONG POSES HELP SELL YOUR CHARACTER TO THE AUDIENCE'

POSE IT OUT

Use a character's body language to showcase their personality. What sort of situations will your character be in? How might they react to those situations? Strong poses will help sell your character to your audience.

ACTION ANALYSIS

When drawing poses, references always help. Looking at moving images (rather than static ones) can help you to understand movement better, such as how a character gets into and out of a pose.

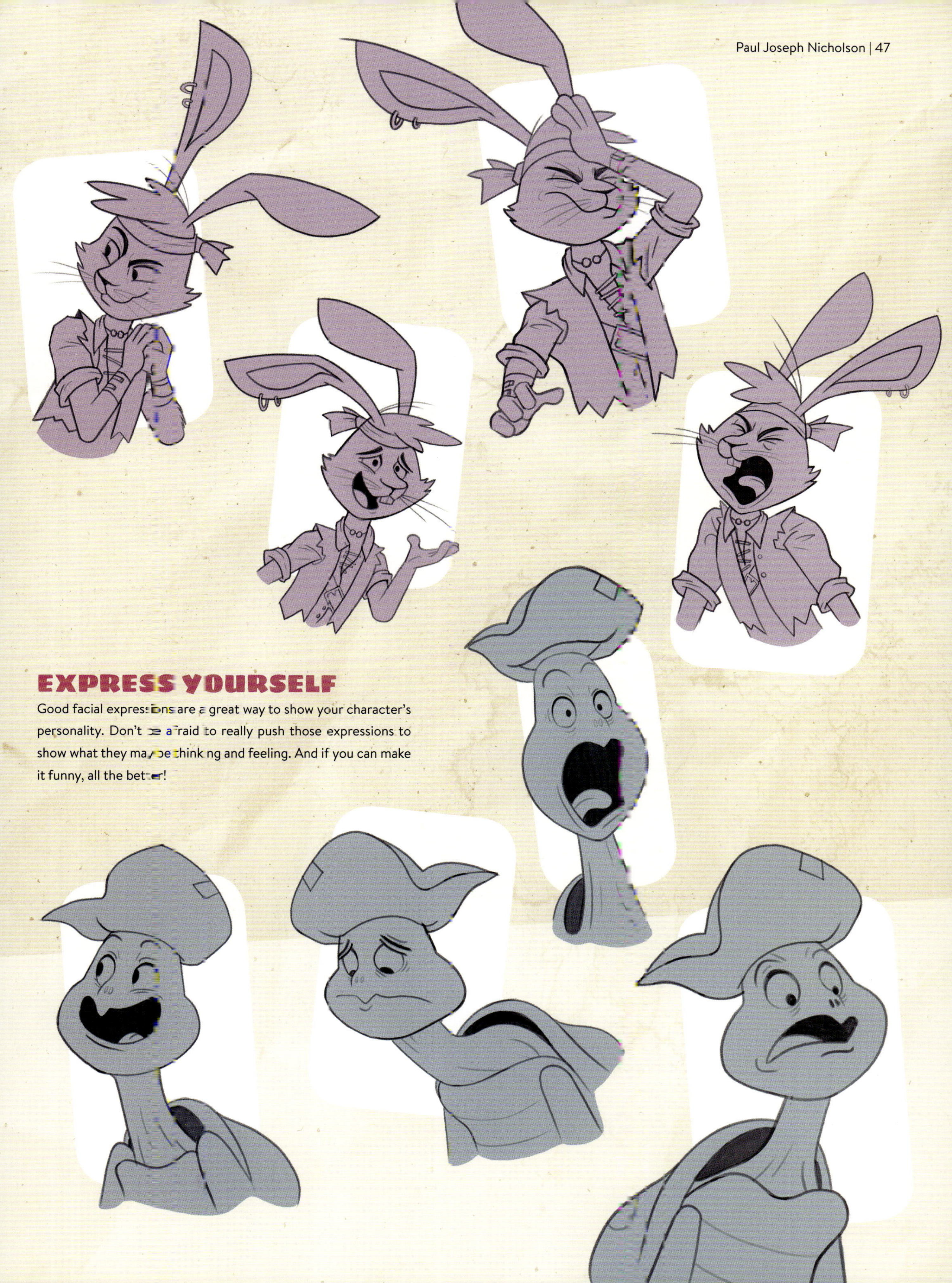

EXPRESS YOURSELF

Good facial expressions are a great way to show your character's personality. Don't be afraid to really push those expressions to show what they may be thinking and feeling. And if you can make it funny, all the better!

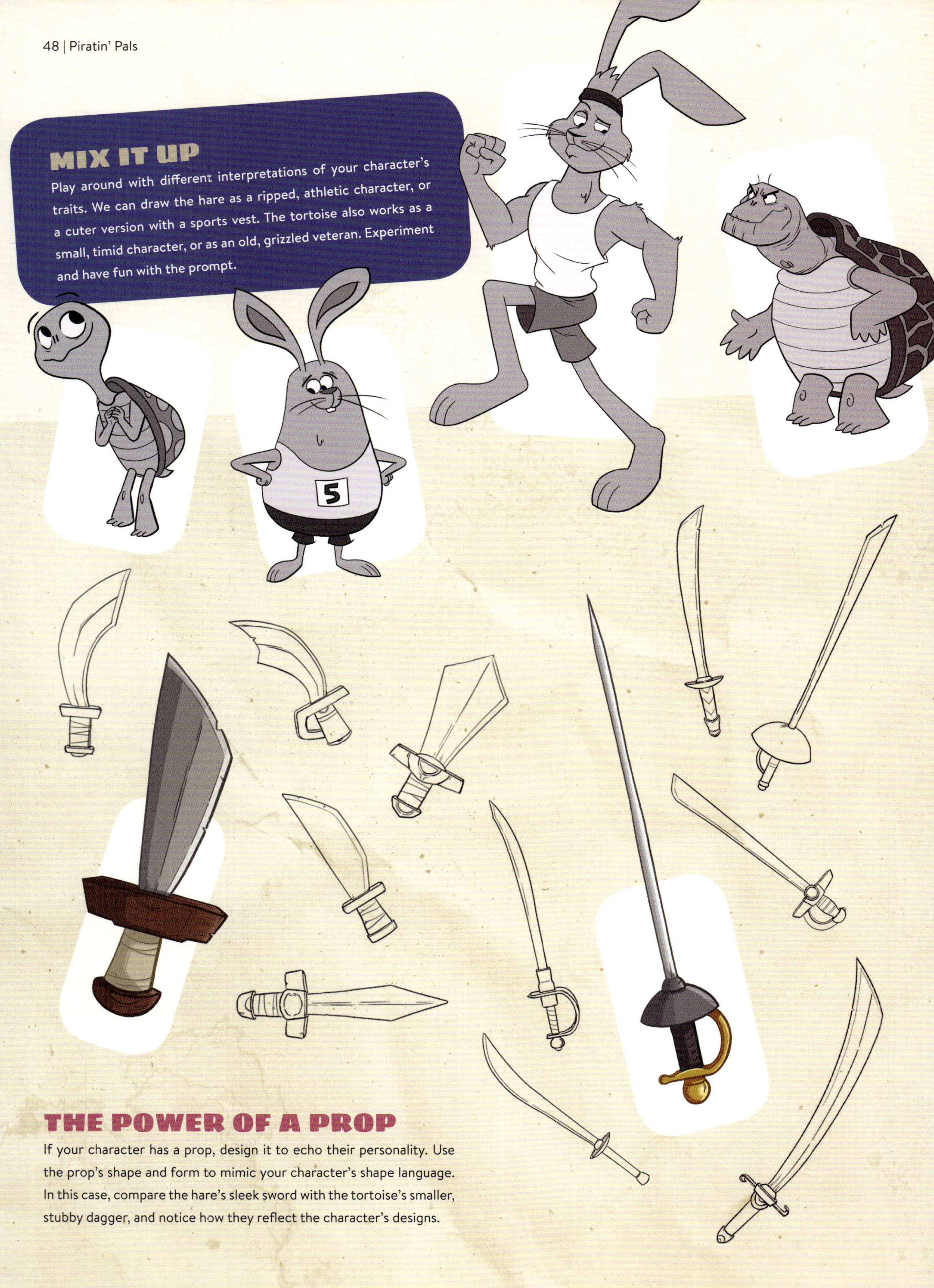

MIX IT UP

Play around with different interpretations of your character's traits. We can draw the hare as a ripped, athletic character, or a cuter version with a sports vest. The tortoise also works as a small, timid character, or as an old, grizzled veteran. Experiment and have fun with the prompt.

THE POWER OF A PROP

If your character has a prop, design it to echo their personality. Use the prop's shape and form to mimic your character's shape language. In this case, compare the hare's sleek sword with the tortoise's smaller, stubby dagger, and notice how they reflect the character's designs.

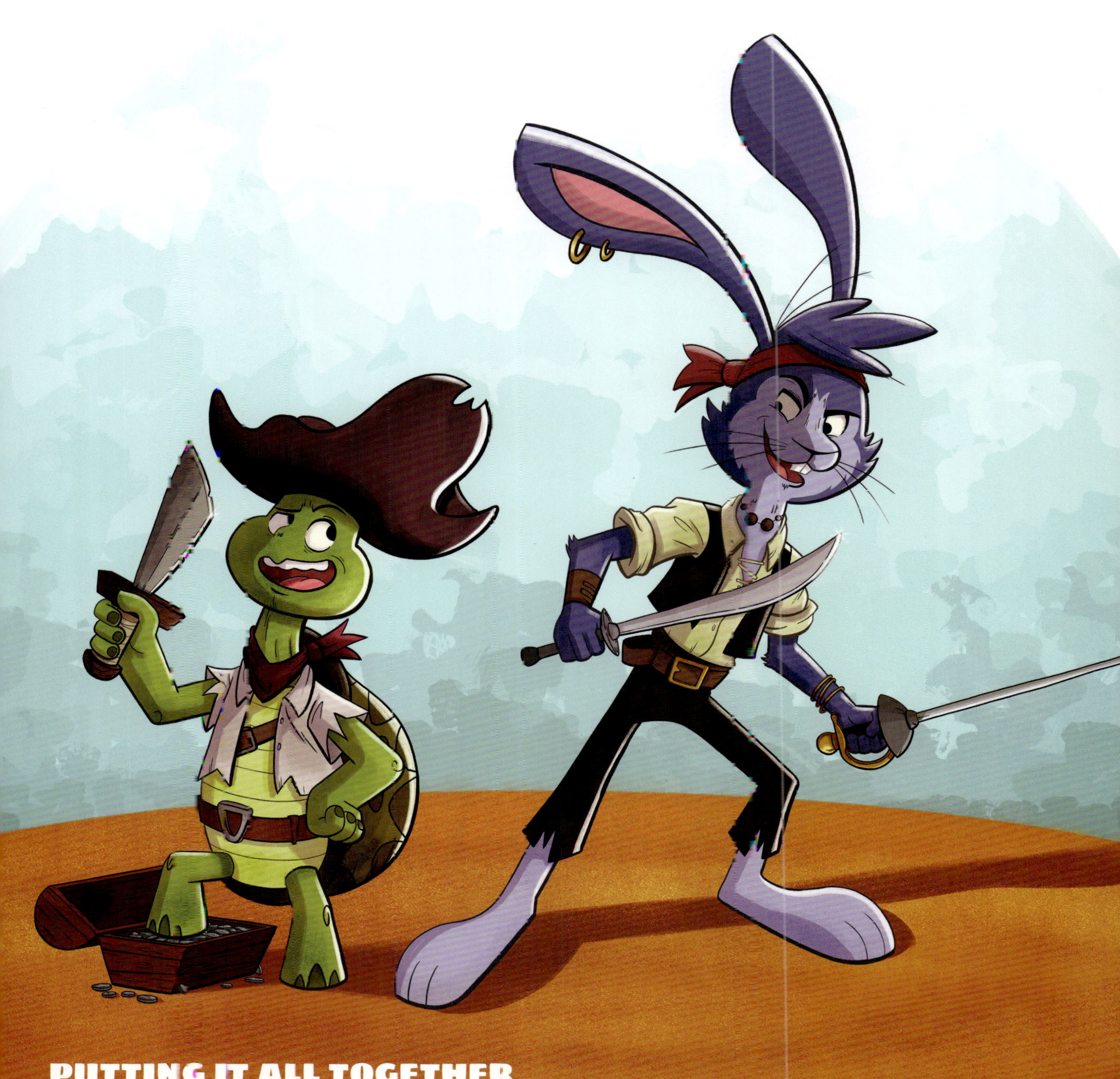

PUTTING IT ALL TOGETHER

Finally, we can put everything we've covered in this tutorial together to create two characters that convey genuine personality in their poses, expressions, and clothing. Our hare and tortoise are ready to set sail and plunder on the high seas!

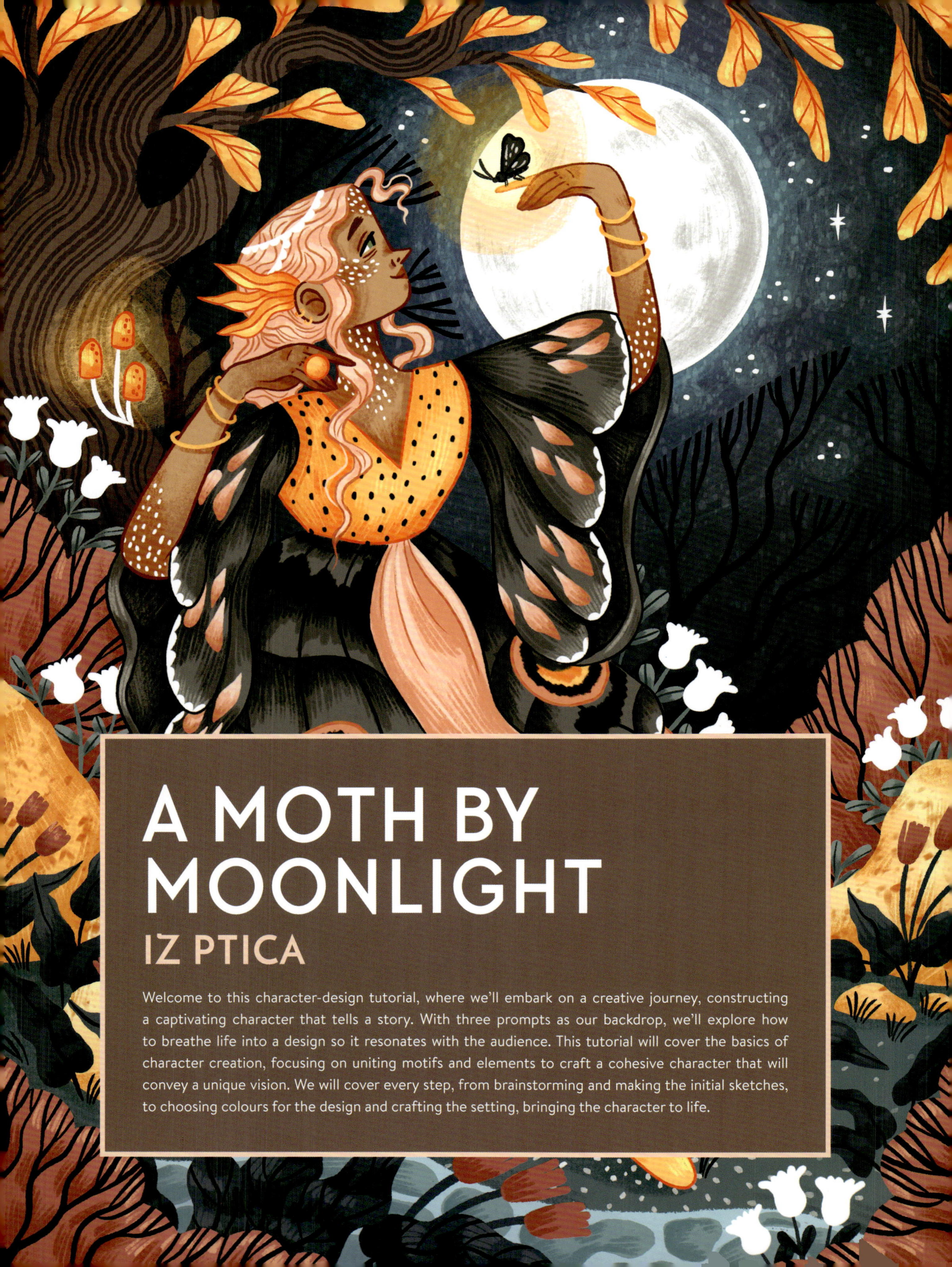

A MOTH BY MOONLIGHT

IZ PTICA

Welcome to this character-design tutorial, where we'll embark on a creative journey, constructing a captivating character that tells a story. With three prompts as our backdrop, we'll explore how to breathe life into a design so it resonates with the audience. This tutorial will cover the basics of character creation, focusing on uniting motifs and elements to craft a cohesive character that will convey a unique vision. We will cover every step, from brainstorming and making the initial sketches, to choosing colours for the design and crafting the setting, bringing the character to life.

BEYOND THE PROMPTS

Here are the three prompts we'll be working with: nature, party, and tiny. When working with such broad concepts, there's an opportunity to incorporate your unique vision into a character. Uncover the motifs hidden within the prompts through brainstorming and let your imagination flow naturally as inspiration guides you. While doing so, remember to stay aligned with the main prompts, using them to guide your thoughts. Think of this process as moving from the outside in, resulting in a character that feels more unique and authentic. The more specific we get, the more efficient we are in creating life-like characters that tell unique and memorable stories.

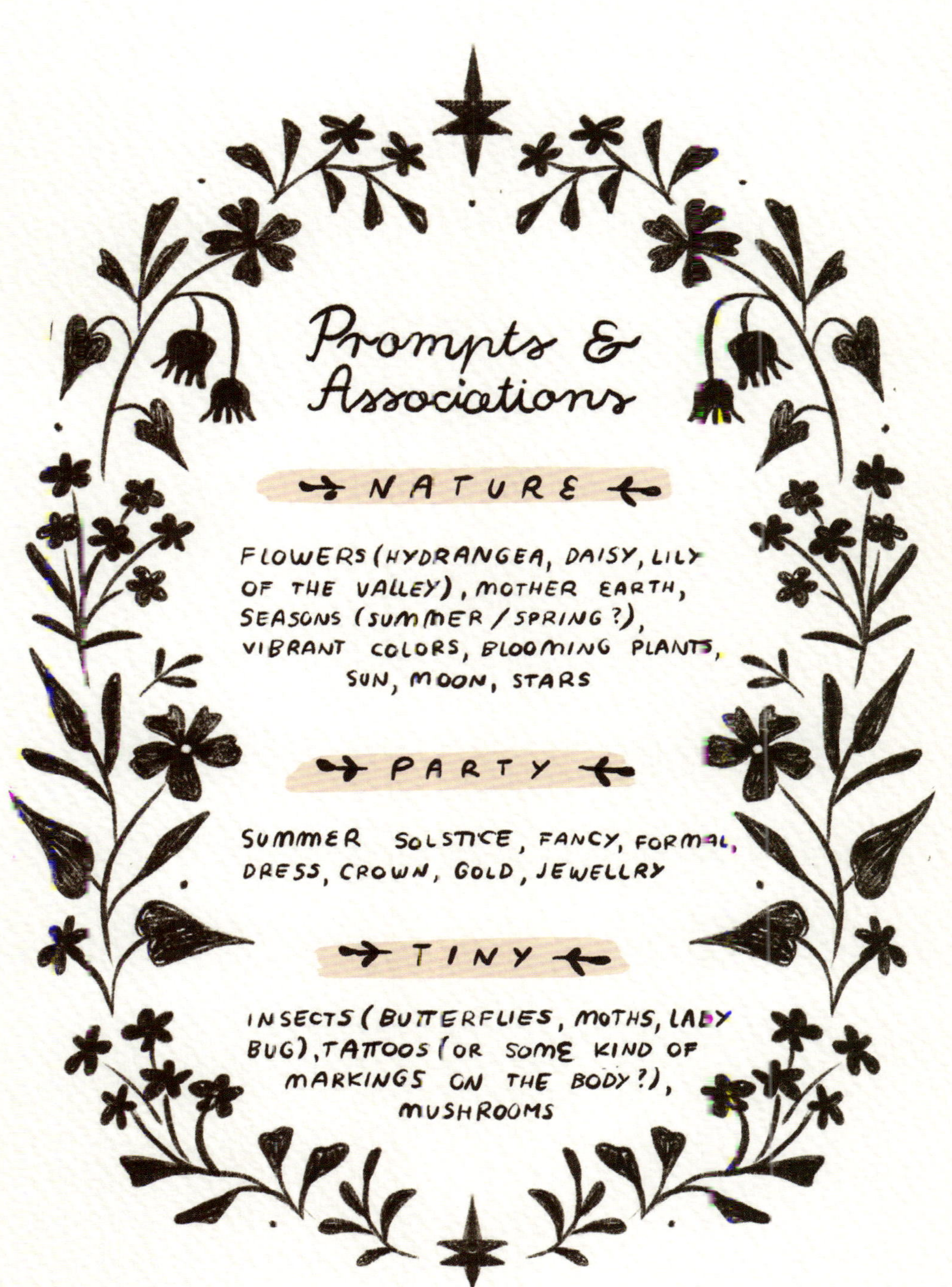

Final image © Kaja Kajfež

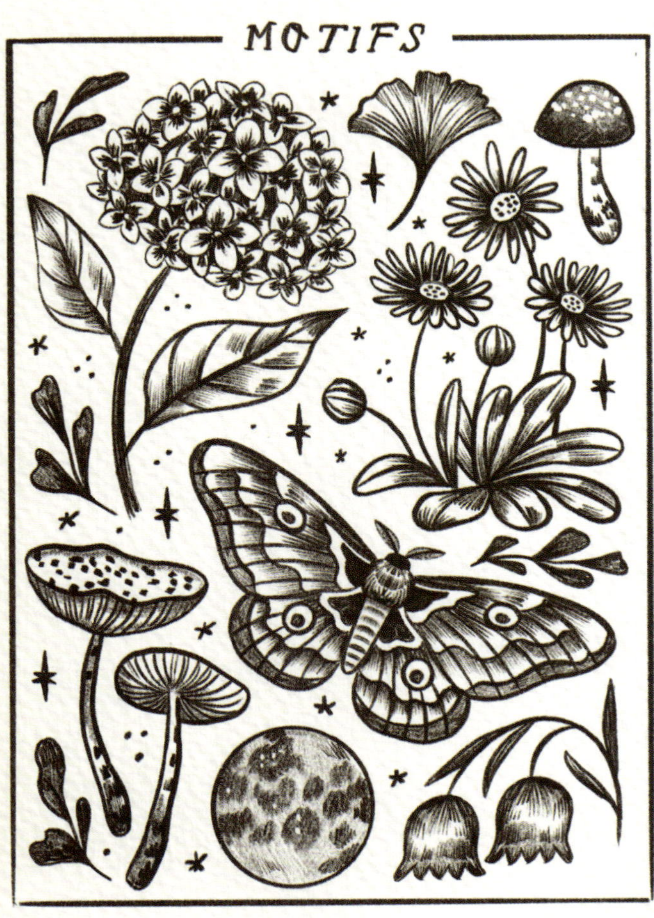

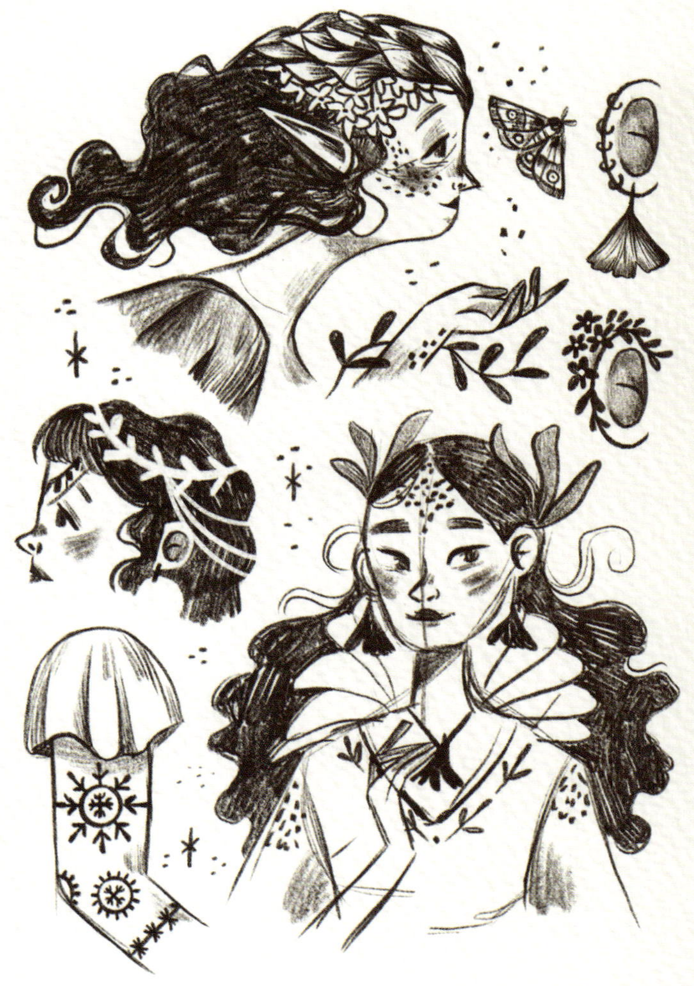

'NOTICE WHAT VISUALLY CAPTIVATES YOU AND IMAGINE HOW THESE ELEMENTS CAN SHAPE YOUR CHARACTER'S ESSENCE'

MOTIF MASH-UP MAGIC

Once you've delved into the motifs through brainstorming, bring them to life through sketches. Notice what visually captivates you and imagine how these elements can shape your character's essence. I find myself drawn to the moth, envisioning it as a starting point for my character development. However, don't forget that the other motifs can serve as a reference, waiting to be incorporated into your design. See where visually developing your ideas will take you – you may find connections you can intertwine to form a good basis for building your own original character.

THE INITIAL SKETCHES

Next, we can begin to play with our ideas so far and incorporate them into an actual character. Try starting with the face – let it reflect the motifs and examine how you can combine your ideas. Feel free to get loose here as there is no right or wrong at this stage. Playfulness can easily take you in all sorts of different directions, but remember to keep returning to the original prompt. Gradually, a story and a character should slowly start to emerge. Take what resonates with you from this process and leave the rest behind.

EXPLORING DIFFERENT DIRECTIONS

During this stage, your aim is to go deeper, working on variations based on the loose sketches from the previous step and developing them further. Feel free to continue experimenting with new elements, but aim to provide them with clearer direction and definition. Focus on one main motif and use a top-to-bottom approach to develop your character. I like to refer to this as the character's defining characteristic, although a single character can have many. Start with just the one and you can always expand upon it later. Now, try out different variants based on the defining characteristic you identified during the brainstorming phase. You now have a more refined foundation for your character. I work on three separate ideas for my character from my motifs: the sun, the moth, and the hydrangea.

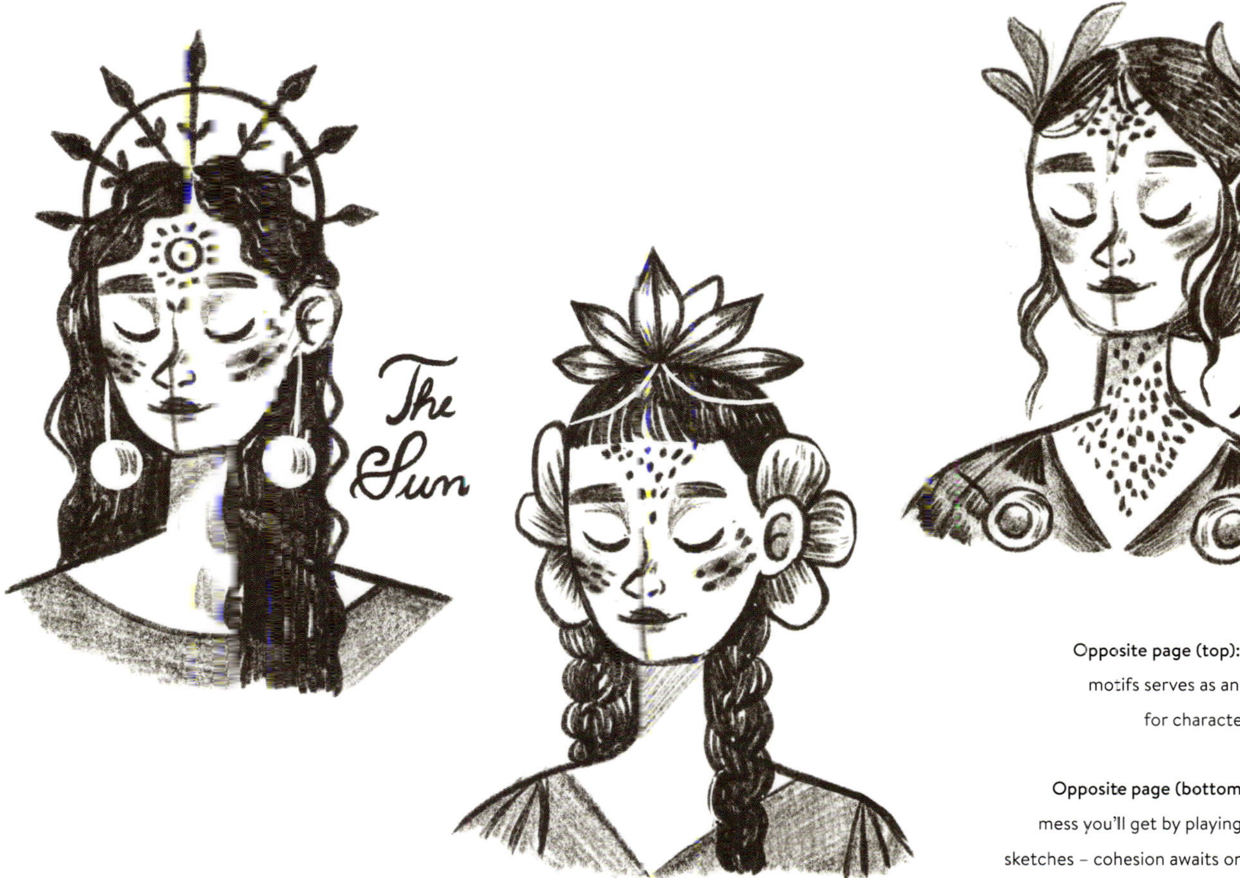

Opposite page (top): Visualizing the motifs serves as an excellent basis for character development

Opposite page (bottom): Embrace the mess you'll get by playing with the initial sketches – cohesion awaits on the other side

This page: Character variants depending on a defining characteristic pulled from the brainstorming phase

PARTY PLANNING

Given my character's features and story was heavily inspired by the prompts, the word 'party' led me to envision a summer solstice theme, an evening celebration. The moth-inspired character seemed like the most suitable choice – I ruled out the flower-inspired and the sun-inspired characters as they didn't fit the evening party vibe as much. Always remember to think logically when making decisions about your character.

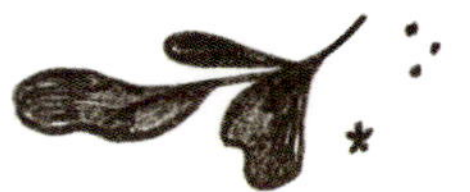

A CLEAR VISION EMERGES

We're through the experimentation phase – now it's time to start defining your character more distinctly. By now, you should have some idea of who your character is: their appearance, behaviour, the world they inhabit, and so on. Work through as many details as necessary, whether by using your imagination or writing them down to create a story around your character. This is what I like to refer to as the story sheet. Additionally, consider defining the style you'll employ and include character enhancers from your brainstorming stage. I move forward with my moth lady, writing a quick one-line story pitch, deciding on the style I want the character to have, and any details I want to add. Pose yourself relevant questions about your character and find visual representations for the answers.

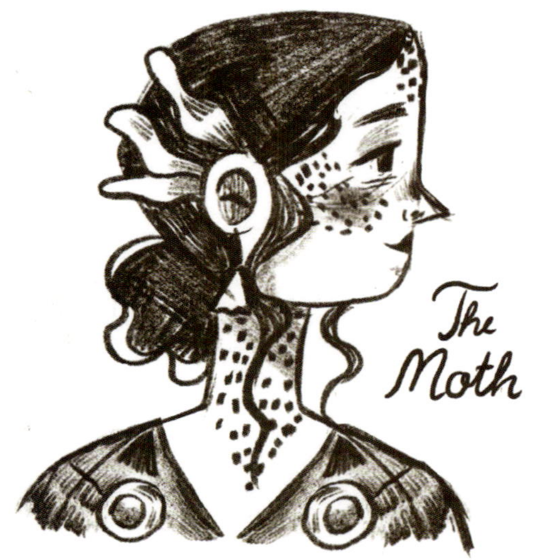

This page (top): Written notes on my more clearly-defined character. You can write as many details as you feel necessary

This page (bottom): Trying to decide on a pose that suits my character

STICK TO THE PLAN

Can your character's body appearance and posture add to the story you're trying to tell? Most definitely! That's why you should take your time envisioning your character in a full-body view, considering how they'll be drawn in terms of body and posture. Pay attention to physical traits, expressions, and body language, ensuring they align with your character's emotional tone. Start with stick figures or basic shape sketches to see what works best for your vision. While some of these initial sketches may not make the final cut, they serve as a solid foundation. Whether your character faces forward or backward, takes action, or adopts a static pose, these decisions significantly contribute to your first full-body sketch. From there, you can refine and breathe life into them.

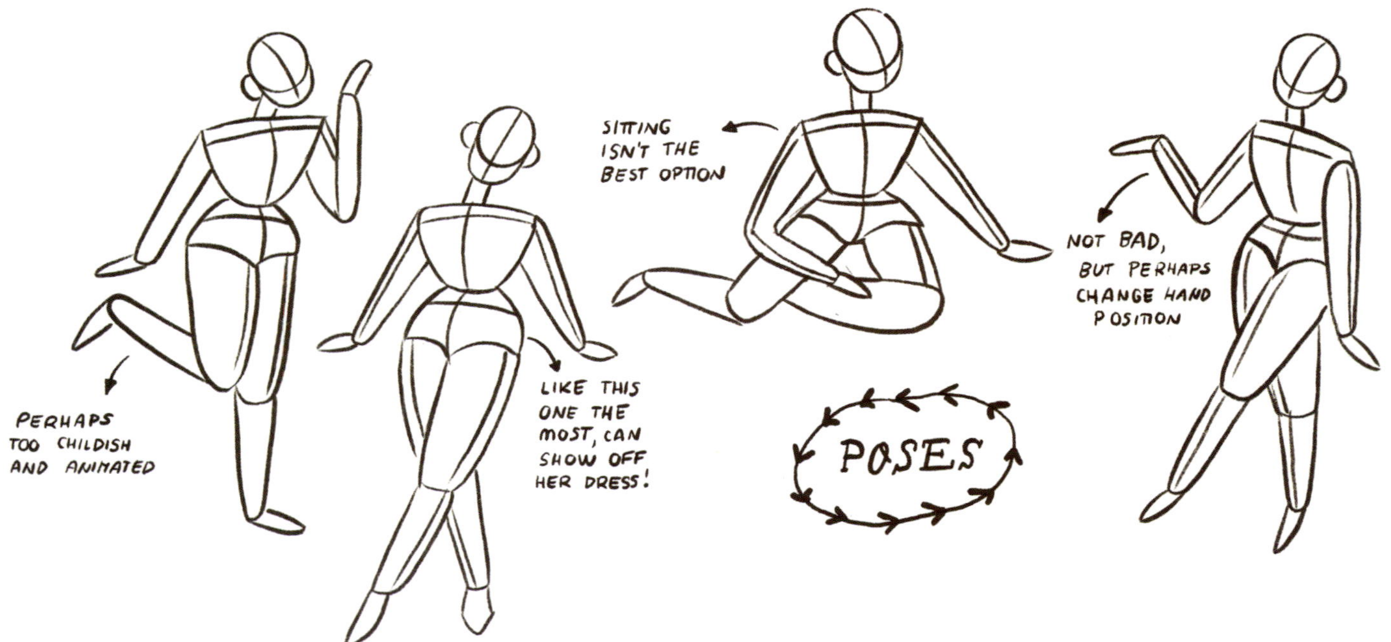

WHY LEARN ANATOMY?

As you can probably guess judging by my sketches, I haven't taken a single anatomy class – but don't make my mistake! Anatomy is absolutely the key for creating believable characters and a basic knowledge will save you some trouble along the way. As you gain insight into the human body's structure, proportions, and movement, you'll feel empowered to depict a broader range of characters. Your characters will become more expressive, allowing them to convey emotions and actions convincingly. Even in stylized or fantastical settings, your anatomy know-how can bring a lot to the table.

DRESS FOR SUCCESS

Your character's clothing and style should extend from their overall look and back story. Give this aspect of character design some time and love because it's a powerful storytelling tool. The right clothing can breathe life into your character, making them relatable, one of a kind, and unforgettable. Get creative with a few sketches or check out some references for inspiration. Remember, your brainstorming sheet, motif sketches, and story sheet are valuable tools throughout the design process – they've got your back! Also, don't go for the most straightforward option – rather than a plain dress design and separate wings, I move forward with a dress that combines the two, giving my character a more unique feel.

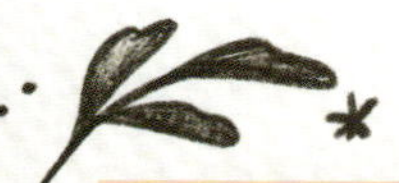

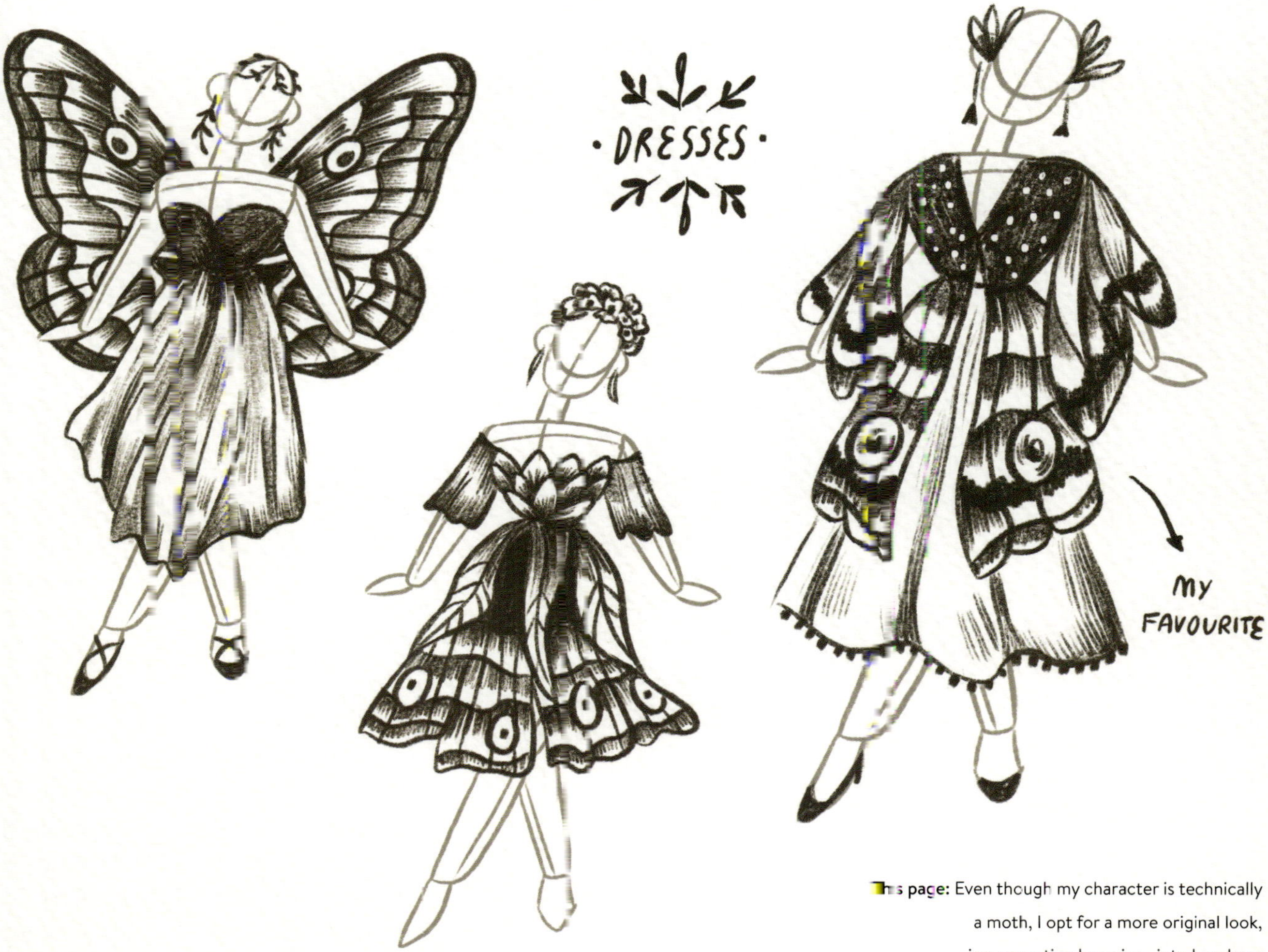

This page: Even though my character is technically a moth, I opt for a more original look, incorporating her wings into her dress

LIKES AND YIKES

Well, this can be a messy step – throw everything you've thought about and done to this point, all the bits and pieces you've been working on, onto one character. Give it a face and let it brave the storm. Will it be good? Probably not. Should you be worried? Not in the slightest.

Why? Because now you have a visual representation to help you pinpoint what's not working and why. Trust the process. Write your 'likes' and 'yikes' about the character, give thanks, and then throw this first attempt in the bin!

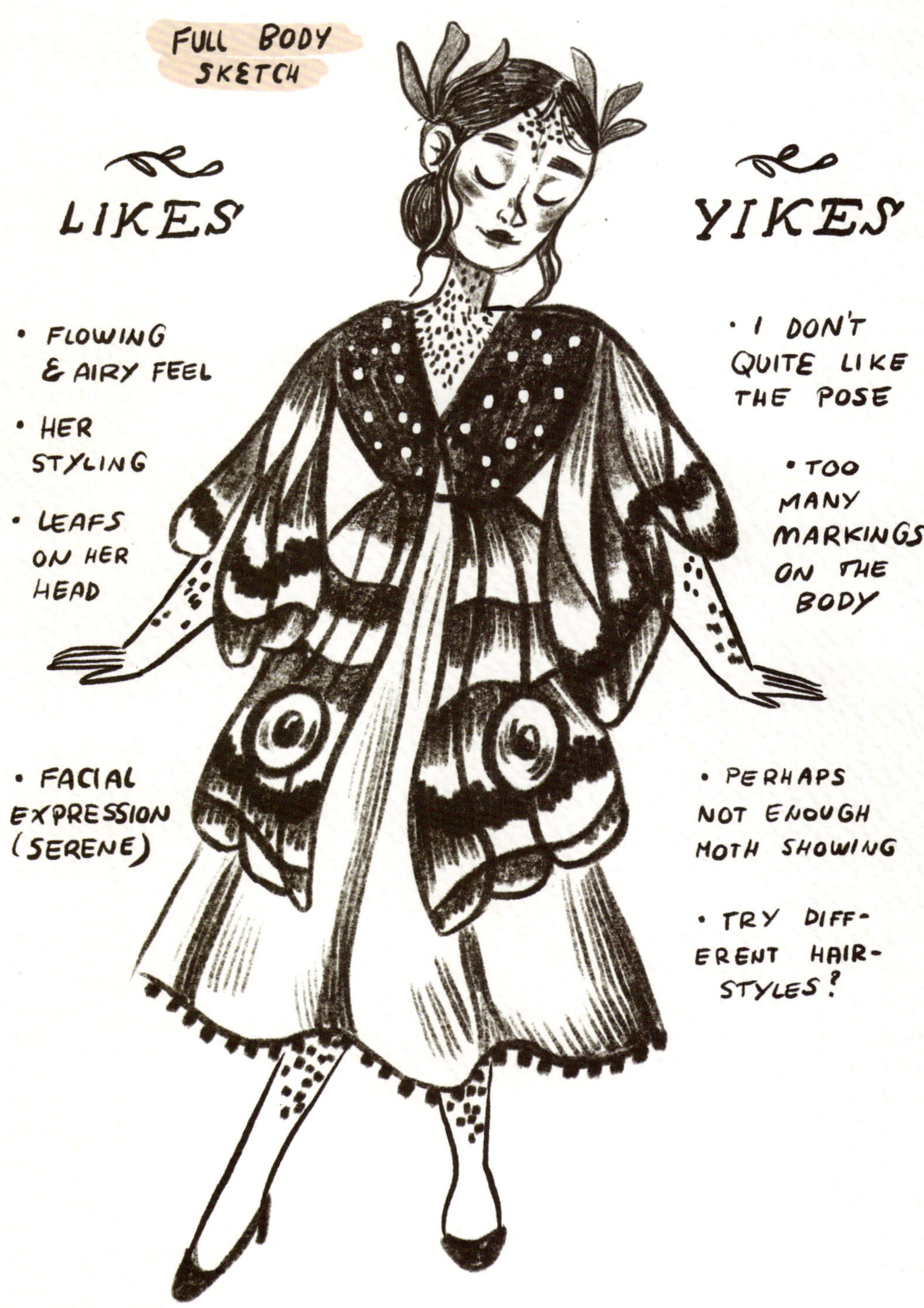

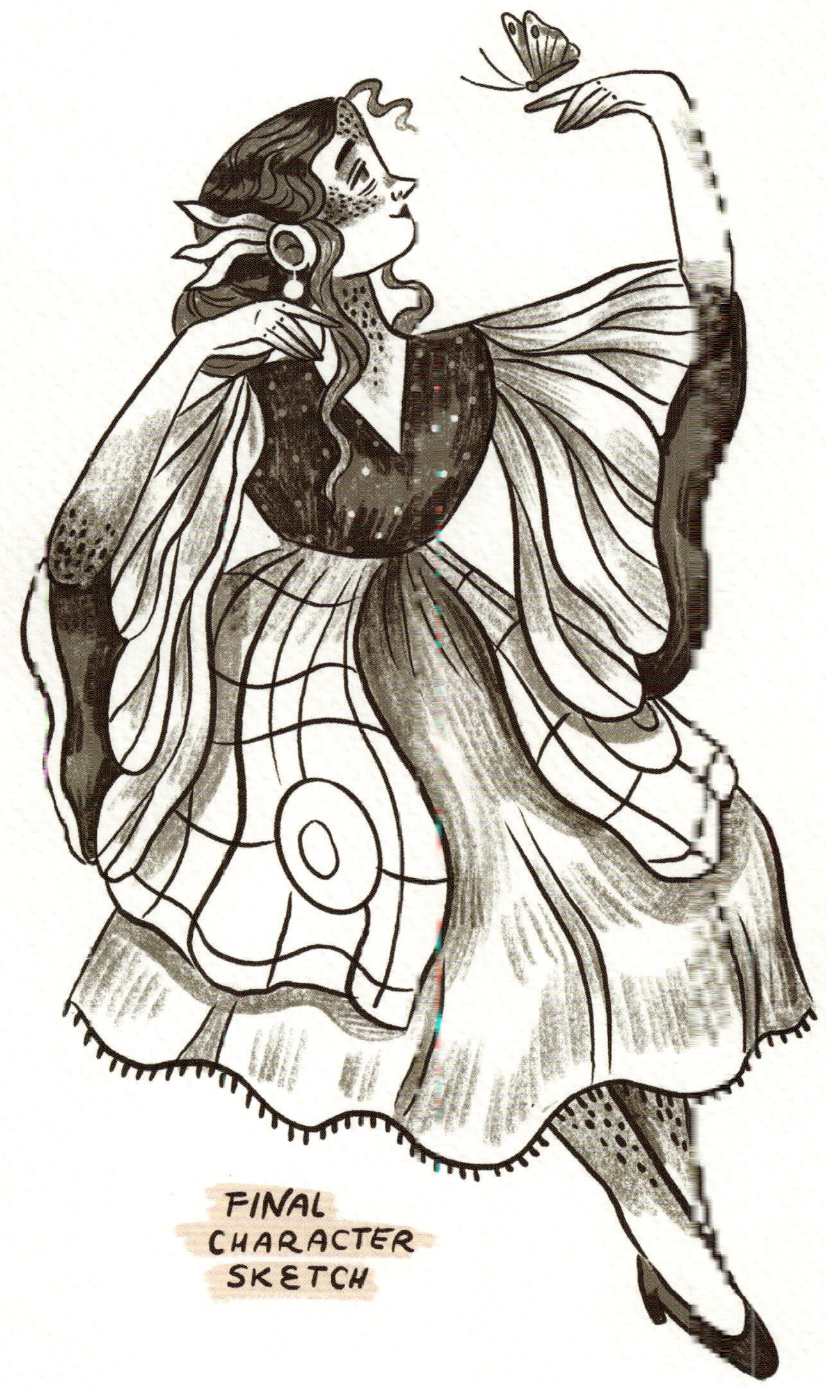

Opposite page: Make a list of your character's highlights and low points – and be honest!

This page: The final sketch is less detailed, but more complete

A GOOD SKETCH IS A GOOD FOUNDATION

After considering all your likes and dislikes from the full-body sketch, refine it until each major character-defining characteristic is clearly readable. From my experience, a solid sketch can save countless hours of going back and forth, refining or coming up with things on the fly. Once you've got a good sketch, you're half-way there. My final sketch may lack some of the detail of the earlier iterations, but it shows a livelier presence, with its dynamic pose and interaction with the moth.

Congratulations, you've made it to this important milestone! You have a fully developed character, created by following the prompts and incorporating your unique motifs and details. Embrace this achievement and prepare for the next step – your character is now ready to embark on a colourful journey.

'GATHER REFERENCES FROM THE NATURAL WORLD, WHICH WILL OFFER A PLETHORA OF UNEXPECTED OPTIONS, PALETTES, AND PATTERNS'

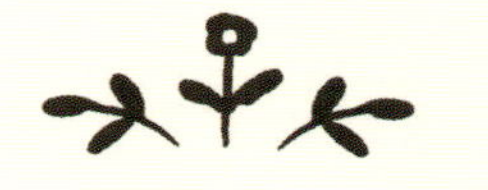

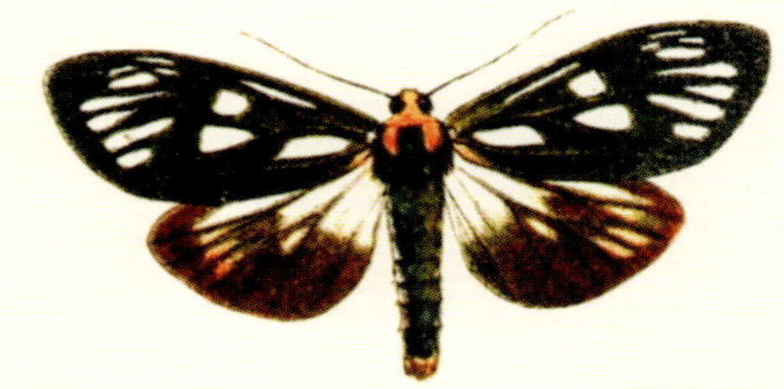

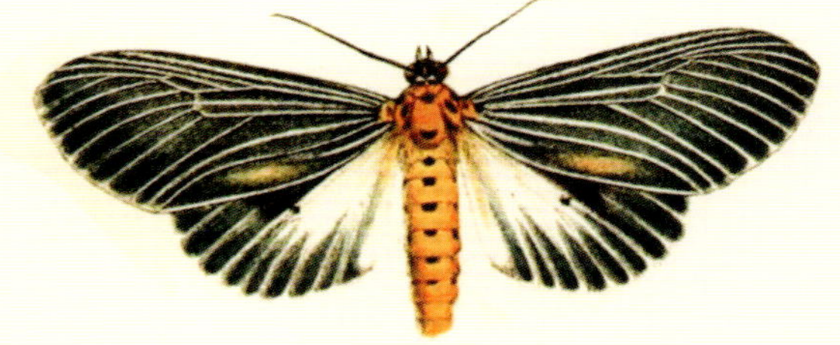

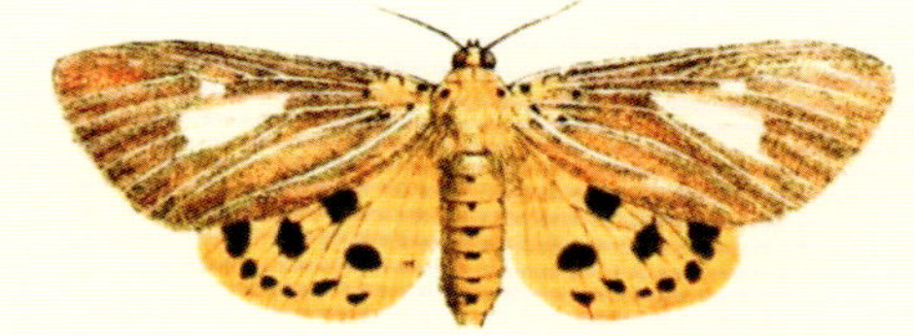

REFERENCES CAN SURPRISE YOU

It's time for the whole process to take a colourful turn. During this phase, I encourage you to gather references from the natural world, which will offer a plethora of unexpected options, palettes, and patterns. Mix and match them as needed, allowing your creativity to blossom. However, don't forget to revisit the original prompts once more to check if there are any colourful inspirations staring right back at you. Consider breaking some rules and challenge yourself to step away from the obvious choices. For example, I challenge myself not to use green for my character, the colour most associated with nature.

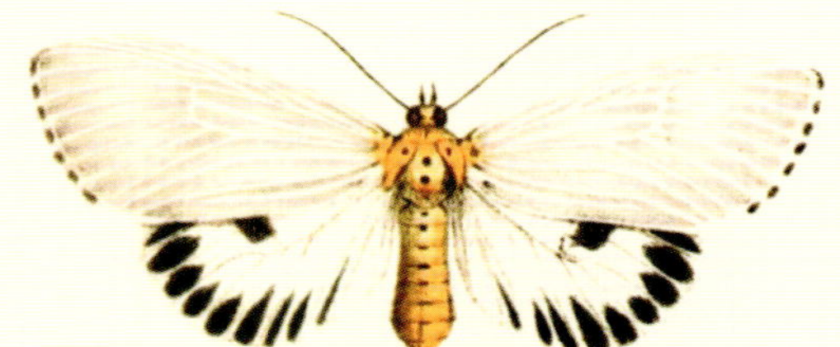

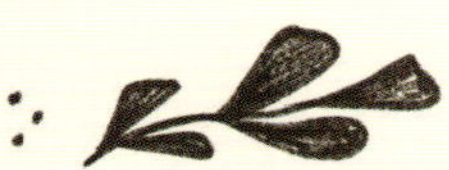

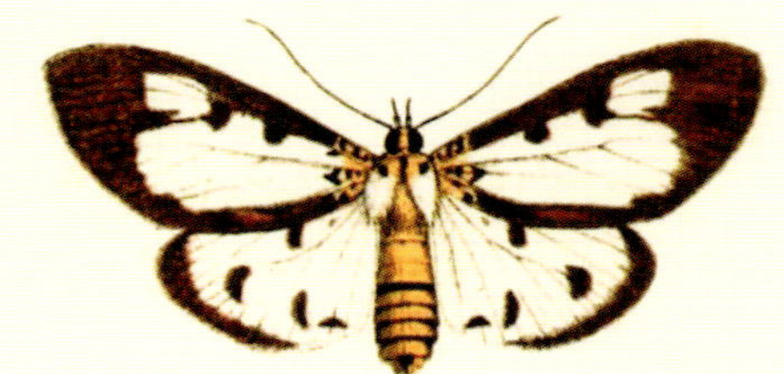

RESTRICTING THE PALETTE

Using a limited colour palette in character design can be really exciting. With fewer choices, you get to be more creative and try out new colour combinations you might otherwise not even think of. Each colour becomes more meaningful, which can add personality to your character. The restricted palette gives your character a distinct style that makes them stand out and appear memorable to others. Don't be afraid to keep it simple and experiment with limited colours – it can lead to some quite unique results.

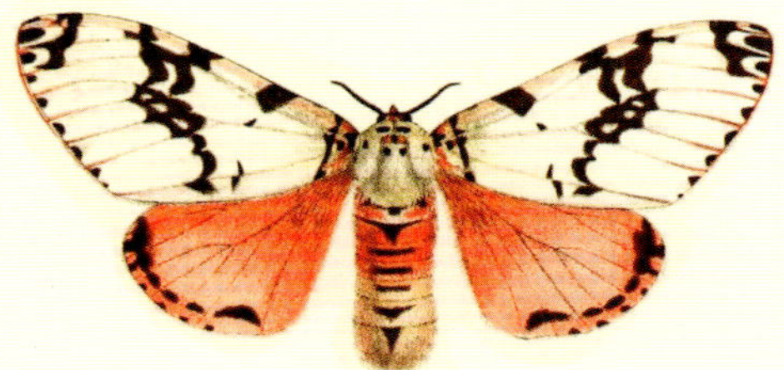

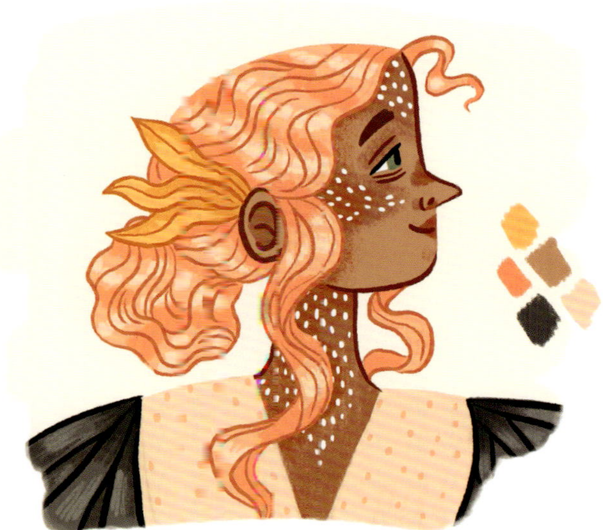

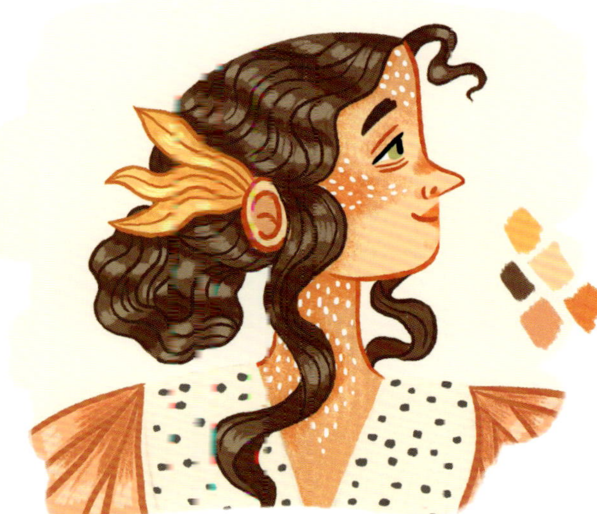

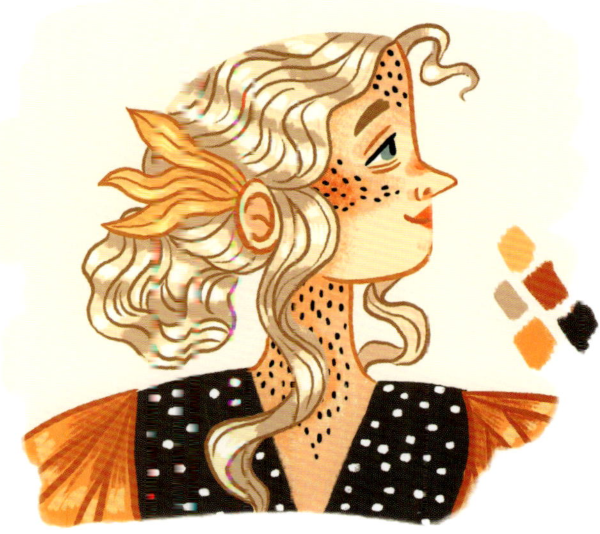

PICKING A PALETTE

The colour palette always makes a massive difference to your design. Those of us who've dipped our toes into the vast field of colour theory know how colour can captivate our brains. With various hues, combinations, backgrounds, and ratios, colours hold the power to shape characters, evoke emotions, and tell captivating stories. With this in mind, gather diverse colour palettes from your references and observe how your character's appeal and impression of them shift with each change. A small sample area of your character, like the bust, is ideal for testing multiple palettes. Look to the emotions that colours evoke when choosing a palette. If you're keen on delving deeper, exploring books on colour theory and psychology of colour can be very helpful.

REVISE AND REPEAT

Once you've chosen your palette, stick with it throughout the entire process of laying out the base colour. This ensures your character remains cohesive and you won't have to struggle or over think your choice. I explore how playing with the hues and their ratios in the overall illustration makes a difference to my moth character over several sketches, and then try my favourite on a full-body drawing. Sometimes, palettes don't fully work when translated to the entire piece – but no worries, you should still have a few palettes from the previous step ready to test out. An 'aha!' moment will arrive – trust me.

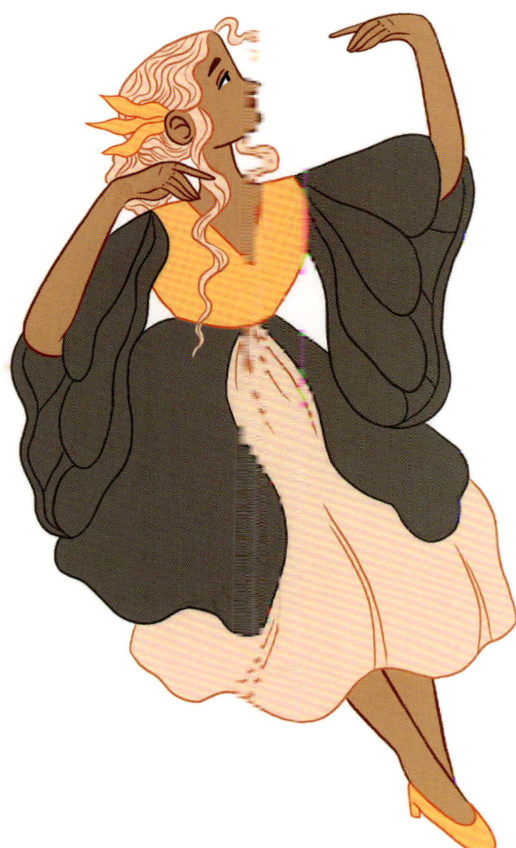

Opposite page:

I focus on a theme closely related to my character, but explore palettes beyond the main topic of nature

This page (left):

Testing out a few different palettes to determine which works best for my character

This page (right):

Test your colour palette on the entire piece to see if it works or feels off

CHARACTER IN A CHRYSALIS

Welcome to the final stage of your character creation: the rendering phase. No matter the style or technique you choose, aim to retain as many storytelling elements and motifs as possible. Whenever in doubt, refer back to the prompts, your brainstorming sheet, story sheet, and gathered references. Have fun during this stage – you might discover an additional element that hadn't crossed your mind before! I bring back all my additional details at this point: the tiny markings on my character's body, golden jewellery, and evolve the moth-inspired dress into a gorgeous cape.

Remember, every detail you add or subtract must serve the same purpose: to breathe life into your character.

USING YOUR LEFTOVERS

Before we move onto the final render, I encourage you to build a world around your character and place them in a captivating setting. Creating worlds can be just as thrilling as crafting characters. If you're lacking inspiration, return to your brainstorming list once more. As you gather everything in one place, you'll quickly see how many motifs and references you've already used can jumpstart the creation of your character's world. Use them to begin sketching your character's surroundings.

I surround my character with plants, mushrooms, and the colours of my earlier explorations. This integration of brainstormed elements will infuse my character's environment with depth and authenticity.

This page (top): My fully rendered character with all the additional details added

This page (bottom): Use brainstormed elements from the first stage to craft your character's world

Opposite page: The finished piece

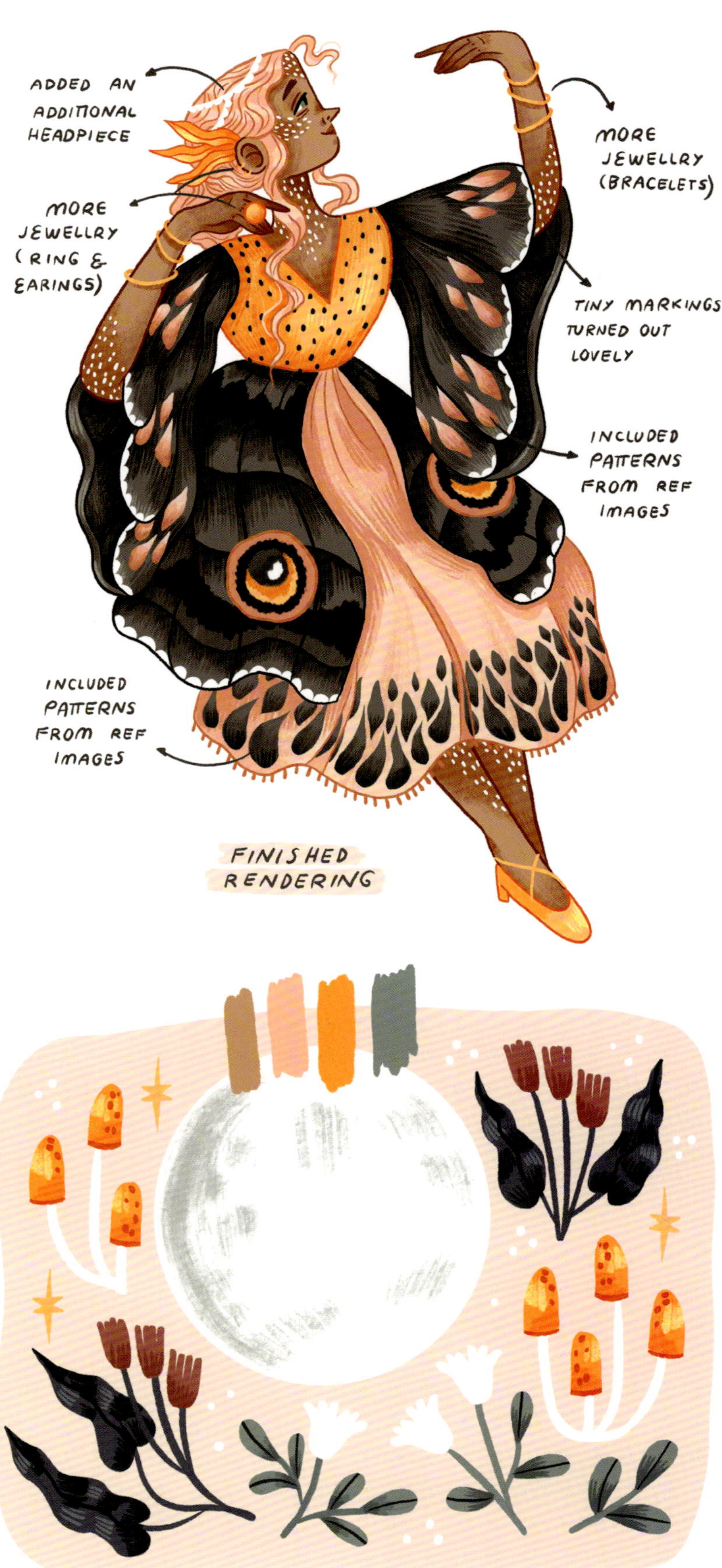

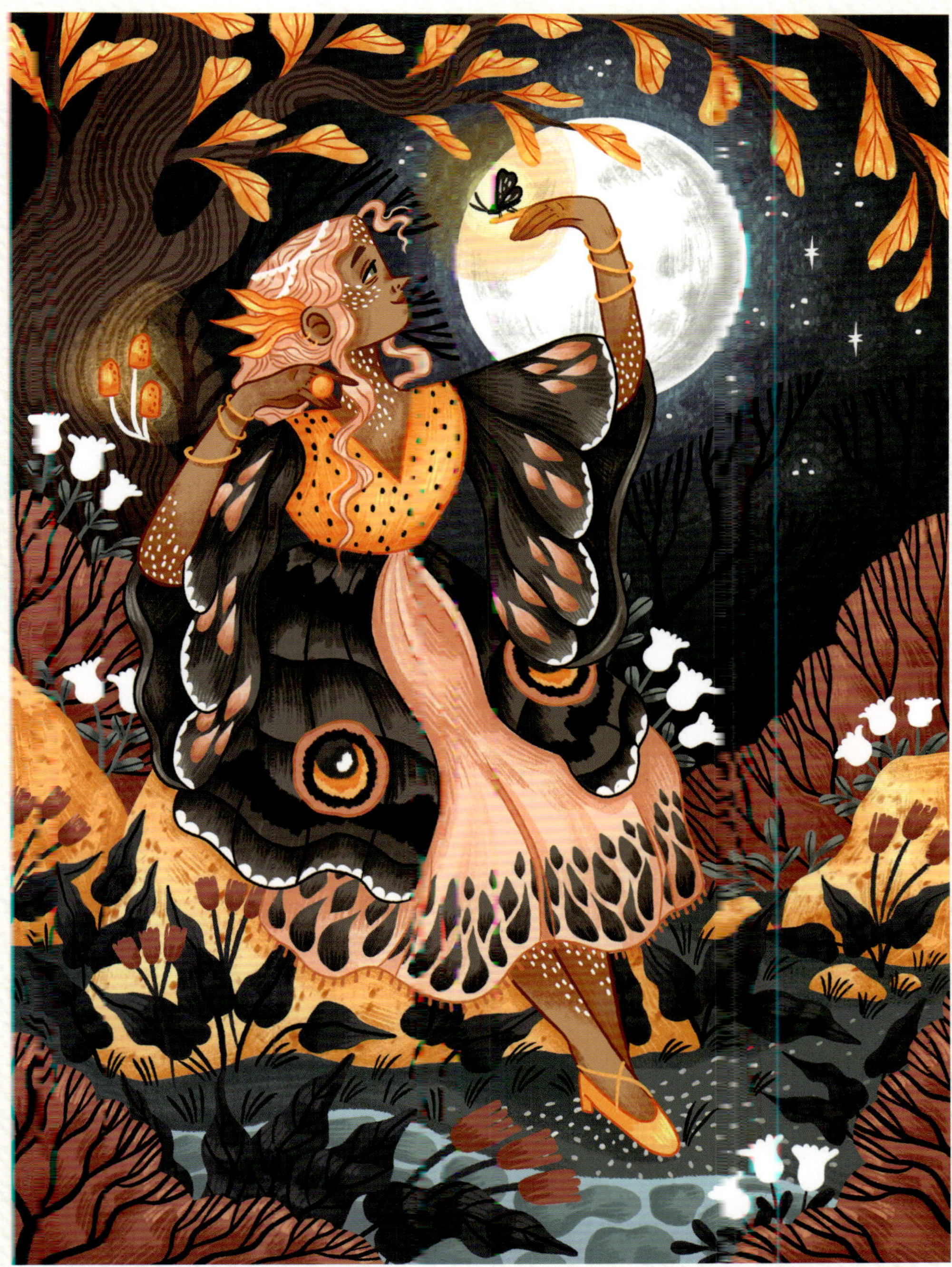

THE MOTH BY MOONLIGHT

Now, for the really fun part: enrich your world with captivating details and colour! However, we need to remember a few key aspects. Firstly, ensure your character is integrated seamlessly into the world around them. Secondly, maintain consistency in the colour palette between your character and their surroundings. This will prevent your character from appearing randomly placed within the scene and enhance the overall cohesion of the world you've crafted.

And with that, we've created a beautiful new character from a simple, three-word prompt. I hope you've enjoyed the process – feel free to customize these steps to your liking, as each creator has a unique approach. Best of luck and stay creative!

Final image © Kaja Kajfež

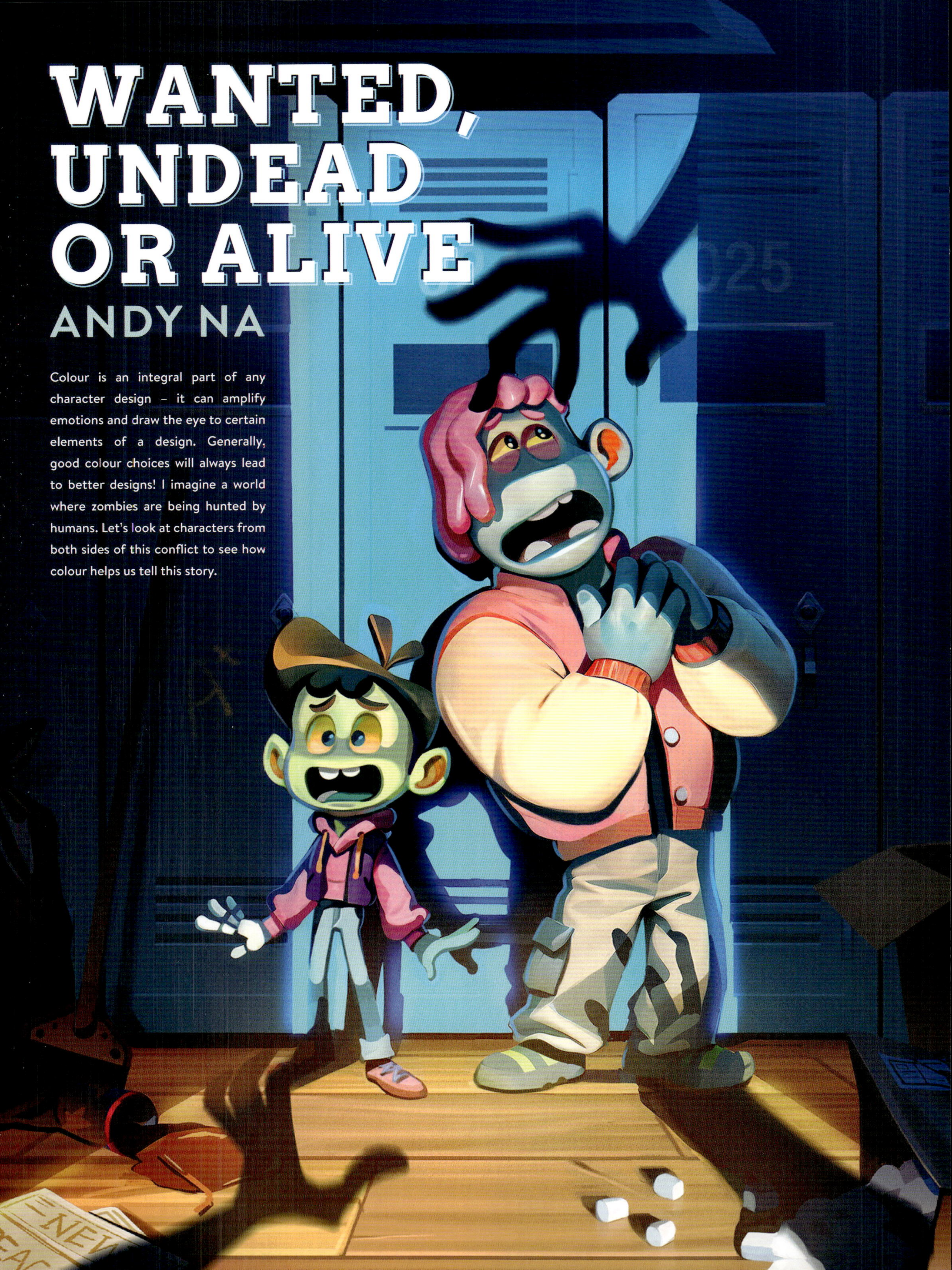

WANTED, UNDEAD OR ALIVE

ANDY NA

Colour is an integral part of any character design – it can amplify emotions and draw the eye to certain elements of a design. Generally, good colour choices will always lead to better designs! I imagine a world where zombies are being hunted by humans. Let's look at characters from both sides of this conflict to see how colour helps us tell this story.

A FRIENDLY NEIGHBOURHOOD HUNTER

Let's start with the zombie-hunting humans. For this first character, I choose blue for her hair and then, to make the hair stand out, I colour her clothes orange and red, which are similar to her skin tone. The skirt is green as this pairs well with the orange of her top. I use the blue accent colour on her weapon – this is an important part of her character, so I need it to stand out from the clothing. Finally, to show she's a little insane, I paint her eyes pink.

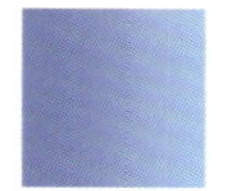

Hair
(accent colour)

Eyes
(accent colour)

Clothes
(main colour)

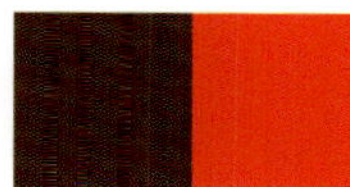

Shoes

THE MINI MOBSTER

This character is a small gang boss who orders the other humans about. I choose pink for his suit, to show he isn't much of a threat on his own. He doesn't like to get involved with the dirty work of killing zombies, so I colour his gloves white and give his face a pale, clean complexion. His traditional-coloured shoes tie the character back to the idea of being a mob boss.

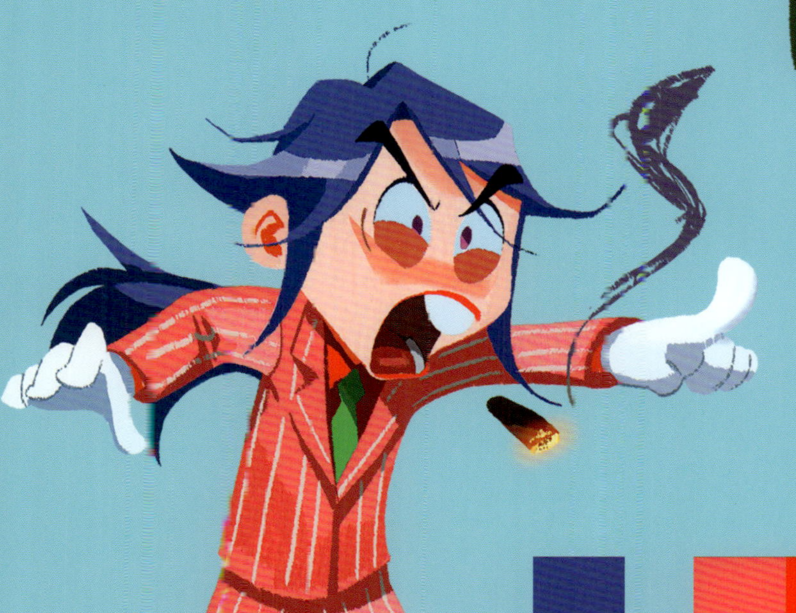

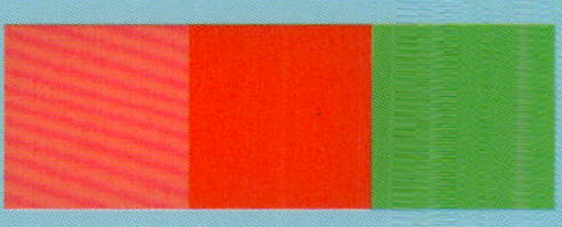

Hair

Clothes
(main colour)

Necktie
(accent colour)

Gloves

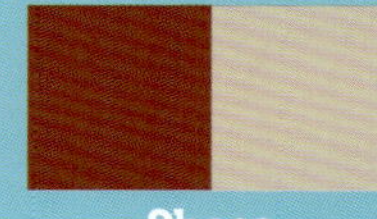

Shoes

CREATE MOOD WITH COLOUR

I place the zombies in a school scene, where they are being hunted by the humans. The scene I'm creating takes place at night, so I choose colours that will express that. Blue creates a cold atmosphere and brown provides a warm tone that works well in contrast. Combining two contrasting colours will balance the painting and make it look richer overall.

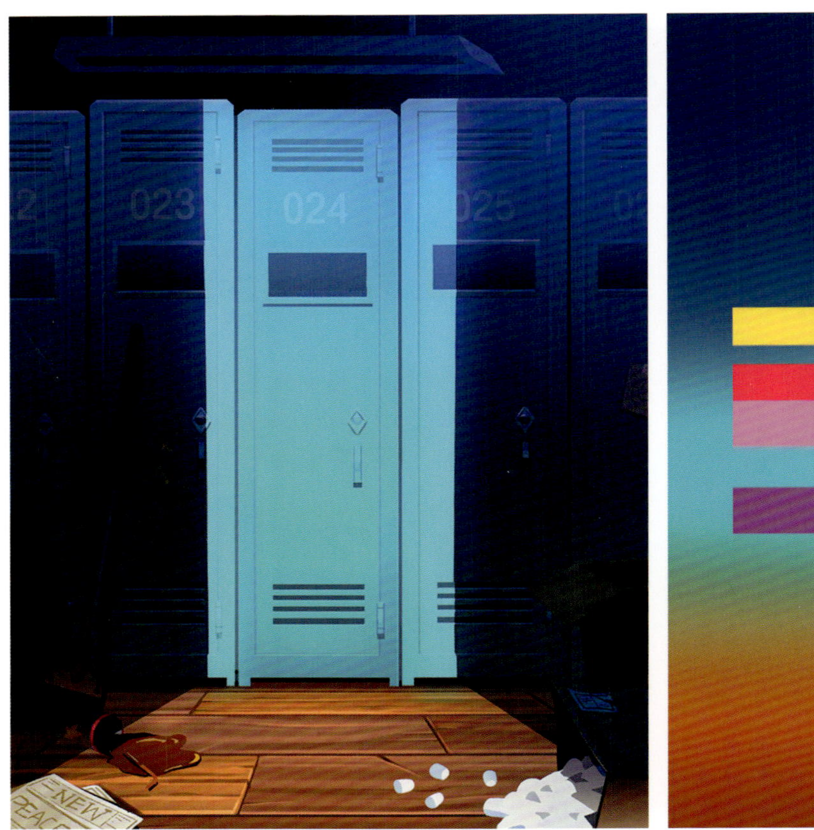

'COMBINING TWO CONTRASTING COLOURS WILL BALANCE THE PAINTING AND MAKE IT LOOK RICHER OVERALL'

STANDING OUT

The character's should be clearly separated from the background and stand out, even with a quick glance. Although the characters have blueish skin, similar to the background, the colour of their clothes differentiates them from the background. The reds, pinks, and purples are distinct from the blues and browns of the school corridor.

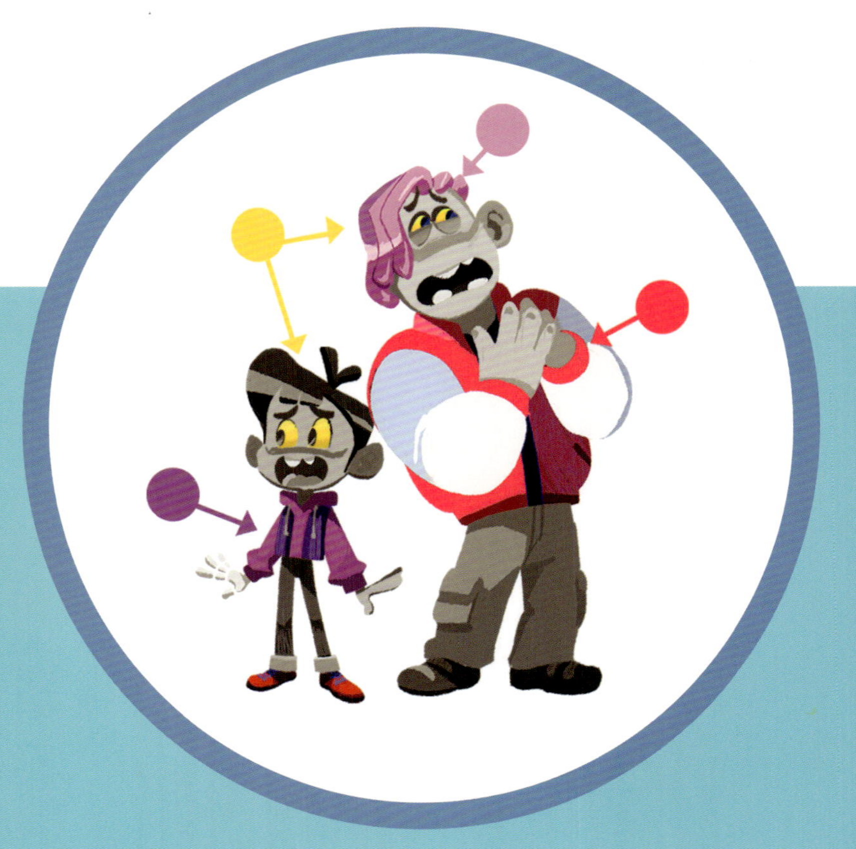

COLOUR COMBOS ARE KEY

Practise using cold and warm colours to create a harmonious look in your paintings. Use cold colours for shadows and warm colours for the light. Remember, the same colour can be used for many different situations and to create multiple moods. Adjusting the saturation and tone will help you to find unique results.

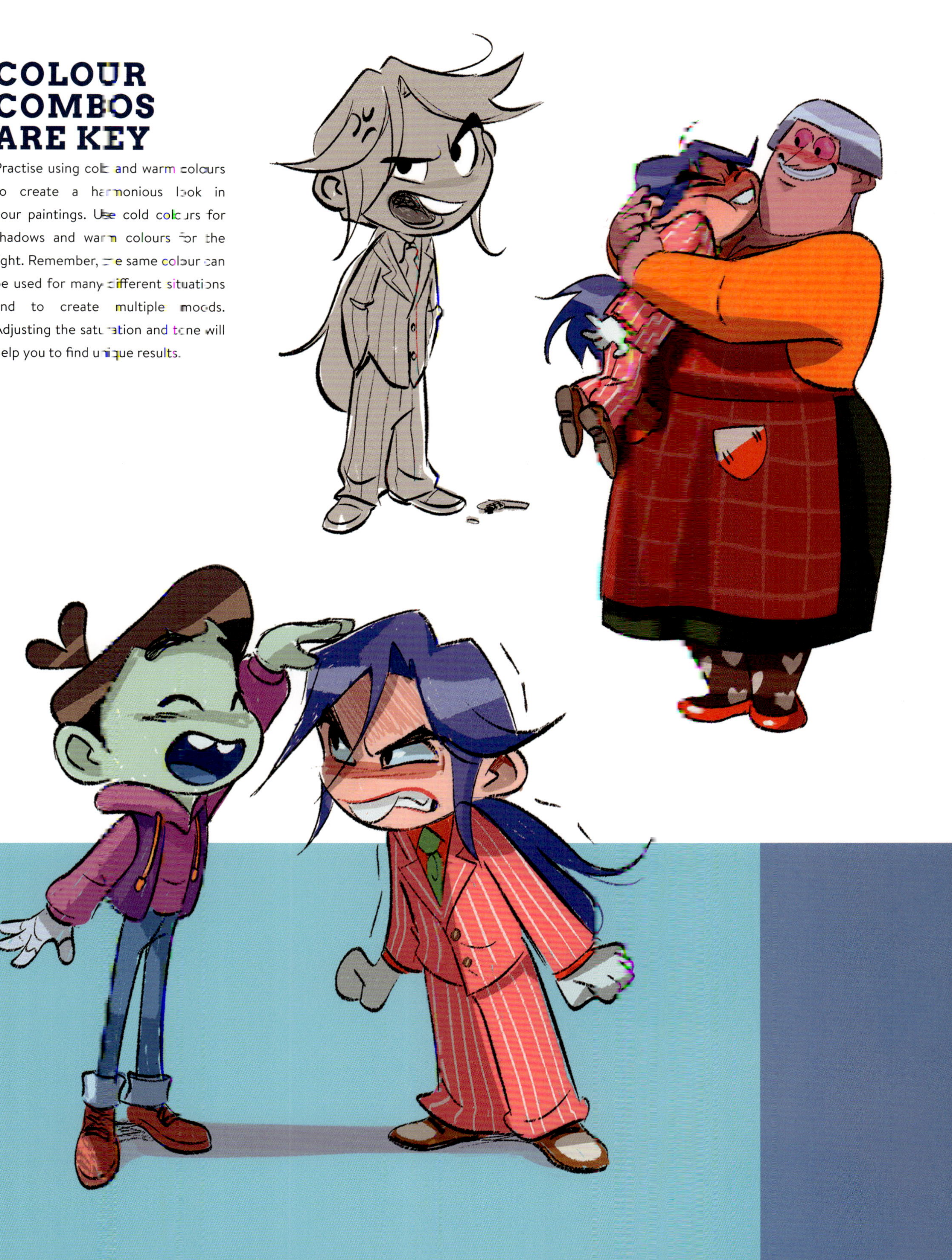

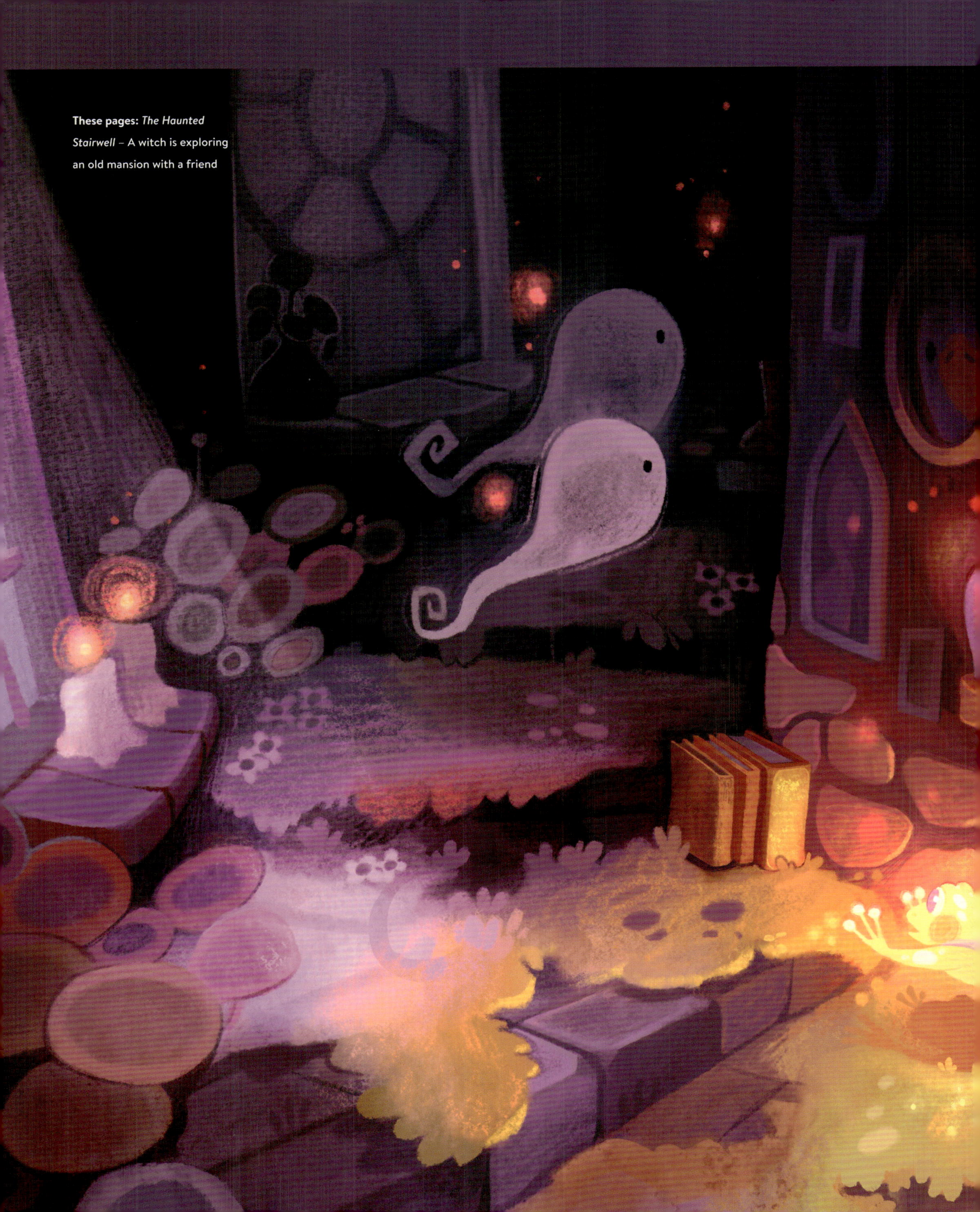

These pages: *The Haunted Stairwell* – A witch is exploring an old mansion with a friend

POOPIKAT

Kate Pellerin (aka Poopikat) is a Canadian illustrator, based in Toronto, who combines illustrating children's books with other freelance work and teaching at Seneca Polytechnic. We caught up with Kate to chat about how she manages her time across all of her different projects, the evolution of her art style, and where the name Poopikat came from.

'HOPEFULLY I'M MAKING A DIFFERENCE TO SOMEONE ELSE'S ART CAREER'

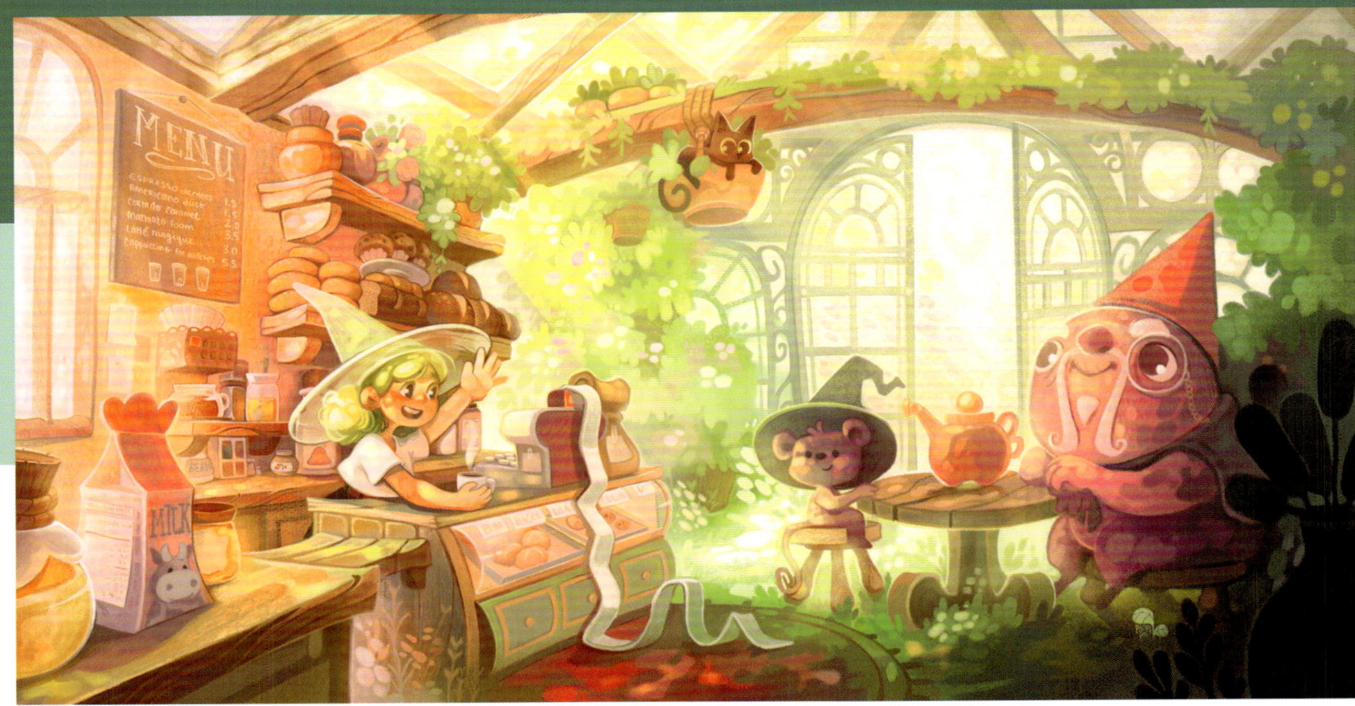

Hi Kate, welcome back to *CDQ*! Can you tell our readers a little about your art journey so far?

Hi! Thank you so much for having me, it's such an honour to be featured here. I would say my art journey resembles a squiggly line. I started drawing when I was young, inspired by Ghibli films and anime. From the start of high school and through my first couple of years at university, I painted more contemporary work, which has no correlation with what I'm doing now. I was a bit lost as to what I wanted to do, and I didn't really enjoy creating art much at all. A few years later, I decided to attend Seneca Polytechnic (where I actually teach now), and that's where I found my love for drawing again! I took a children's book class and fell completely in love with the idea of storytelling, character design, and so much more! Since then, I've been trying to improve my art in service of my goals. I'm currently working on visual development for kid's animation, magazines, and a couple of new books.

It must be an interesting experience teaching where you were once taught. What's the best thing about teaching other artists?

It really is, hah! It's odd seeing teachers that once taught me and calling them my colleagues, but overall, it's really fun. The best thing about teaching other artists is seeing their progress as they start to understand concepts and techniques. To see someone go from A to B and to have an 'I get it!' moment is so satisfying and makes me feel so happy that I've helped a bit in their art journey. I also find it very fun to teach overall. Us freelancers don't get many chances to talk with others face to face, so it's nice to have these interactions while teaching. And hopefully I'm making a difference to someone else's art career at the same time!

This page: *The Greenhouse Bakery* – This is a drawing of a magical coffee shop, operating in a greenhouse in the midst of summer

Opposite page: *Flower Basket* – A traditional drawing exploring paper cuts and a more muted colour palette

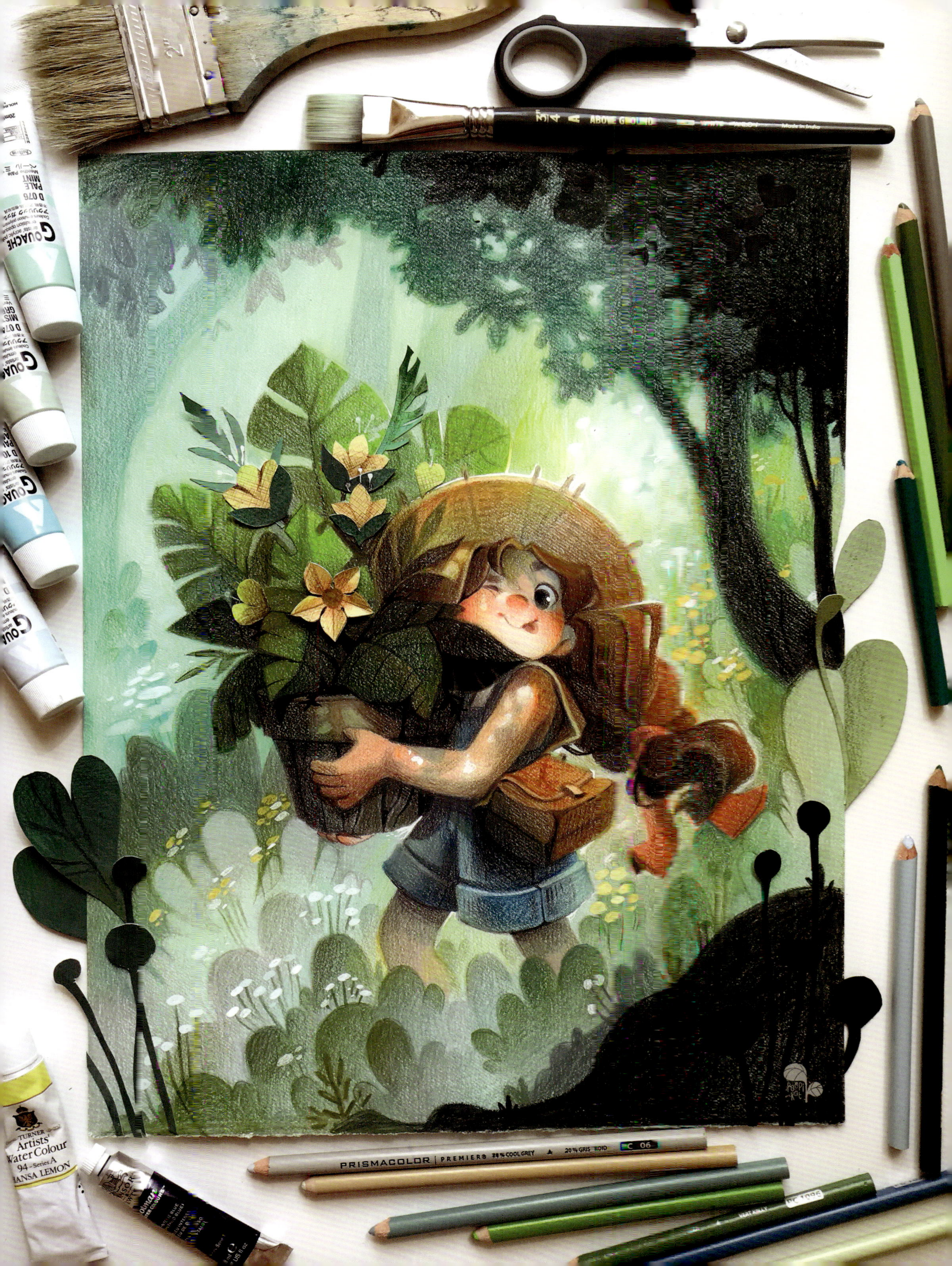

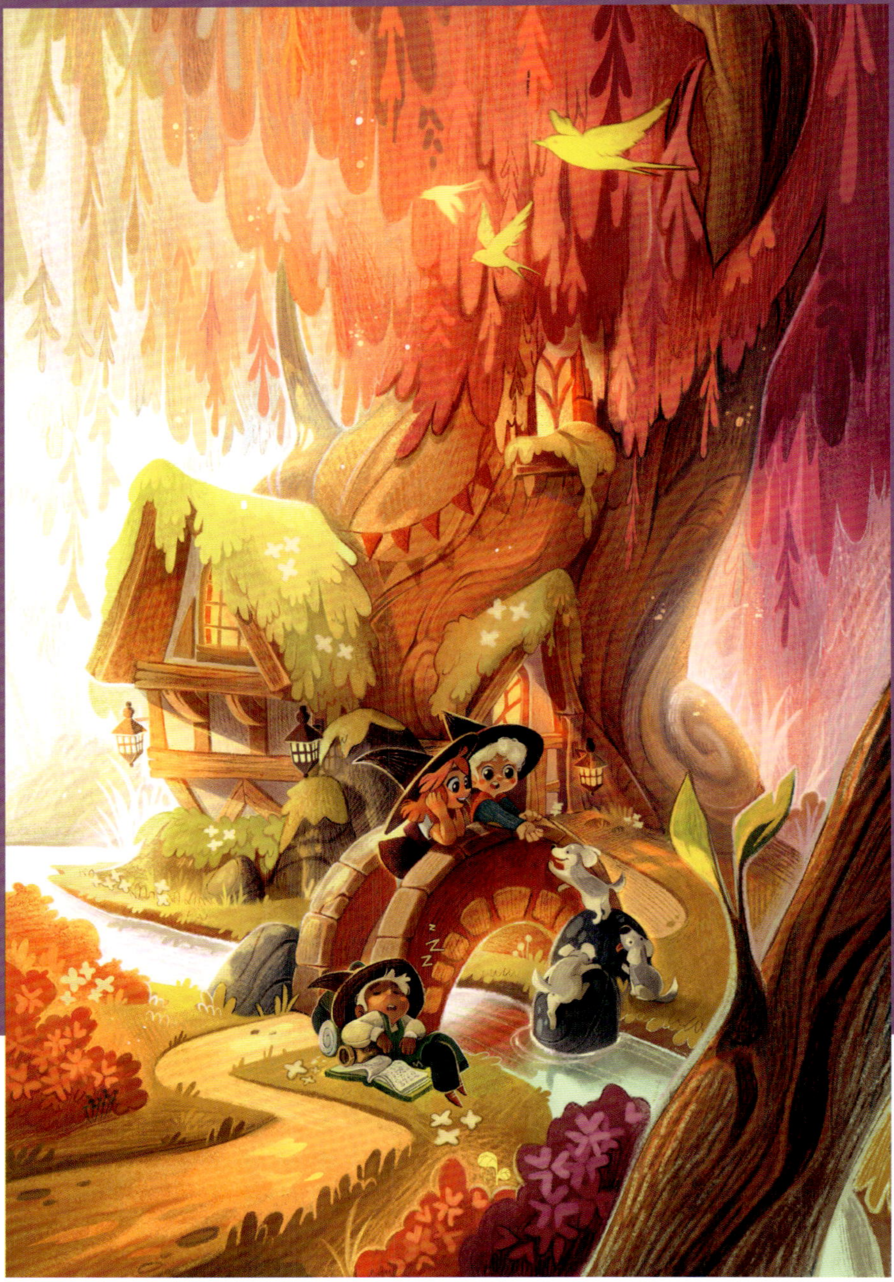

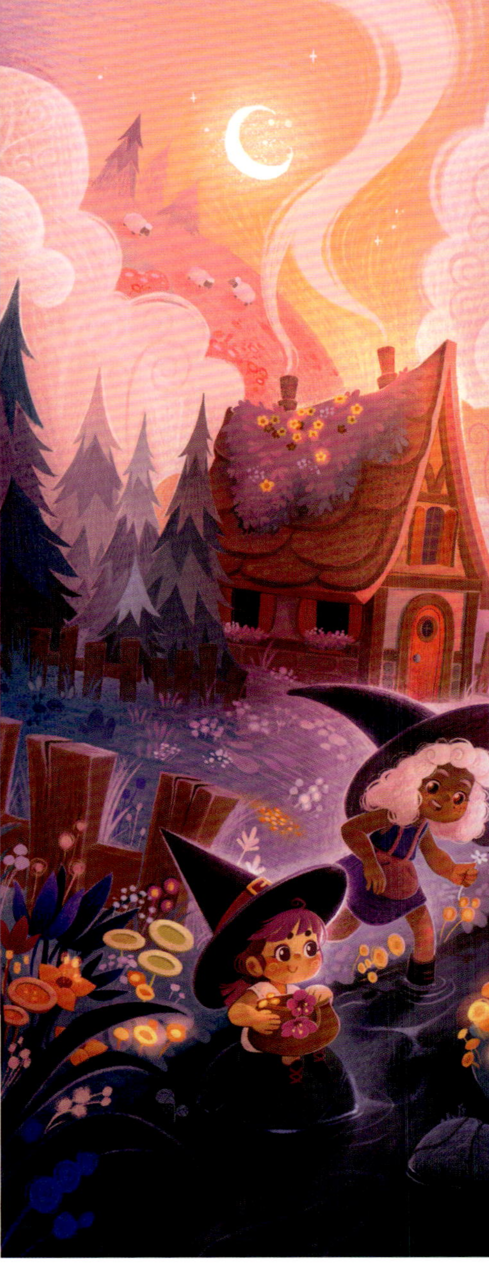

We often speak to freelance artists who, like yourself, have lots of different projects on the go - do you have any tips for managing your time across so many different projects?

I think the biggest thing is to have an agenda of some sort. I used to broadly plan my days, but then I transferred to using the app Notion which has been amazing for me – you can do just about anything with it. I have my weekly schedule and then a checklist of things that needs to get done. I then have a 'current project' checklist with dates and deadlines to keep track of what's coming up.

I also think limiting the projects you have on the go to four or five things at once is a good idea – if you put more than that on your plate, you'll overwhelm yourself. Finally, to keep myself from procrastinating, I do my client work in the morning when I'm really in 'work mode' and leave my own personal work for after lunch when I feel a bit more tired. I feel like structuring my days like this has really helped me to get things done and to never miss a deadline.

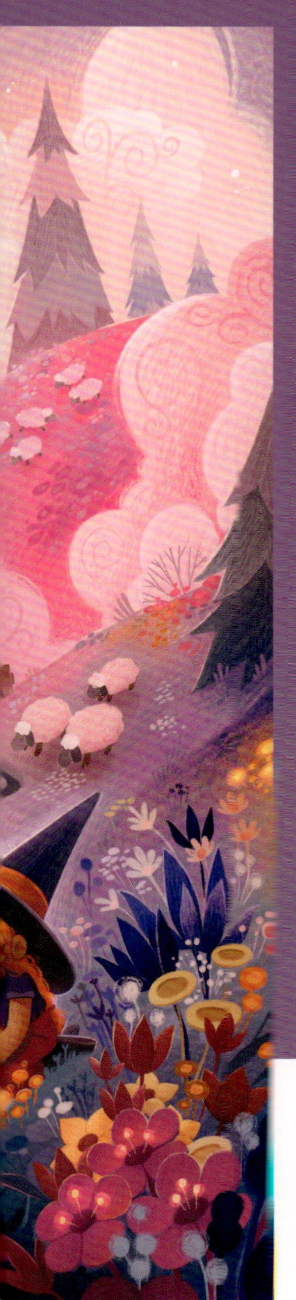

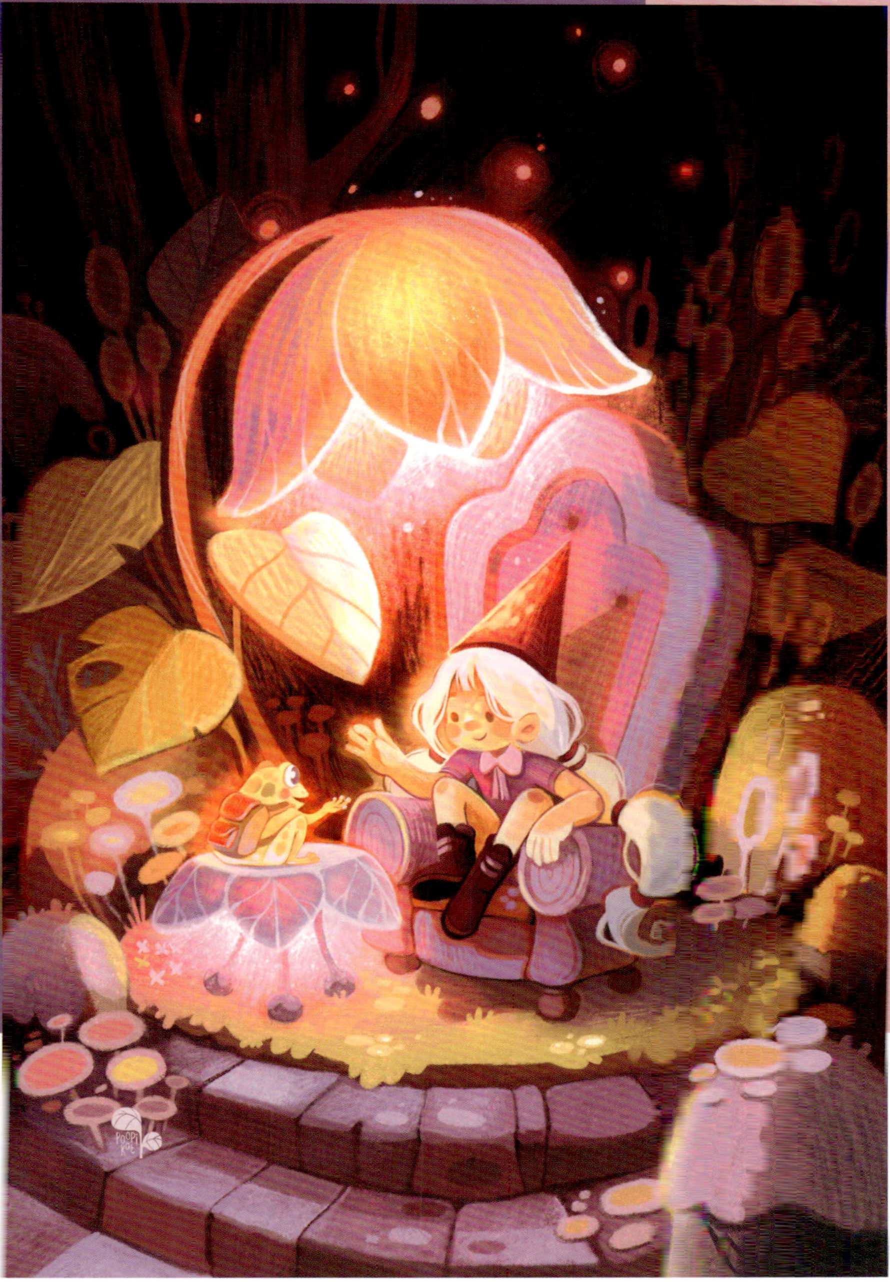

What advice do you have for artists who would like to work on children's books?

Know your audience! The first thing to consider is which age groups you're interested in designing for. There are so many different types of children's books, ranging from board books, to picture books, to teen graphic novels, and many more. Once you've figured out which direction you want go, start drawing your characters in an appropriate style. For example, my work goes between picture books to middle grade in some instances.

My next piece of advice is to study the books you want to draw. Go to your local bookshop and look at how other illustrators draw their characters and craft their pages. Keep seeking out inspiration from others.

And last but not least, take the time to learn visual development. It is so important as it will teach you how to create interesting characters, draw them over and over again, and create props and worlds that will aid your story. I always work on visual development before starting any project to ensure that my characters have a world of their own. Remember to start small and take baby steps towards bigger things.

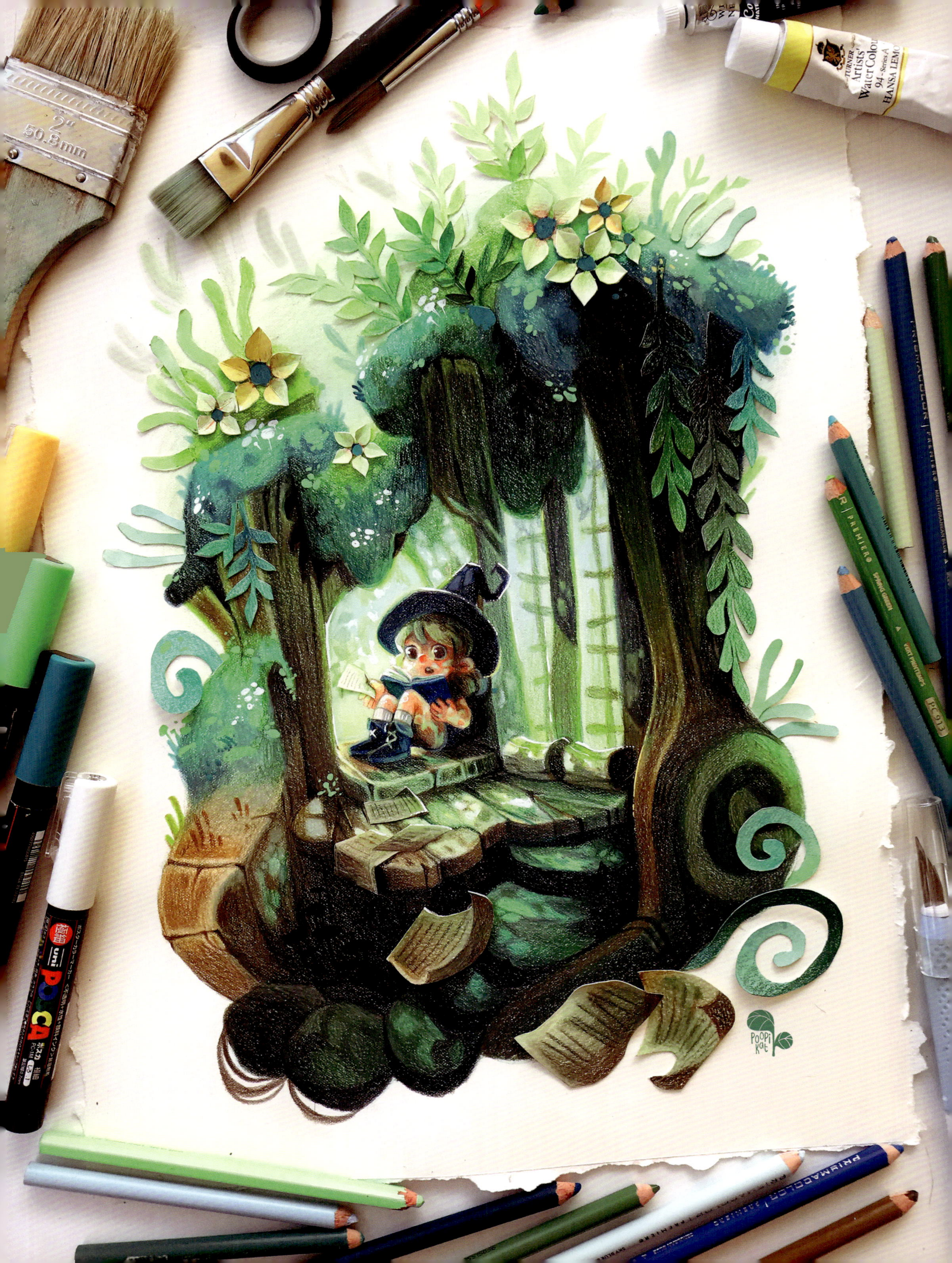

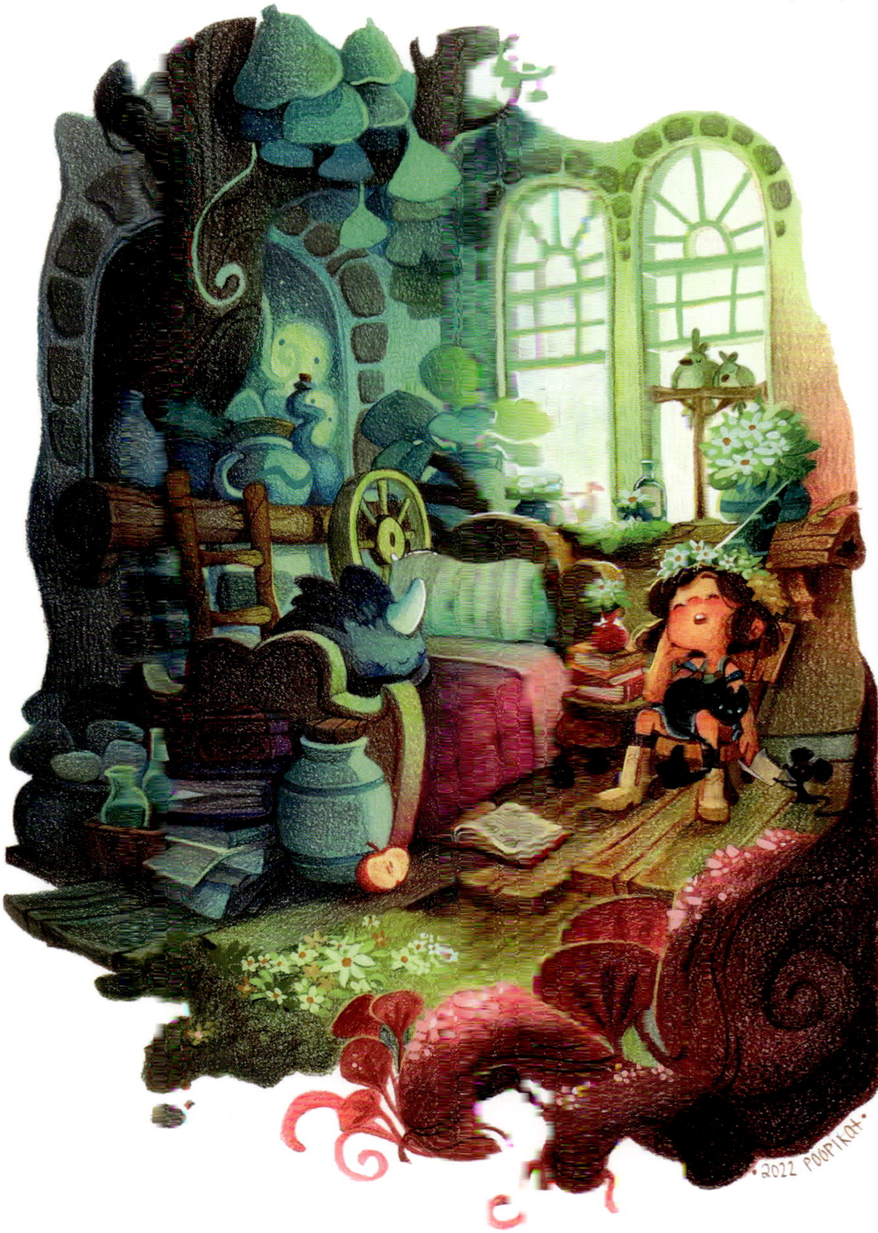

How important is social media for an artist nowadays?

Oh, this is an interesting question! Honestly, it depends on what you're aiming for. If you solely want to become a children's book illustrator, then just showing that you are alive by posting a few photos here and there online is good. You don't need a million followers to be well integrated in the book illustrator world – some amazing book illustrators have barely any followers and are so much more advanced than I am. I do recommend having a portfolio website though, and at least one other social media account to showcase your best work.

If you're trying to open a shop to sell things (like prints, stickers, brush packs, and so on) then growing your online presence would definitely be important.

Do you prefer working with traditional materials or digitally?

I love working with both. At the moment, I wish I had more time to work traditionally and create more pieces that way, but due to client work it's been a bit tough. I prefer doing client work and visual development digitally as it's easier to change, erase and play around with my concepts than if I were to do them traditionally. Also, in most cases, I start my traditional drawings digitally by sketching on my iPad and figure out my colour palette that way. Once I'm happy with a design, I try my best to transfer the line art to paper by using a grid to help me, and then I move onto colour. When it comes to the actual production of a drawing, I do love to use traditional media. My preference changes over time – sometimes I will get bored with one, and then I move on to the other, and keep alternating that way.

How has your character-design process changed over time? Is your style still evolving?

My style has changed quite a bit, I think. I've improved my overall shape design, which is something I struggled with a lot. At first I was only able to do certain types of characters but now I feel confident enough to create all kinds, which is so much fun. Style is something that definitely keeps evolving, for everyone, as long as you are actively trying to better your skills. For example, I feel as if my characters have become more fun, in terms of their poses and expressions, and my rendering has started to feel a lot more detailed in the last year or so, especially when working traditionally. However, I'm still at a point where I want to get better – there are still so many aspects of my art that I can improve.

Opposite page: *The Open Book* – This has to be one of my favourite pieces. I wanted to work on some close-up features and really enjoyed the process and overall composition

This page: *Emma's Bedroom* – This is a drawing I made for a friend of mine – it also opened so many new doors for me

Where do you find inspiration for your characters and the colourful worlds they inhabit?

I'm someone who's heavily influenced by nature. I lived in the natural world for a long time before coming to the city, so it's always been a part of me. I love the different shades of greens, the sounds, and the air. This is most likely why the Ghibli film *Princess Mononoke* has been a favourite of mine, ever since I was a young girl. I have always tried to imagine little characters running in the wild, doing their own things, which has inspired me to create the drawings you see today. Another source of inspiration is music, specifically music scores from films I've seen or games I've played. A good example of this would be the music score from the game *Ori and The Blind Forest*, or from the movie *How to Train Your Dragon*. Other things, like bright and sunny days and the changing seasons, have always been sources of inspiration for me, too.

Finally, we have to ask – where did the name Poopikat come from?

Hah, the infamous question! When I was studying in Italy for a year, I couldn't bring my cat Noëlle along with me, so she stayed with my mom. I missed her a lot – she's my first pet and we are very close. When I first rescued her, she had little accidents, so I called her my 'little poopy cat'. Anyway, when I was in Italy, I started creating digital art again for the first time in what felt like forever – that's when I started my Instagram account, under the name Poopikat. I chose 'Poopi' because I missed Noëlle, and Kat as an abbreviation of my name, Kate.

Thanks for chatting to us Kate! Do you have any upcoming projects we should be looking out for?

Of course, thank you so much for having me. I've just finished a picture book which will be coming out very soon. I'm very excited about that. I'm also working on another book, and another TV series, but I can't share too much info about that yet. Otherwise, stay tuned to my social channels for more information in the months to come. Thank you so much for this interview, it was so much fun!

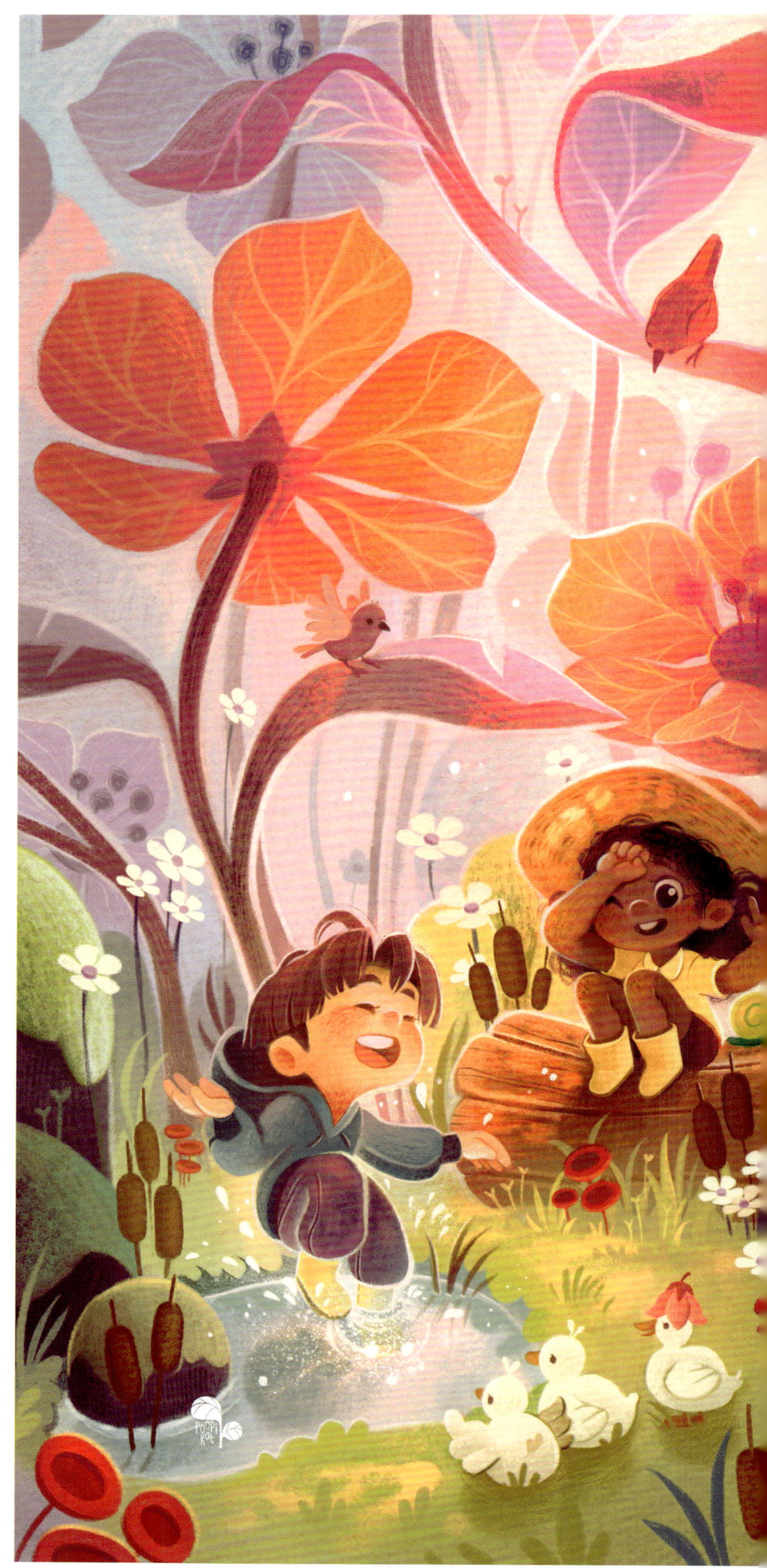

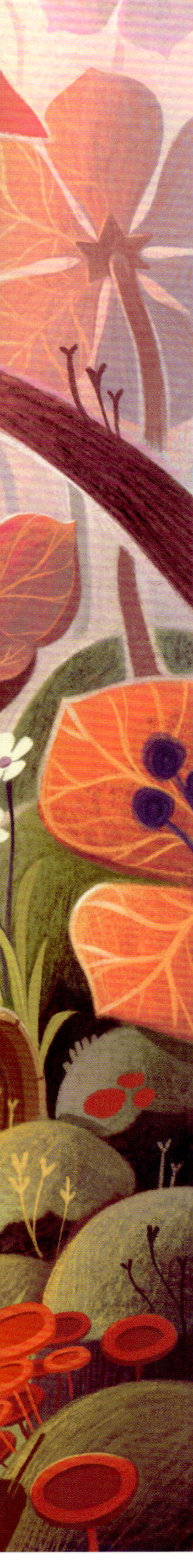

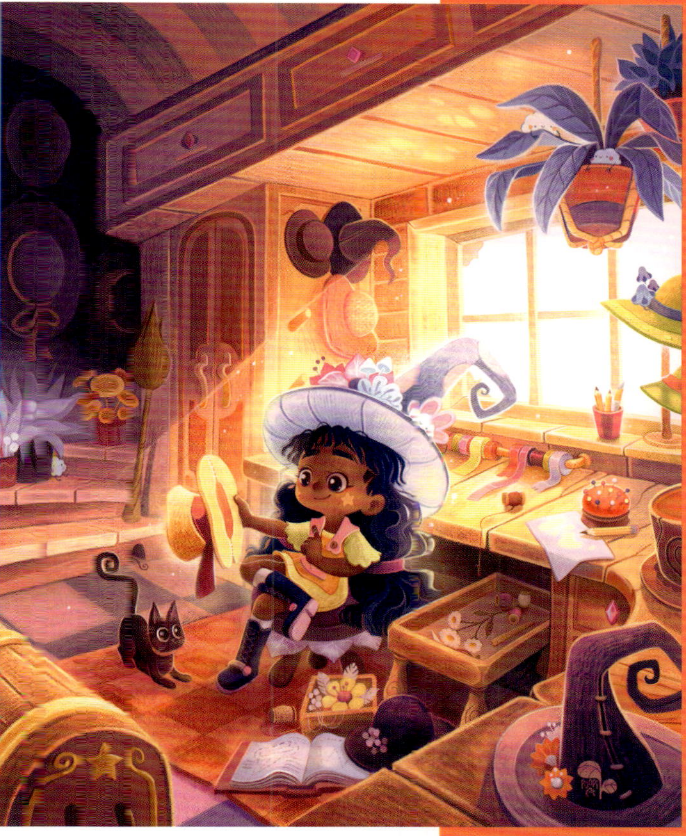

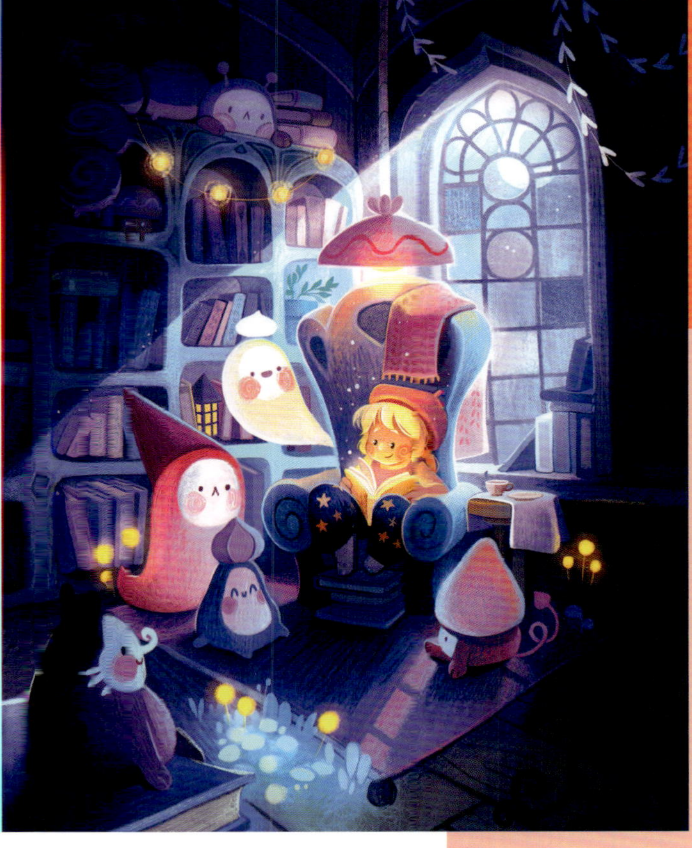

'I LIVED IN THE NATURAL WORLD FOR A LONG TIME BEFORE COMING TO THE CITY, SO IT'S ALWAYS BEEN A PART OF ME'

Opposite page: *Playful Rain* – Two kids enjoying a fabulous spring day together

This page (top): *The Hat Shop* – This drawing was so much fun to create. It was partly inspired by *Howl's Moving Castle*

This page (bottom): *Storybook* – I felt like having a few more creature characters, so this nighttime piece came to mind

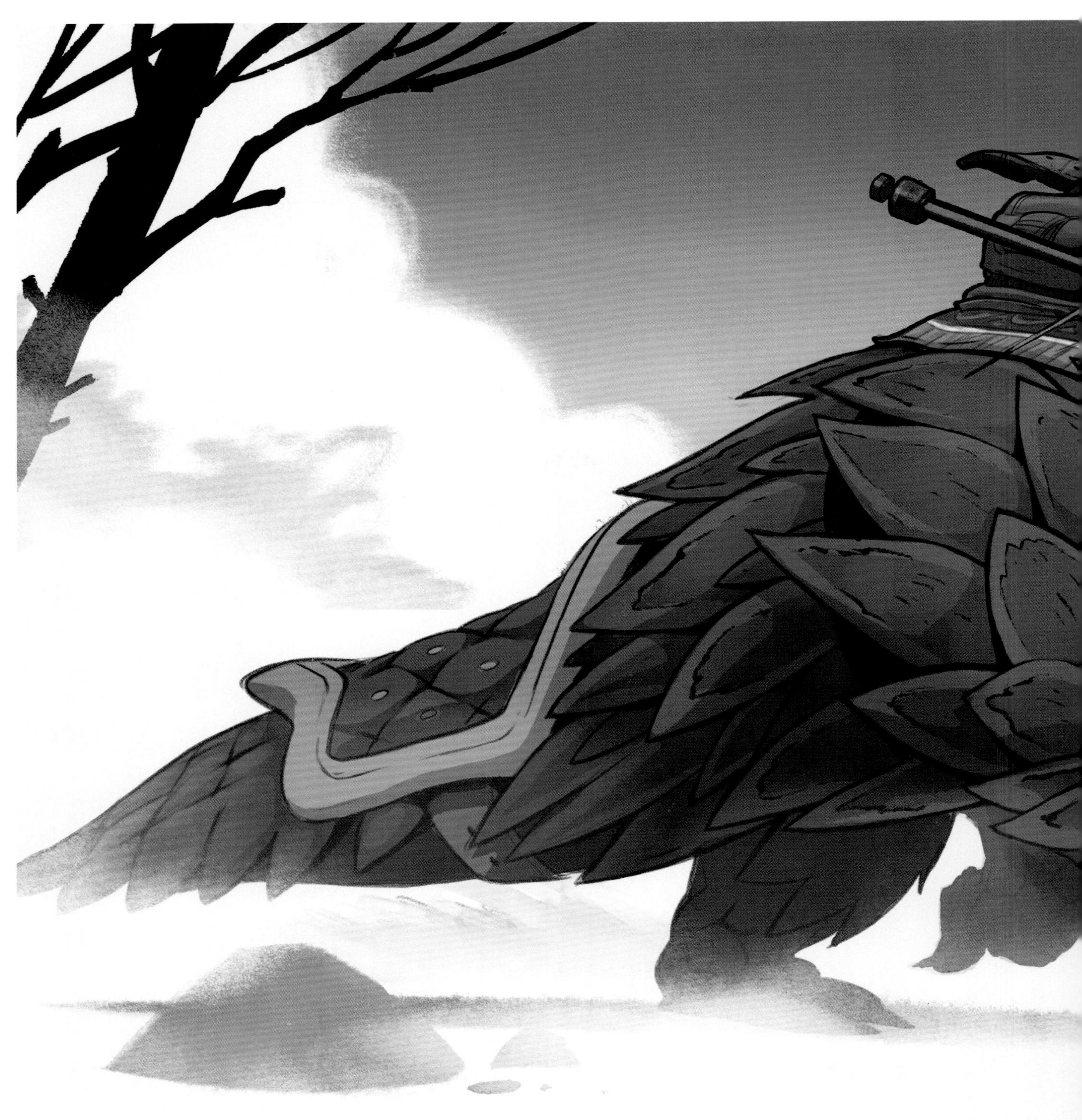

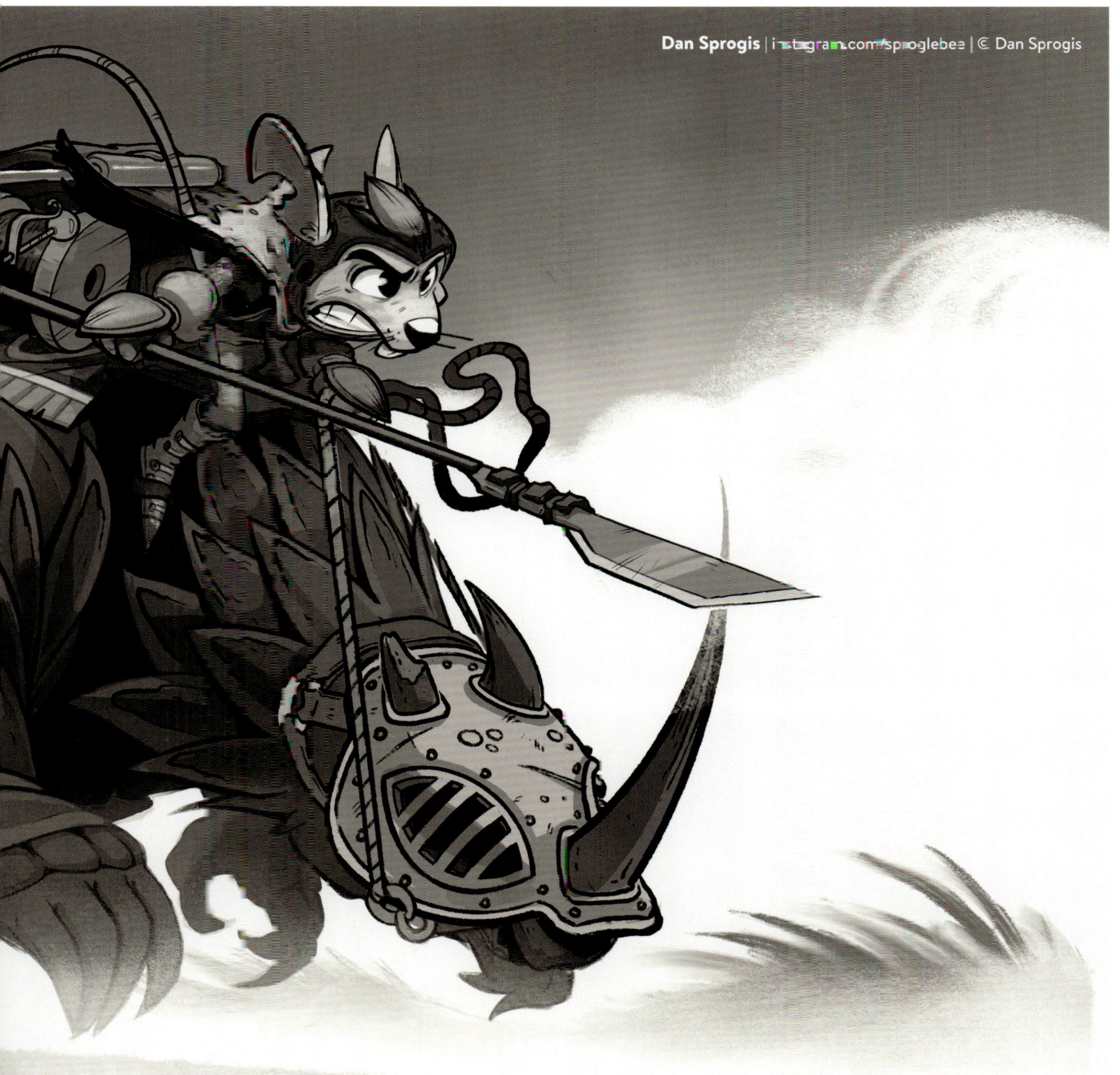

THE GALLERY

In the gallery we present a fresh selection of art from talented individuals from all across the industry. In this issue we have pieces from three exciting artists: Dan Sprogis, Kenny Leoncito, and Haiyang Sun.

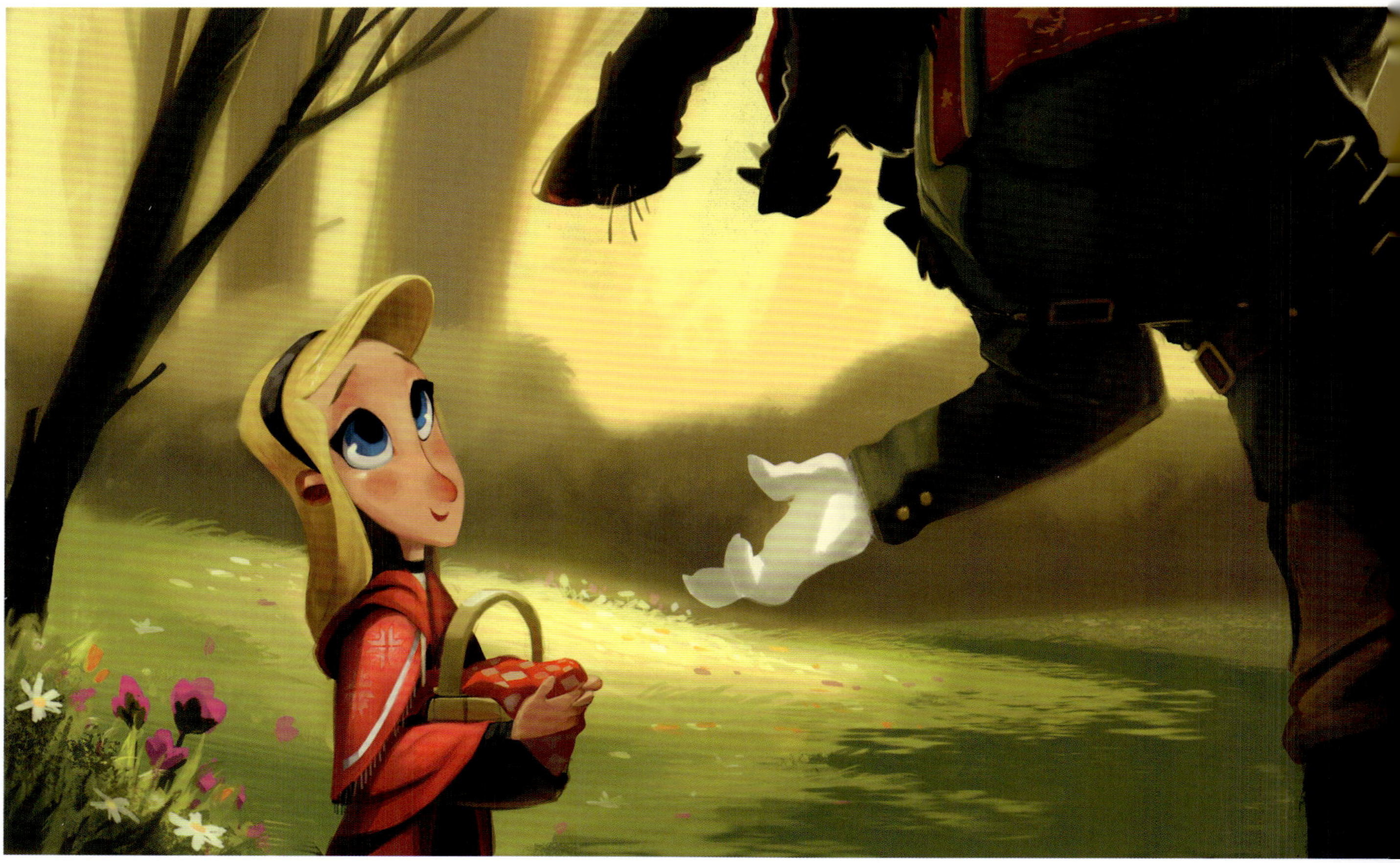

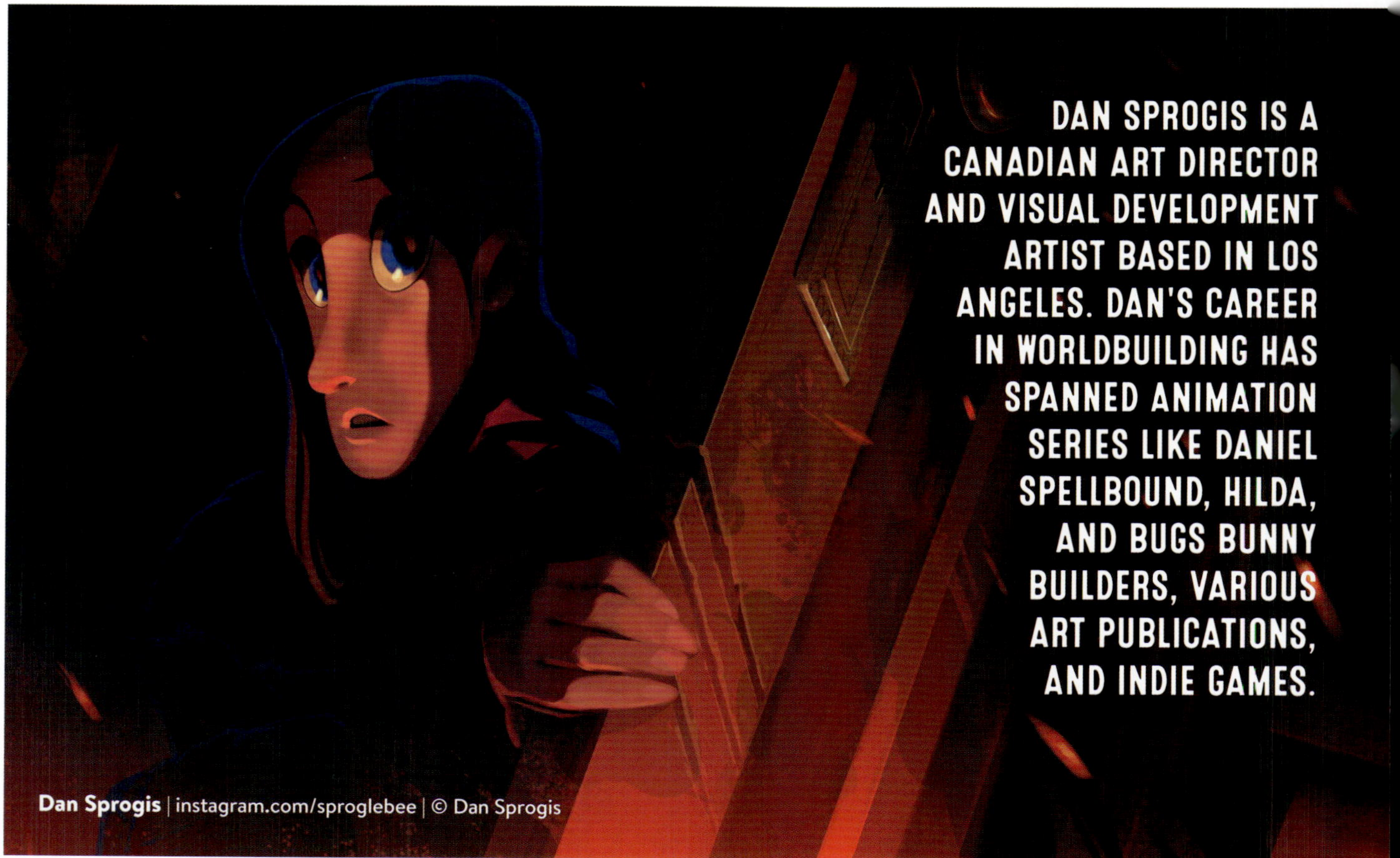

Dan Sprogis | instagram.com/sproglebee | © Dan Sprogis

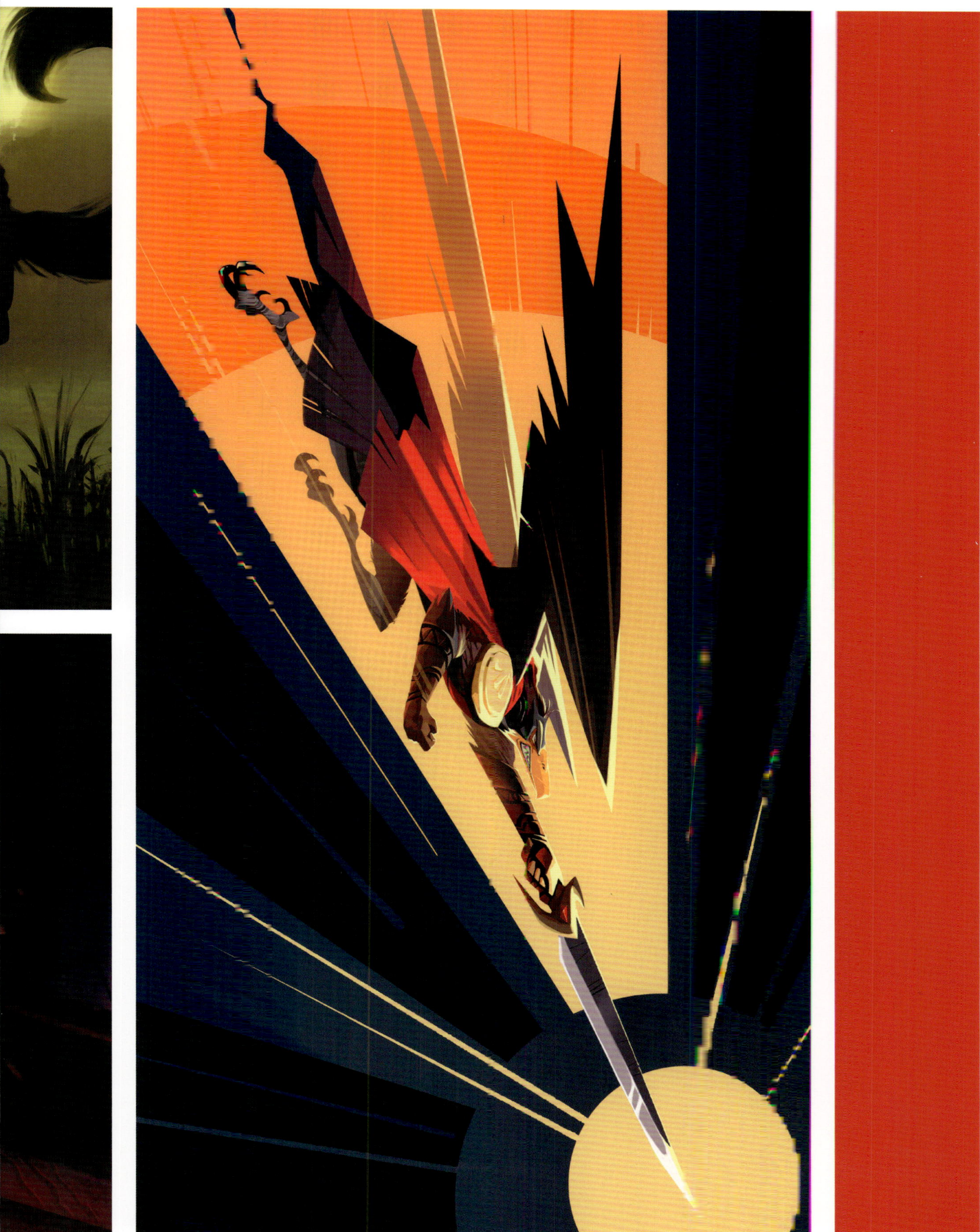

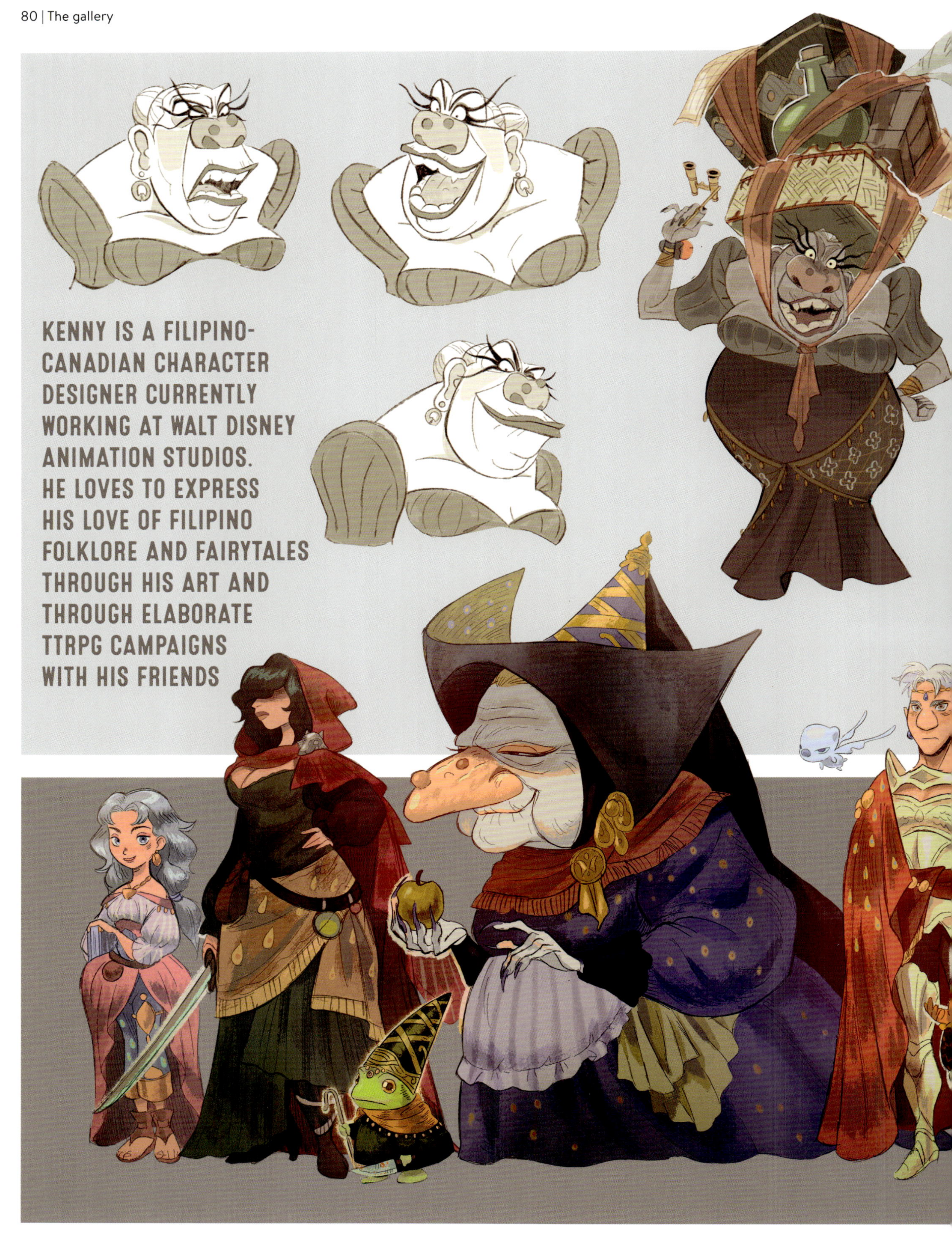

KENNY IS A FILIPINO-CANADIAN CHARACTER DESIGNER CURRENTLY WORKING AT WALT DISNEY ANIMATION STUDIOS. HE LOVES TO EXPRESS HIS LOVE OF FILIPINO FOLKLORE AND FAIRYTALES THROUGH HIS ART AND THROUGH ELABORATE TTRPG CAMPAIGNS WITH HIS FRIENDS

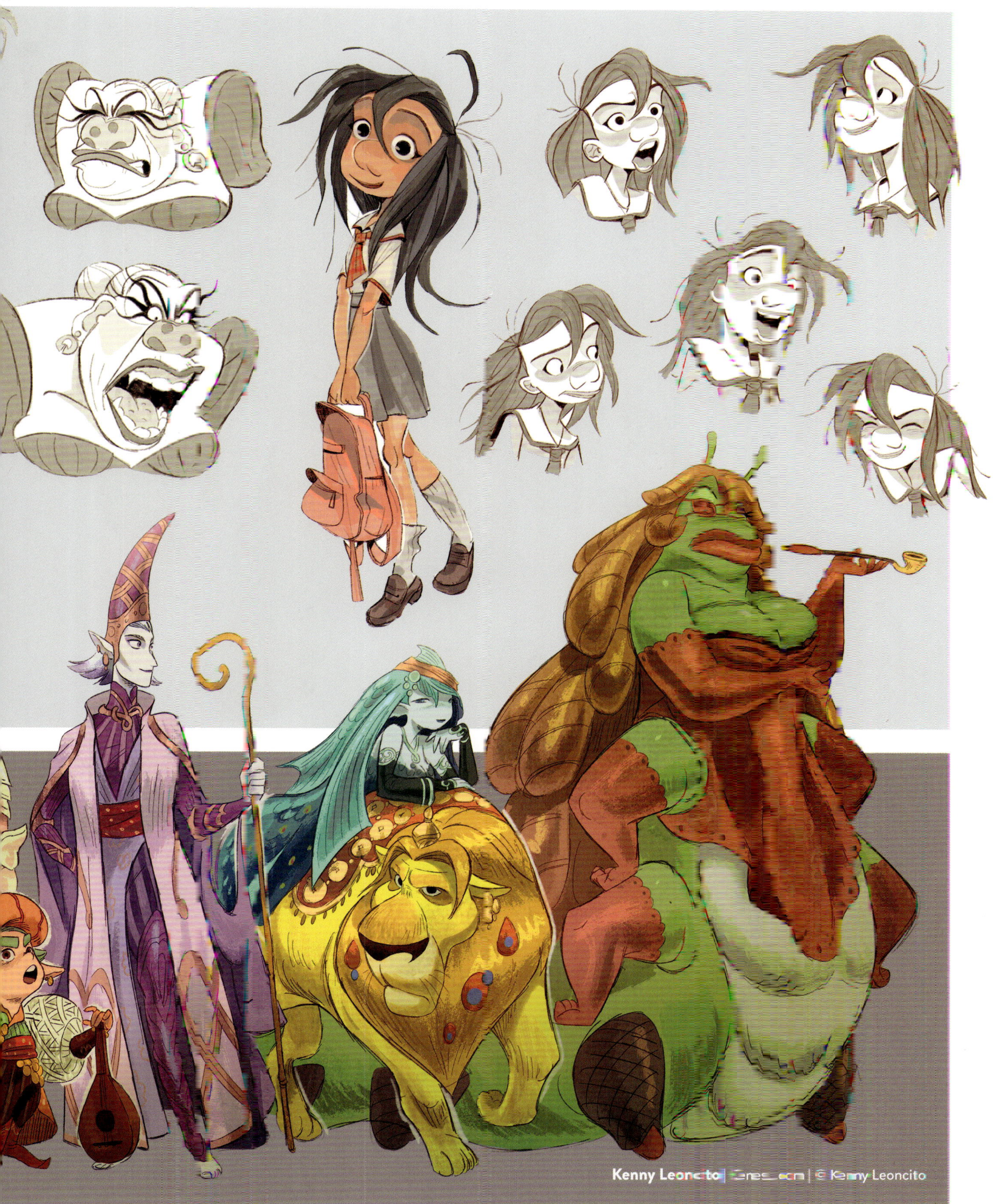

HAIYANG SUN IS A CONCEPT ARTIST, BASED IN THE LA AREA. HE WORKS IN THE VIDEO-GAME INDUSTRY AND HAS PREVIOUSLY CONTRIBUTED TO MULTIPLE AAA TITLES, INCLUDING APEX LEGENDS, CALL OF DUTY: COLD WAR, PERFECT DARK, AND MORE.

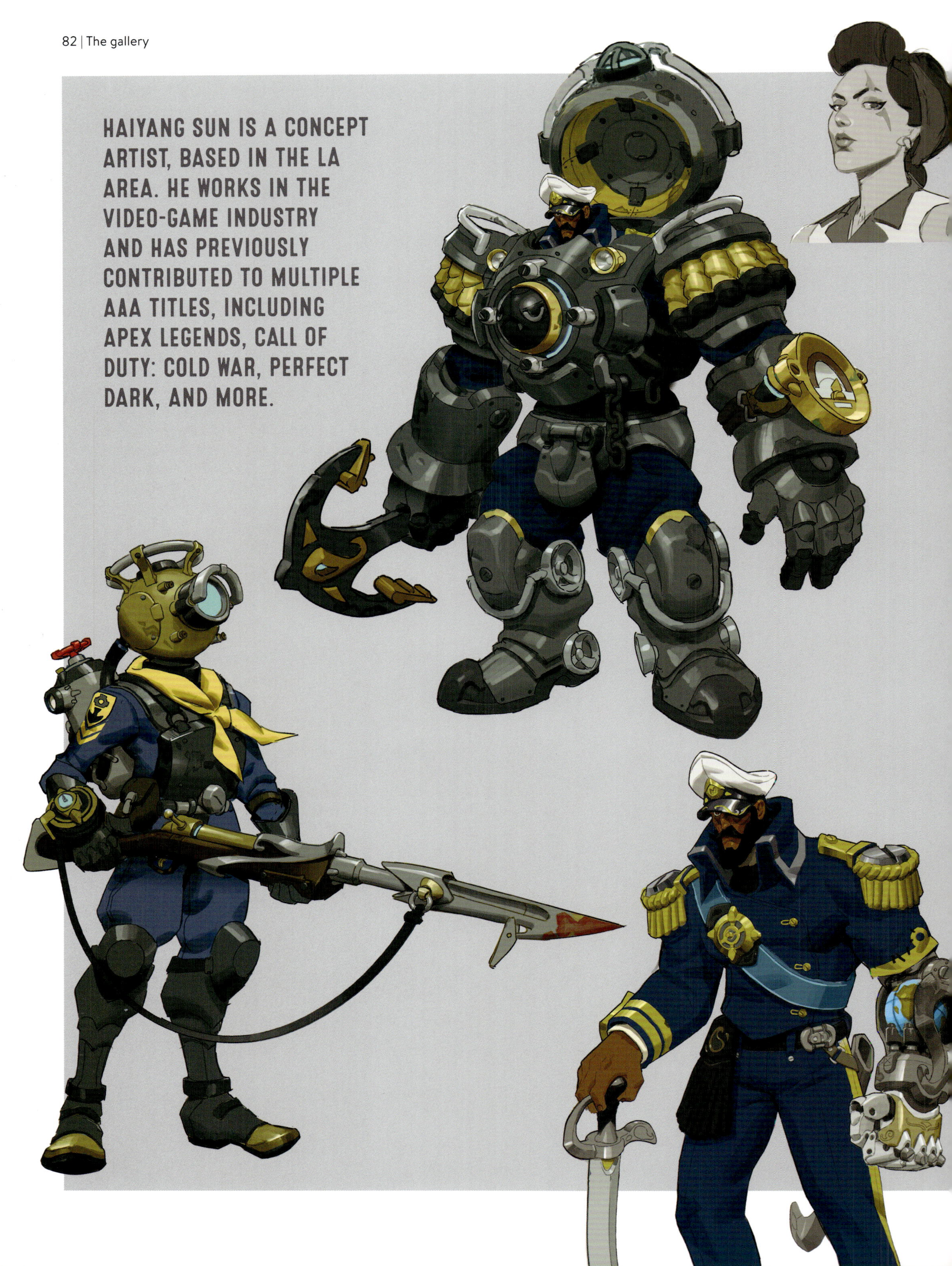

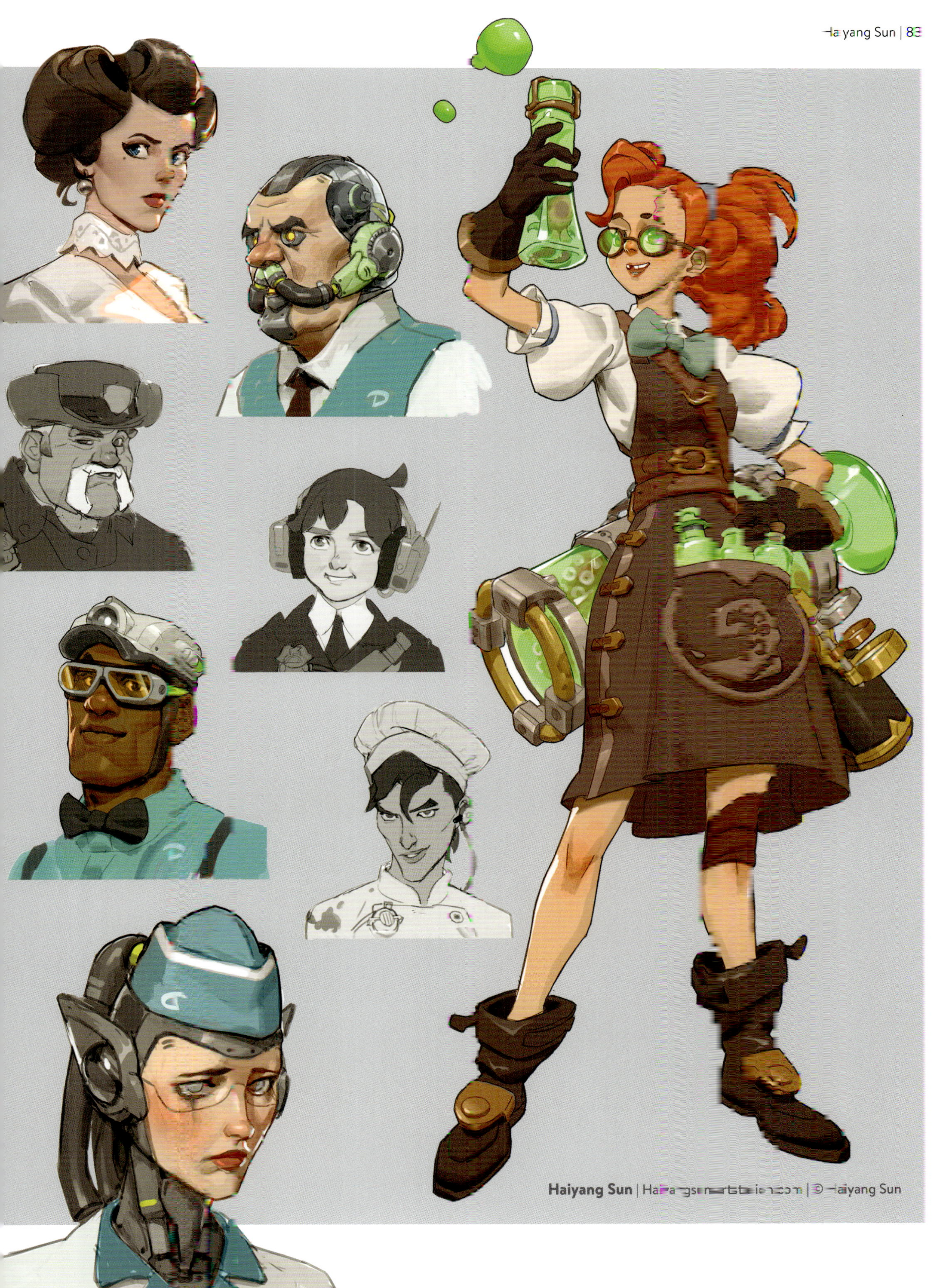

YOU ARE WHAT YOU WEAR

LAURA DUMITRIU

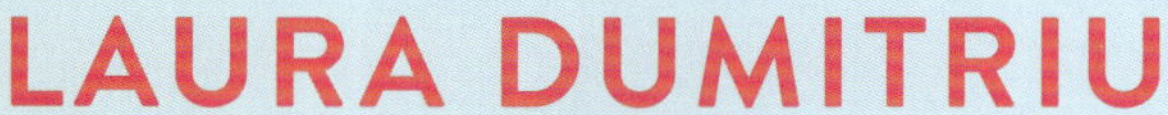

In this tutorial, I will explore how to portray characters with three different looks: sporty, casual, and elegant. We'll look at two characters, Daisy and Lorelei, and delve into the importance of poses and facial expressions in effectively conveying the desired emotions. Additionally, I will share valuable tips to help you approach the sketching process with confidence, enabling you to create quality designs.

BASIC BEGINNINGS

The first thing I do when developing a character is sketch out a basic pose, so I can establish my character's physical appearance: tall or short, large or skinny, and so on. Once I have a rough sketch, I start cleaning it and adding details to the face. Gradually, a compelling character will start to take shape.

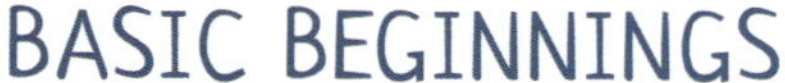

POSE POSSIBILITIES

The first step in creating any character for me is browsing for interesting poses. My favourite websites for this task are Pinterest, Google, and ArtStation. Once I find some inspiration, I sketch a few poses that I like and choose the best one. I take into consideration the mood and emotions I'm trying to portray.

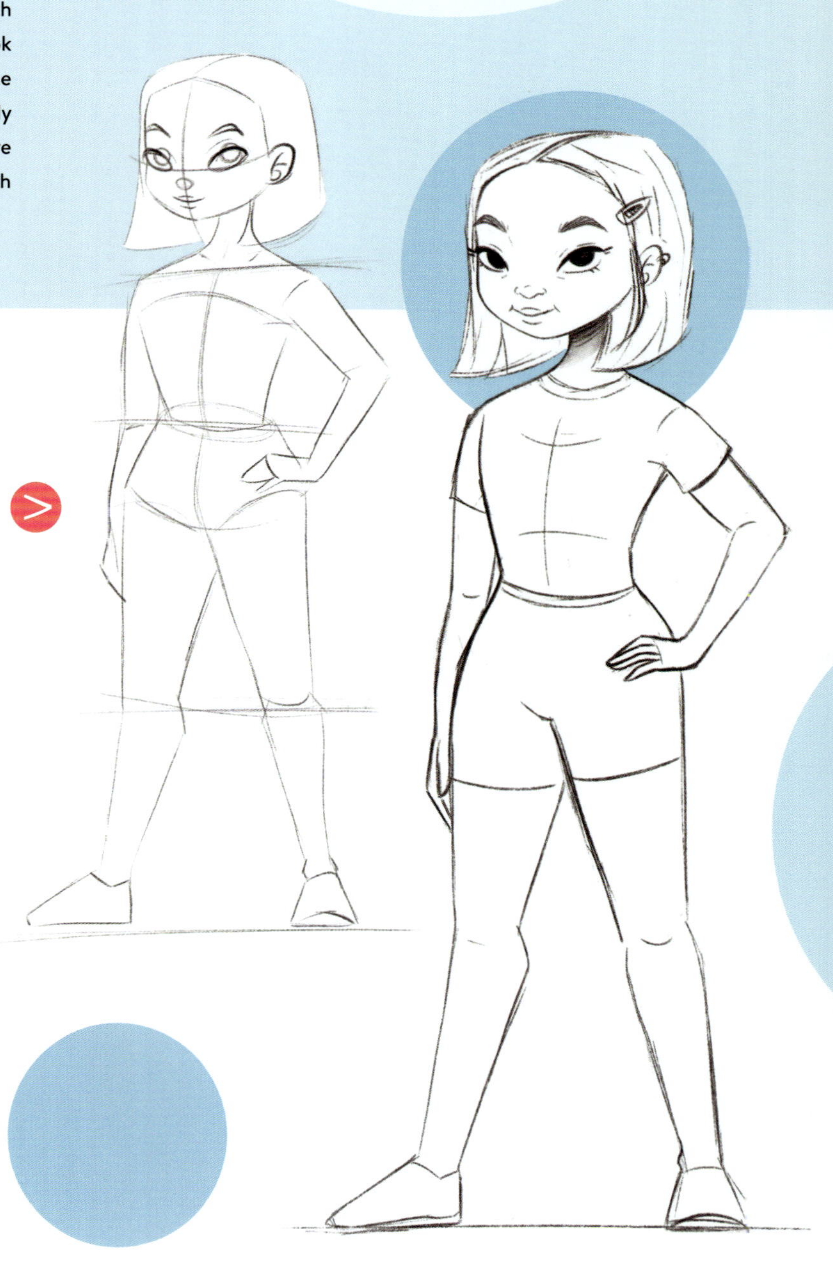">

ATHLETIC IDEAS

Because I'm portraying a sporty look, I choose a pose that's dynamic and shows my character in a stretch. Her facial expression helps to convey that she is exercising. To choose colours, I start with the skin colour, then the hair, and finally the clothes. Everything needs to be in harmony. I add a touch of red to her face to emphasize the effort of her stretching.

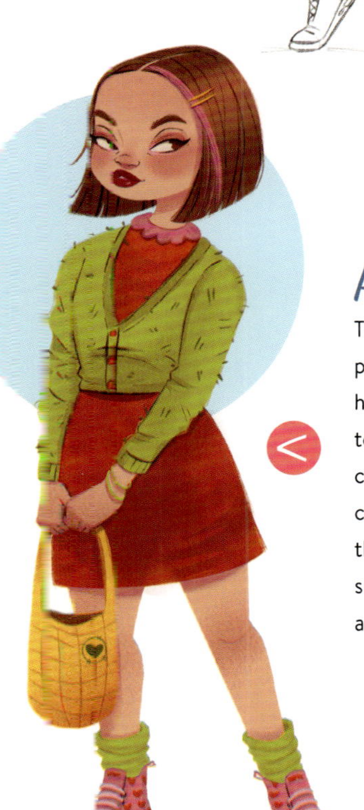

AUTUMN MOOD

The outfit your character wears is an integral part of their design. Clothes work hand in hand with facial expressions and body pose to evoke a mood and create a narrative. To create a casual, autumnal look I choose the complementary colours green and red for the outfit, with pink and yellow accents which suggest playfulness. I emphasize this with a streak of pink in the character's hair.

ELEGANT POSING

To create an elegant outfit, I draw a simple yet dynamic pose. I draw pink lines on the sketch to show the rhythm that the different shapes create, almost opposing each other. These points help make the pose feel alive. When rendering the final image, I use subtle shading to accentuate the delicacy of the dress fabric and the elegant vibe.

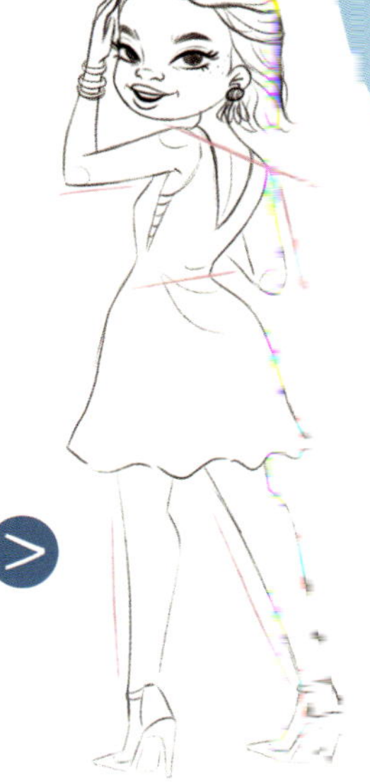

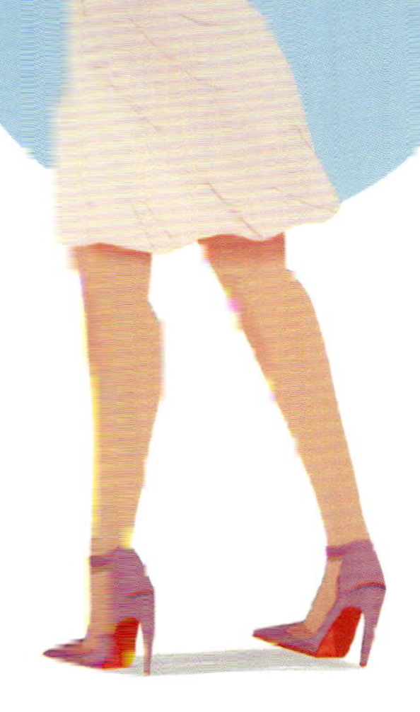

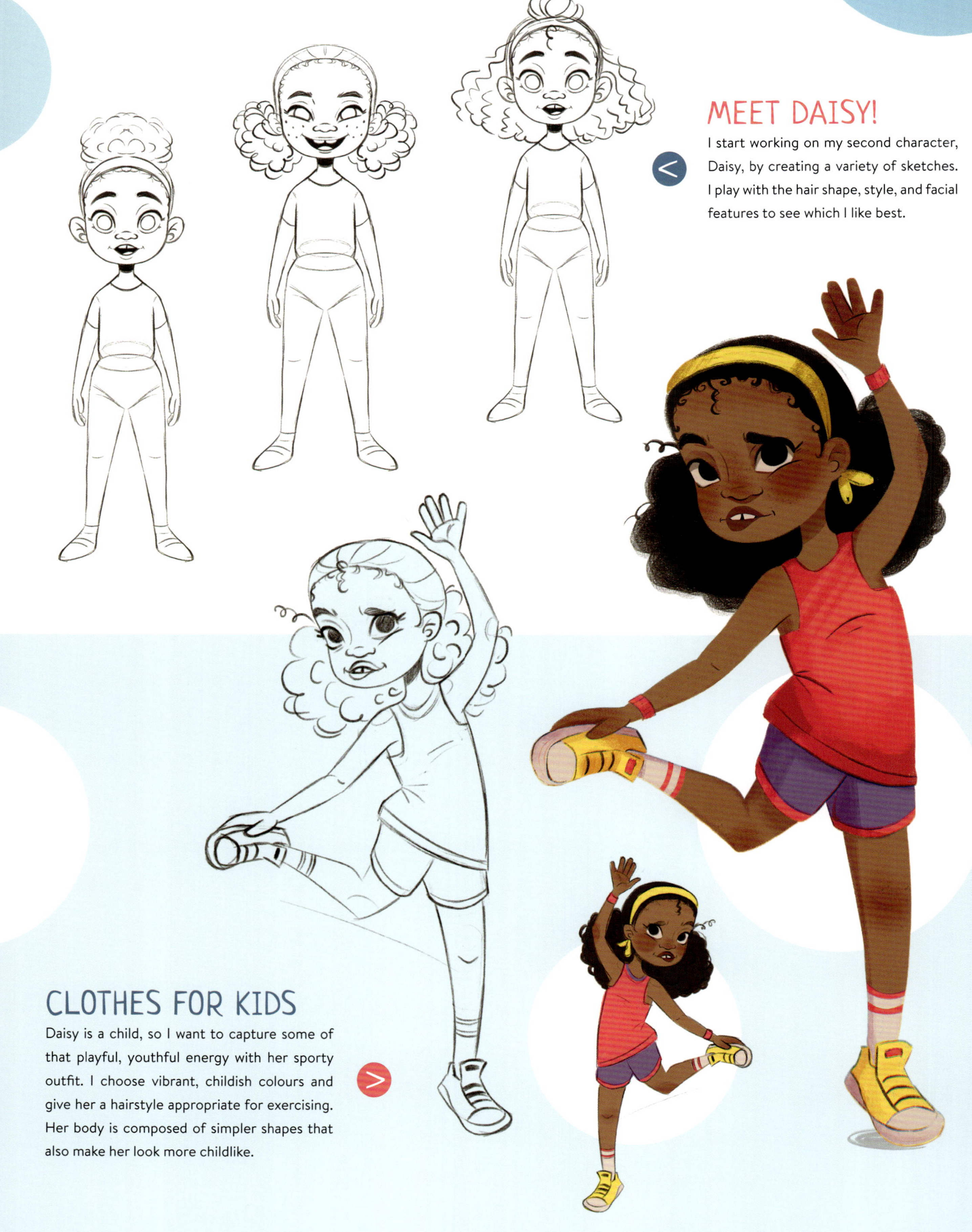

MEET DAISY!

I start working on my second character, Daisy, by creating a variety of sketches. I play with the hair shape, style, and facial features to see which I like best.

CLOTHES FOR KIDS

Daisy is a child, so I want to capture some of that playful, youthful energy with her sporty outfit. I choose vibrant, childish colours and give her a hairstyle appropriate for exercising. Her body is composed of simpler shapes that also make her look more childlike.

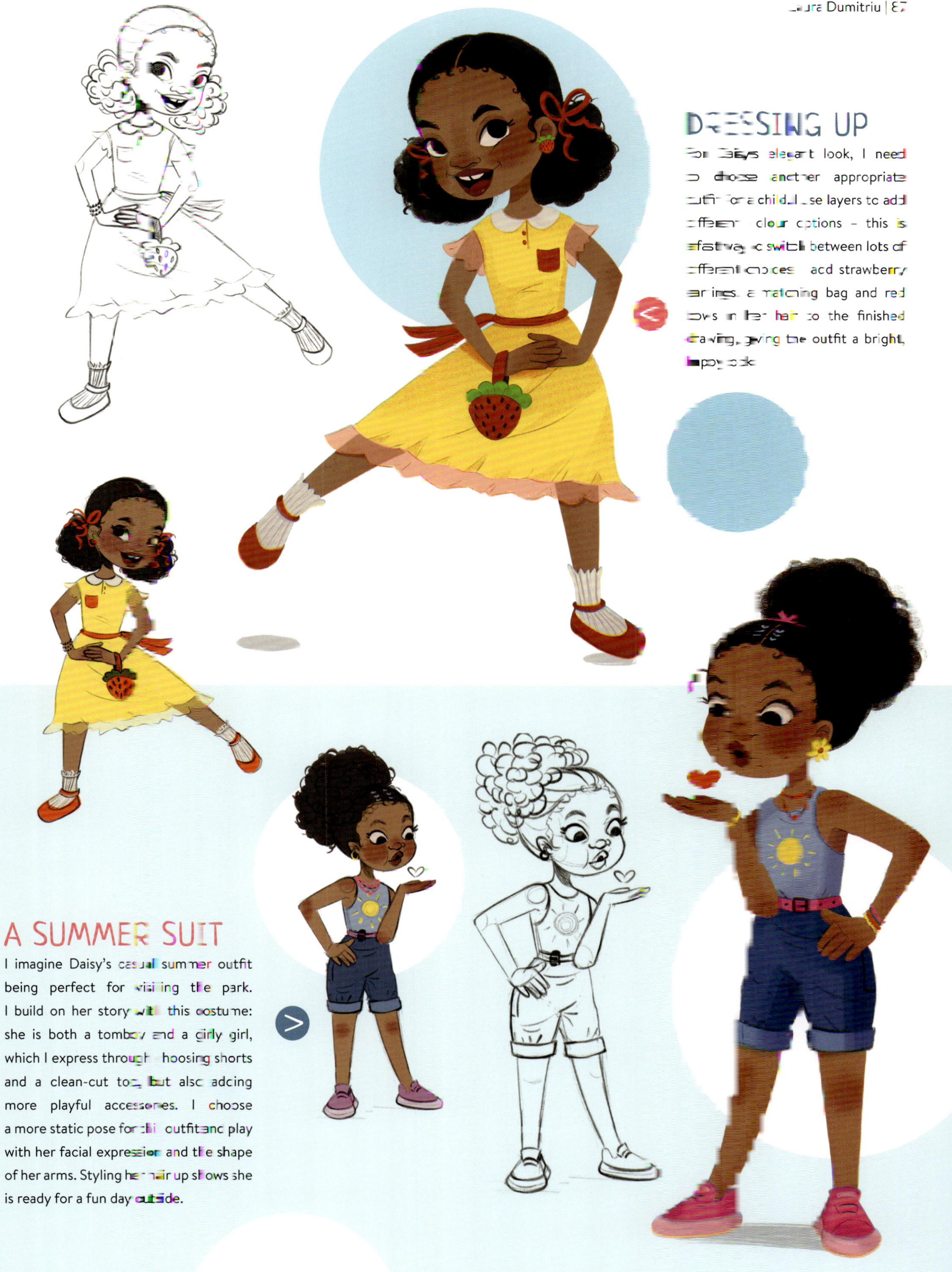

DRESSING UP

For Daisy's elegant look, I need to choose another appropriate outfit for a child. I use layers to add different colour options – this is effective to switch between lots of different choices. I add strawberry earrings, a matching bag and red bows in her hair to the finished drawing, giving the outfit a bright, happy look.

A SUMMER SUIT

I imagine Daisy's casual summer outfit being perfect for visiting the park. I build on her story with this costume: she is both a tomboy and a girly girl, which I express through choosing shorts and a clean-cut top, but also adding more playful accessories. I choose a more static pose for this outfit and play with her facial expression and the shape of her arms. Styling her hair up shows she is ready for a fun day outside.

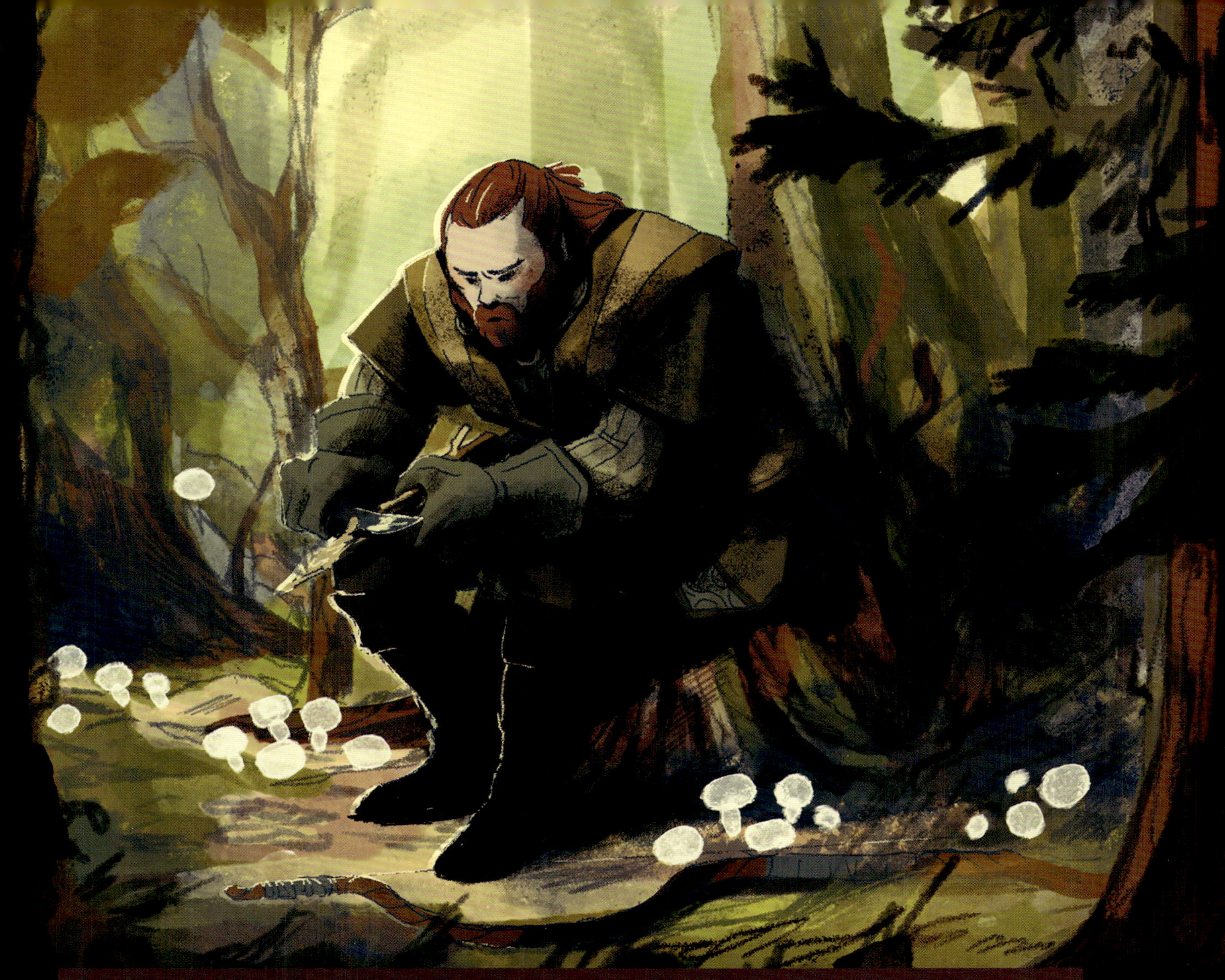

ROBIN HOOD REBORN

ERICA HODNE

When I was first asked to reimagine the classic character Robin Hood, I had my reservations. The character's cultural significance and many existing interpretations made me feel a little scared. I want to honour his heritage, while also giving myself the creative freedom to create my own original take. I also want to have fun with this character, which, in my opinion, is the whole point of character design – there should be joy amidst the pressure.

Robin Hood is such a fascinating character and I am extremely excited to take a deep dive into his history. For this tutorial, I will work digitally, mainly using Procreate and Photoshop. I hope that this digital journey will inspire you – let's embrace the chaotic beauty of character design together!

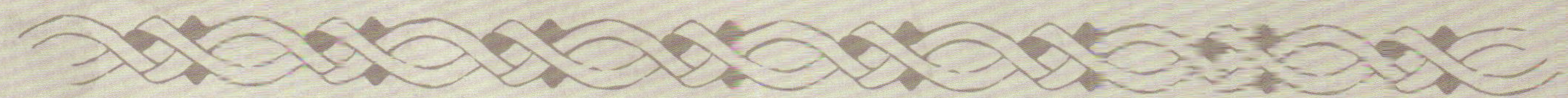

MORE THAN MERRY MEN?

Before I start drawing, I like to dive into the character's history. I investigate the many variations of Robin Hood's story to try to get a feel for the essence of the character so I can truly do him justice. I start off by making a list of facts I find interesting and that I wish to keep in mind as I move forward. For this stage, I like to use a notebook and jot down the elements of the character I'm planning to use. I want my version of Robin Hood to be about more than just green tights and merry men – I think there is depth of character I can use, beyond the obvious tropes.

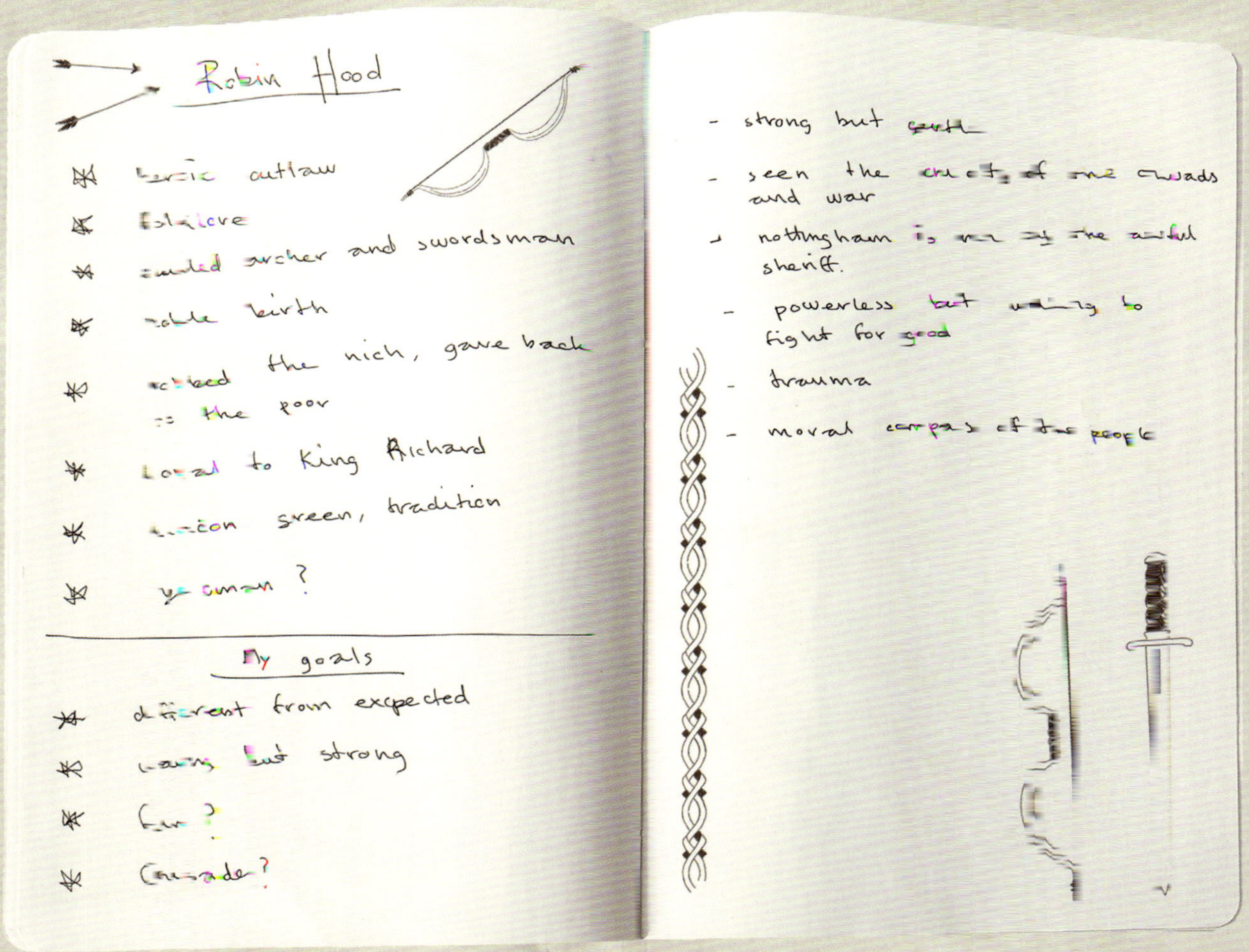

Robin Hood

- heroic outlaw
- folklore
- skilled archer and swordsman
- noble birth
- robbed the rich, gave back to the poor
- loyal to King Richard
- Lincoln green, tradition
- yeoman?

My goals

- different from expected
- caring but strong
- fun?
- Crusade?

- strong but gentle
- seen the cruelty of the crusads and war
- nottingham is run by the awful sheriff.
- powerless but willing to fight for good
- trauma
- moral compass of the people

This page: I write down every fact that fascinates me as I research a character

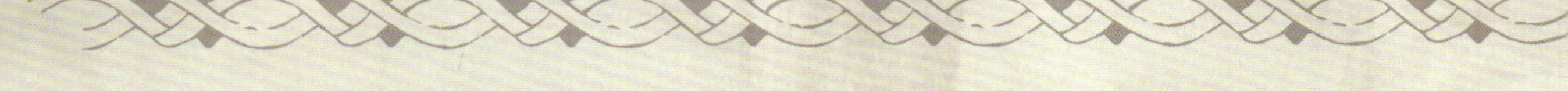

CRAFTING THE STORY

Using a mind map makes it easier to figure out what aspects of Robin Hood resonate the most. Is he just a thief, or is he a beacon of hope? I want to go beyond the superficial and look deeper into his character. Does his loyalty to King Richard seem an interesting facet to explore? Or maybe his skill as an archer, or his past life as a crusader?

I collect the elements I am most drawn to and write them down. I like to let these elements guide my design process. When I feel like I have enough to work with, I write a short story that I believe will give me enough detail to work with.

Robin Hood was born into a noble and religious family in Nottingham and grew up safe within the walls of their grand estate. He was interested in archery from an early age and quickly became the finest shot in all of Nottinghamshire. Once he was of age, Robin was sent to join the crusades, as was expected of a person of his standing. There he had an epiphany – he didn't want to lead a life dedicated to war, hurting the innocent and those less fortunate than himself. Scarred by the horrors he saw on crusade, he deserted the army and returned to Nottingham. He decided he would dedicate his life to fighting for the common people, stealing from the rich and giving to the poor.

This page: A mind map of the elements of Robin Hood's story I want to explore

Opposite page: A collection of head designs, based on my earlier research

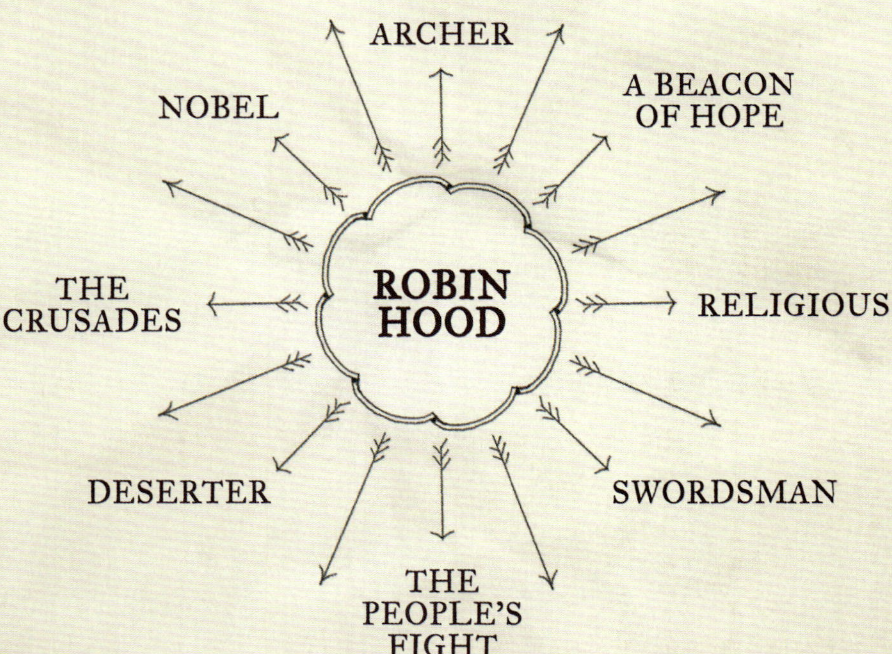

THOUGHTS BECOME LINES

With any character, the initial sketches are so important. Start drawing, allowing your thoughts to freely translate into lines. For this stage of the characterization I like to work with Procreate on my iPad. I love the freedom of being able to draw whenever and wherever inspiration hits me. I start by illustrating a couple of different heads, each representing different visions of the Robin Hood I am looking for. I find faces to be the most important part of the body when I characterize, as I think there is room for so much of the character's source to shine through. The second to last of these sketches particularly resonates with me – it has a certain essence I visualize for Robin Hood. As my notes suggest, it is important to me that Robin has a softness to him, while still showing that he can be stern and strong. Remember, at first stage it's all about exploring and capturing the right feel.

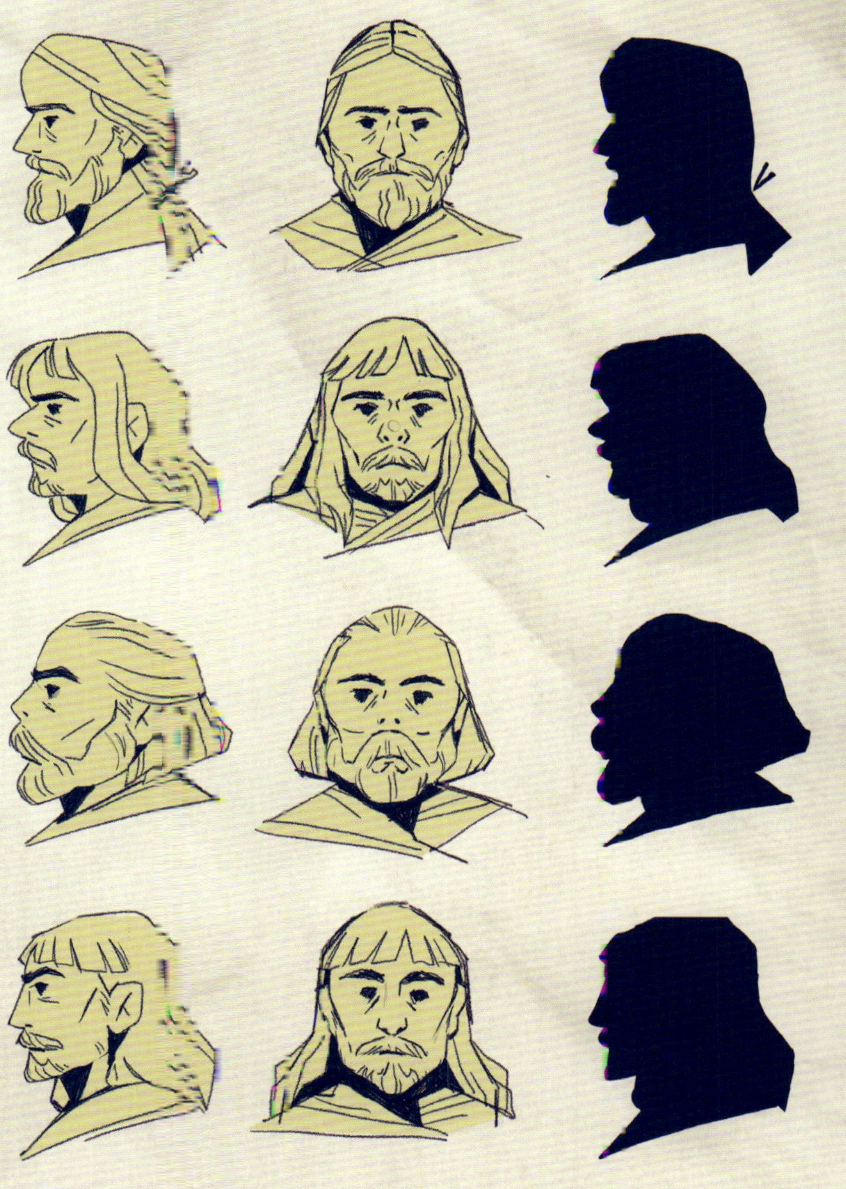

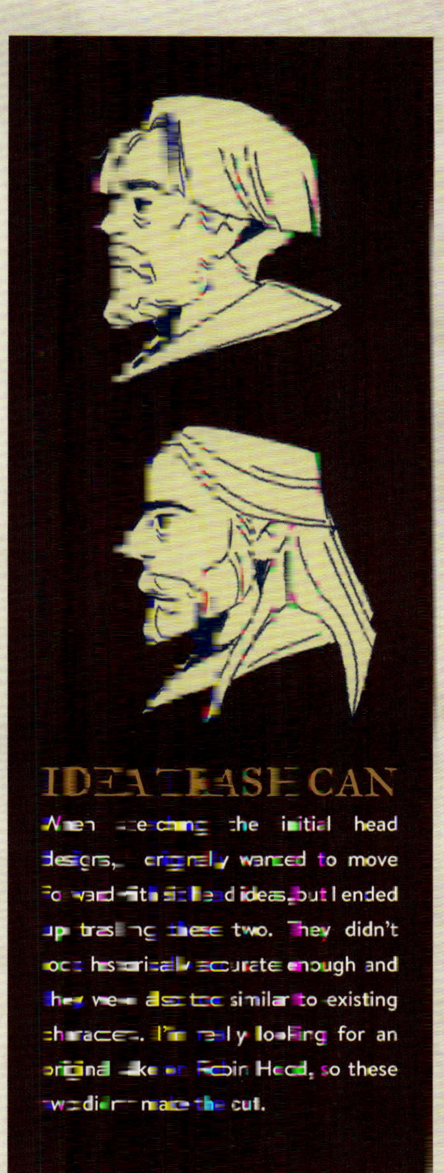

THE SHAPE OF A LEGEND

Defining Robin Hood's physique is a huge part of his characterization. To explore further, I sketch a range of different body types. I include the heads from the earlier step to help narrow down my character choices. My goal is to capture the essence of each character, as they could each be a good candidate for Robin.

There are four physiques that spoke to me: a tall and slender shape, a balanced, muscular form, and two robust shapes, one a little shorter than the other. I think many people may envision Robin Hood as tall and slender, but I want to try a fresh perspective. I find myself gravitating towards the fuller figures. When making a choice I often look for what feels right to me, as well as what suits the research. So, I decide to move forward with the muscular and more balanced silhouette.

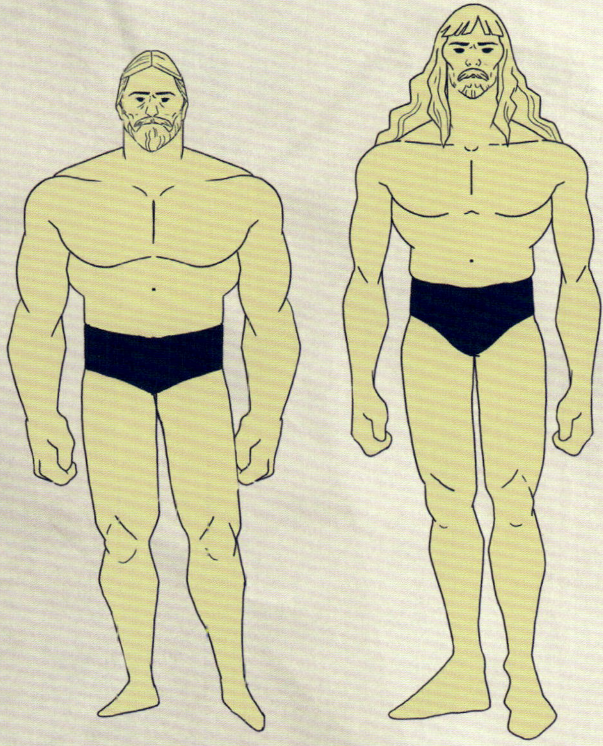

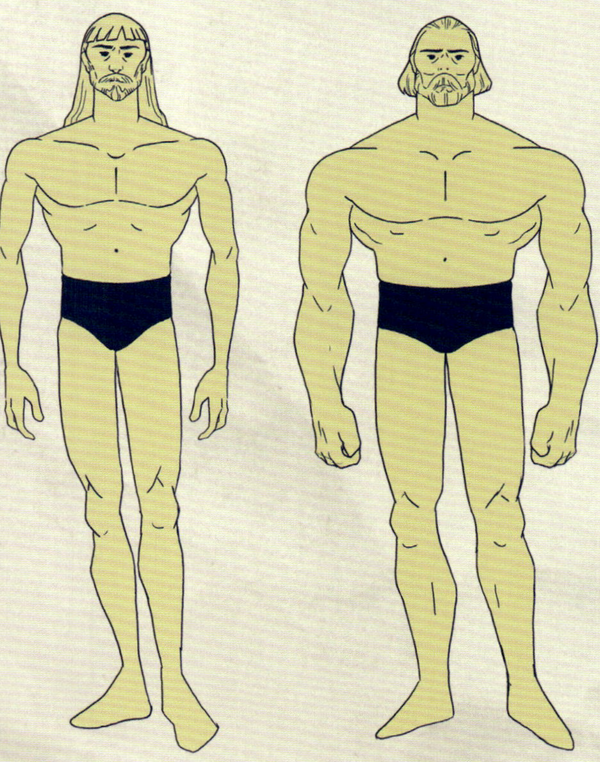

This page: Four different body types that I envision could suit Robin Hood

Opposite page (top): Four illustrations of potential outfits

Opposite page (bottom): Two different takes on bringing my ideas together

TESTING SYMMETRY

When creating bodies and faces, it can sometimes be difficult to make them look symmetrical. If I have this problem, I mirror the character to make sure all the details and proportions match on each side. I then put them together as a whole. This only works superficially, of course. It can look odd, but I find it is a good exercise to measure the character's symmetry.

MEDIEVAL FASHION

Now, to choose the right outfit for Robin. While researching the fashion of the time, I was surrounded by so many different silhouettes and colours. The number of shapes and patterns can be overwhelming, so when I start sketching it's important that I pull out the main elements that catch my eye. I think of things like practicality – where would the character get the clothing from? Does it make sense that he is wearing this particular piece?

From my many sketches, four outfits stand out the most. They are cut together with different shapes, fabrics, and silhouettes that I found during my research. When selecting an outfit, I think the most important thing to consider is whether it truly embodies the character. In this case, the outfit must show the strictness of Robin Hood's past and the freedom of his present.

STOP AND REFLECT

In my experience, design is often filled with doubt. Just when I'm hopeful about a character, I start to second guess my decisions and rethink everything I've done. Here you can see two versions of the same Robin Hood – the initial design on the left was made a month or so before the revised one on the right. Something just felt wrong about my first attempt, it felt too proper and elegant. So I revisit my research and inspirations, in search of a fresh perspective to propel me forward. I think it's important to take a moment to breathe and reflect on the design like this. Create space to move back and forth between designs until you find the one that truly hits different. After having considered both designs, I lean into the less pompous outfit as I think this will lead to a character that feels more genuine.

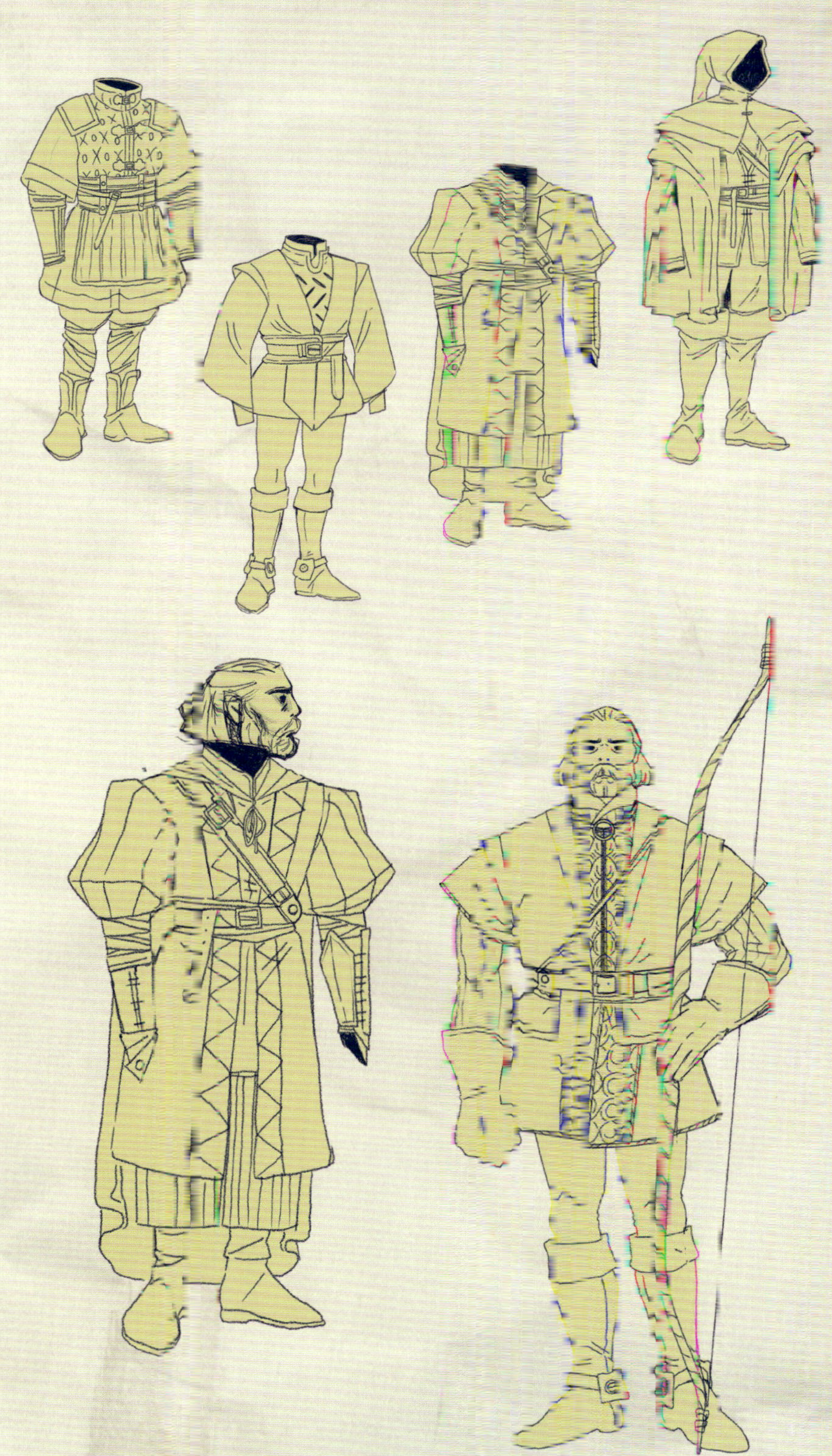

DYNAMIC ACTION

Dynamics play an important role in characterization. For characters like Robin Hood, it's important to see how they will move in action, as it is a big part of their character. I start sketching some action poses to understand the character's range of motion, putting him in three dynamic positions. I find this very helpful as it ensures that the character, particularly one skilled in archery and swordplay like Robin, can be depicted in a range of action scenes. This brings some more clarity to the character's physical limitations.

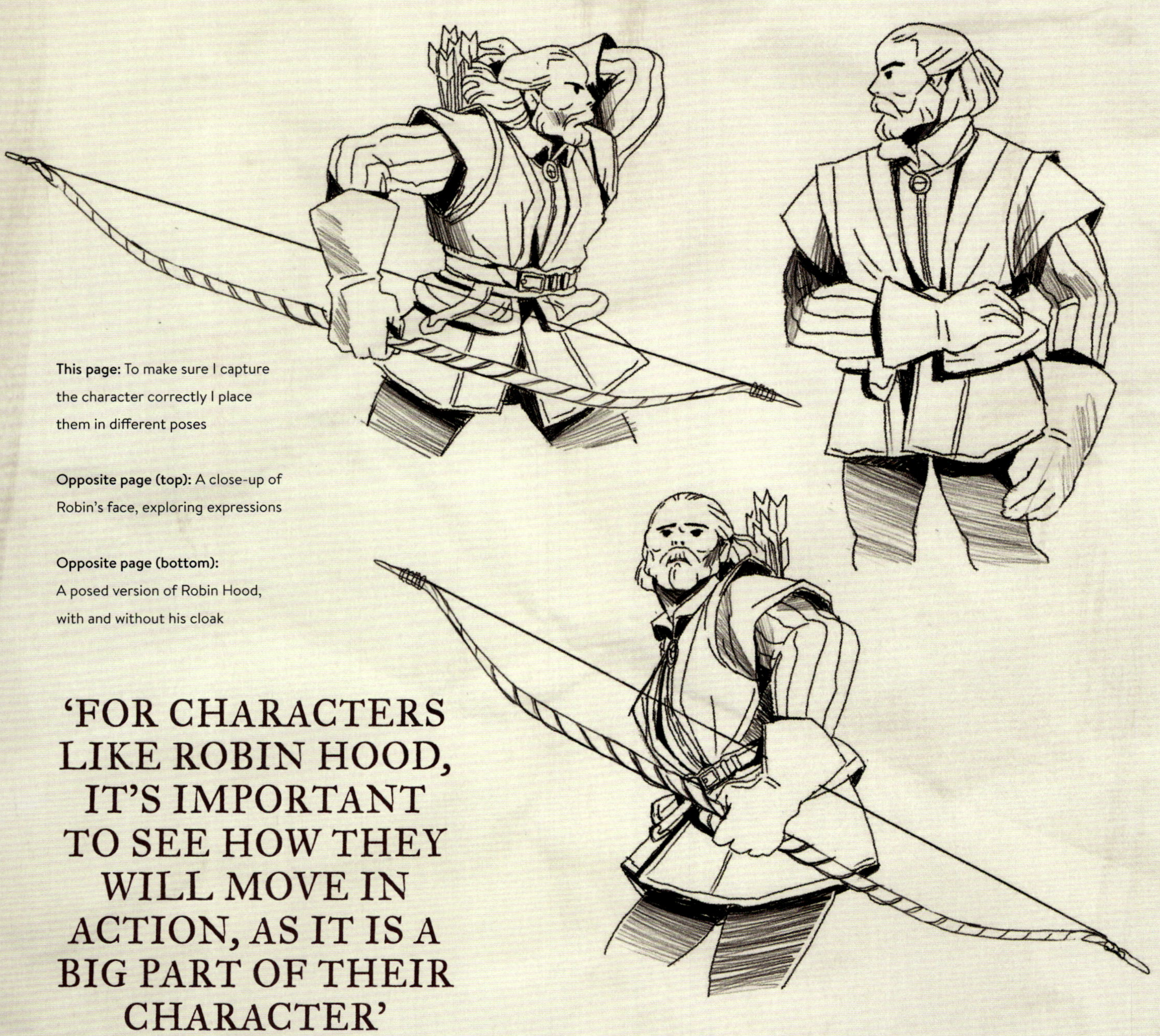

This page: To make sure I capture the character correctly I place them in different poses

Opposite page (top): A close-up of Robin's face, exploring expressions

Opposite page (bottom): A posed version of Robin Hood, with and without his cloak

'FOR CHARACTERS LIKE ROBIN HOOD, IT'S IMPORTANT TO SEE HOW THEY WILL MOVE IN ACTION, AS IT IS A BIG PART OF THEIR CHARACTER'

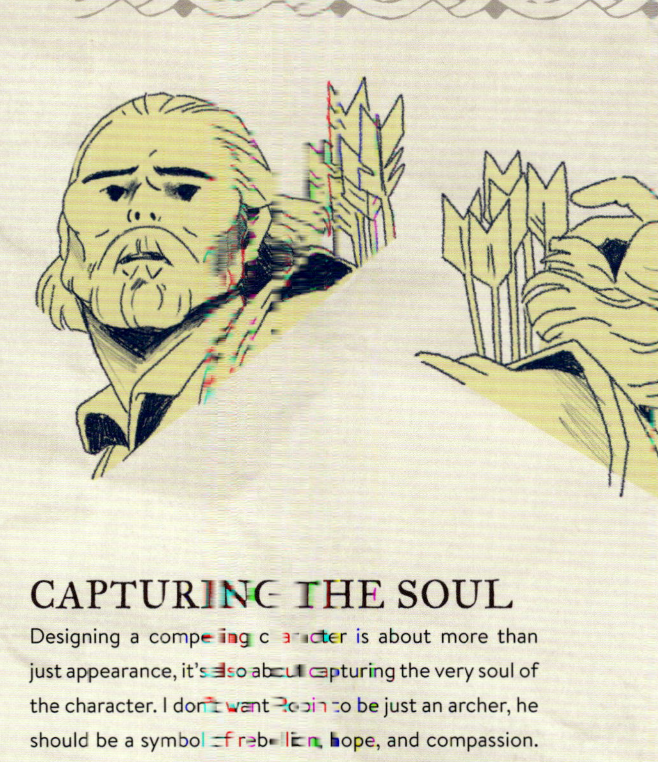

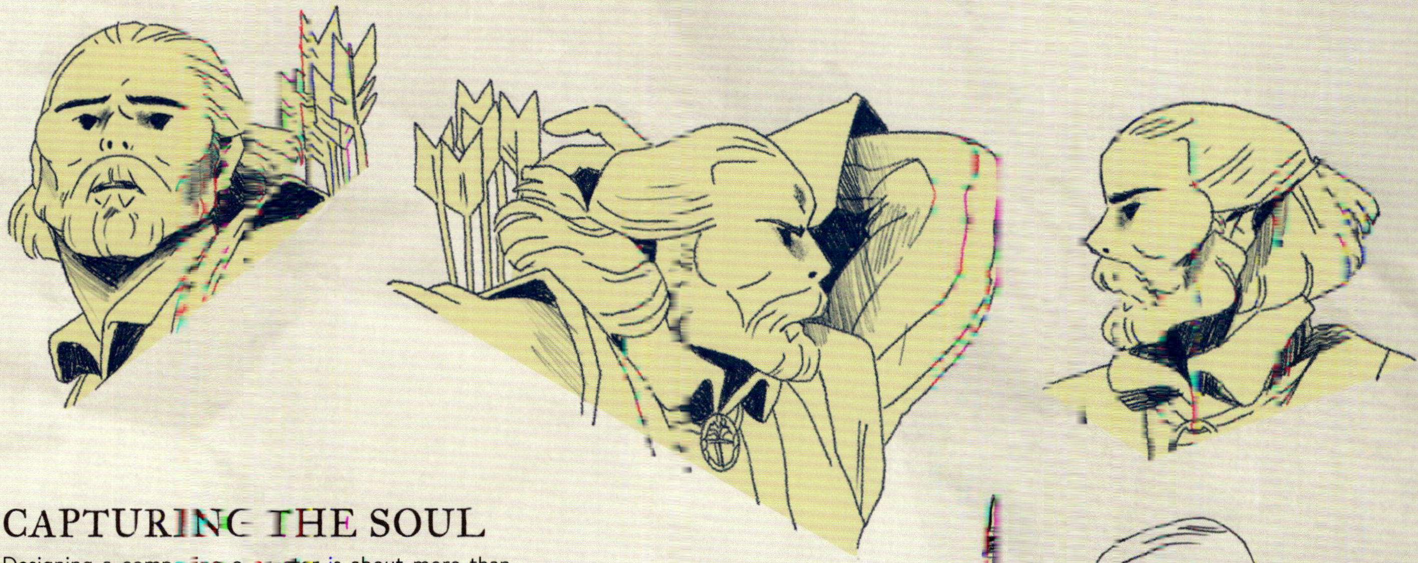

CAPTURING THE SOUL

Designing a compelling character is about more than just appearance, it's also about capturing the very soul of the character. I don't want Robin to be just an archer, he should be a symbol of rebellion, hope, and compassion. It's in the details of my character that I will bring these qualities to life, through subtle expressions in his eyes and eyebrows, or the way his mouth moves to show different emotions. I think Robin's stories are frequently traumatic and I want to reflect that somewhere on his face, perhaps in his eyebrows. It's very subtle, but his brow can communicate a continuous sense of worry. It's this kind of depth of connection during the design process that I believe truly brings a character to life.

ROBIN'S HOOD

We are now at the point of the characterization journey where we should start making final decisions for the design. I finally feel confident that my Robin Hood stand outs, not just for the visuals, but for how his design resonates with the essence of the character. The combination of emotion, narrative, and aesthetics start to come together in a way that looks more like what I'm trying to achieve than my earlier sketches. I sketch Robin Hood wearing a hood and cloak, making sure the focus is still on the character. I now have some good groundwork laid for the final steps ahead.

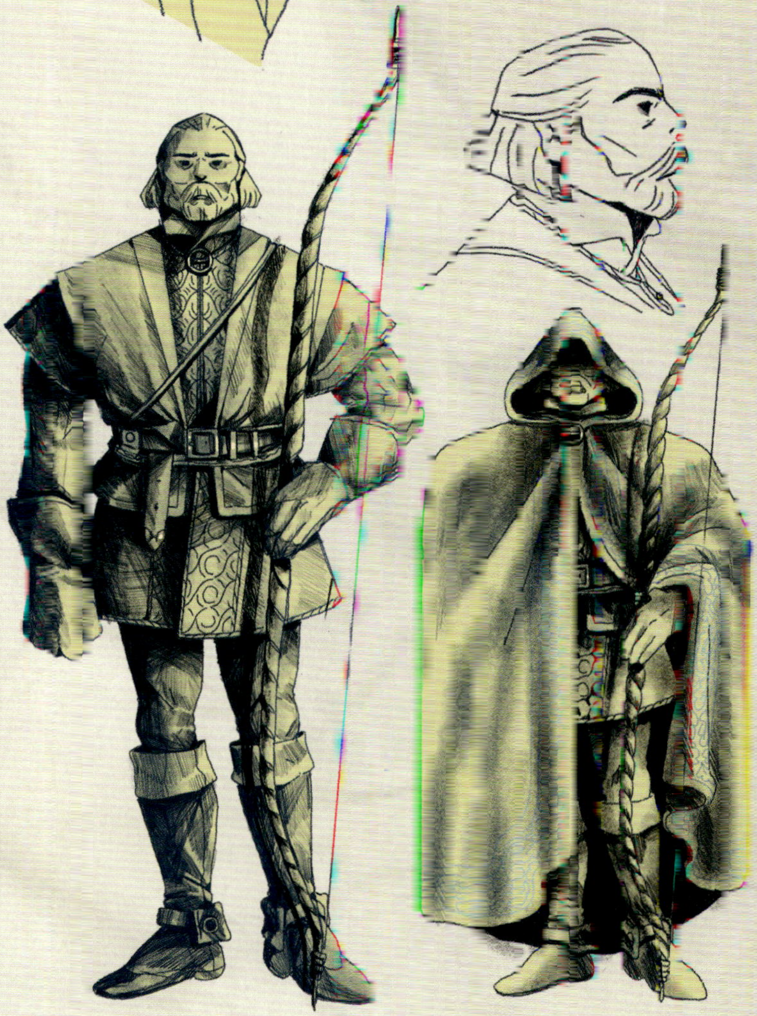

DETAIL AND DESIGN

After making all the big, tough decisions, it's time to dive into the detail of my design, specifically in Robin's clothing. Details are where story is told. They subtly convey status, past experiences, and social ties. Due to his heritage, it seems natural to include patterns and embroidery inspired by the celts. I also want the fabric to communicate his past as nobility and for it to hint at a heritage of forgotten oaths. In this step I hope to infuse each design with parts of Robin Hood's life story, making every element meaningful.

THE SWORD, THE BOLTS, AND THE BOW

I move onto props and accessories, focusing on Robin's weapons of choice. These aren't just the tools of his trade, they are another part of his character – just as the rest of his attire tells a story, so must his armoury. Again, I draw inspiration from Celtic patterns, each weapon showcasing designs that resonate with Robin's heritage and his ties to tradition. These designs not only hint to the historical context, but also connect Robin with his position as both a nobleman and an outlaw.

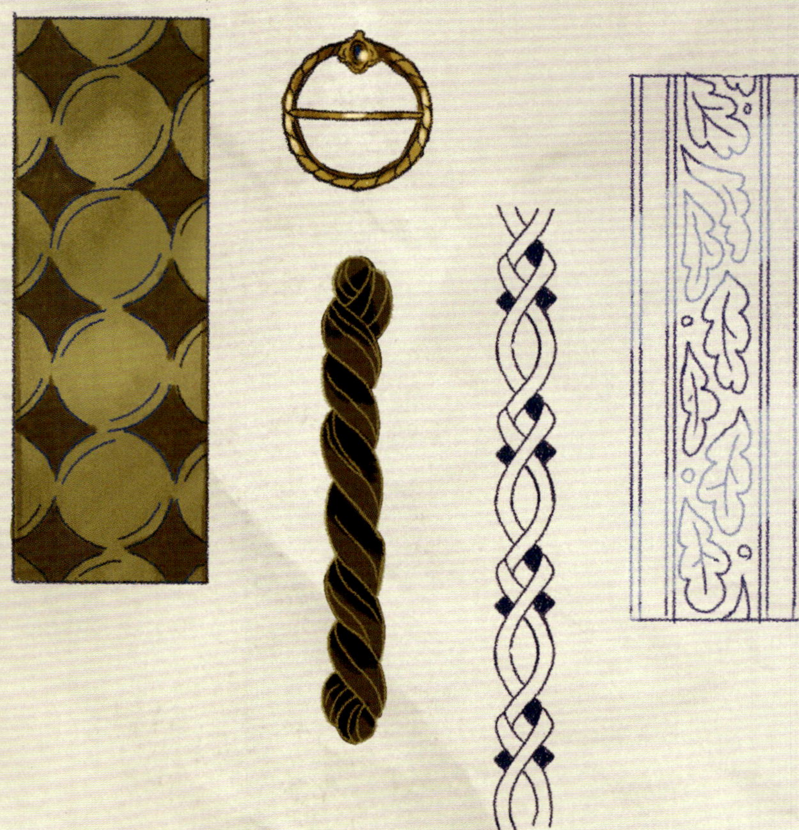

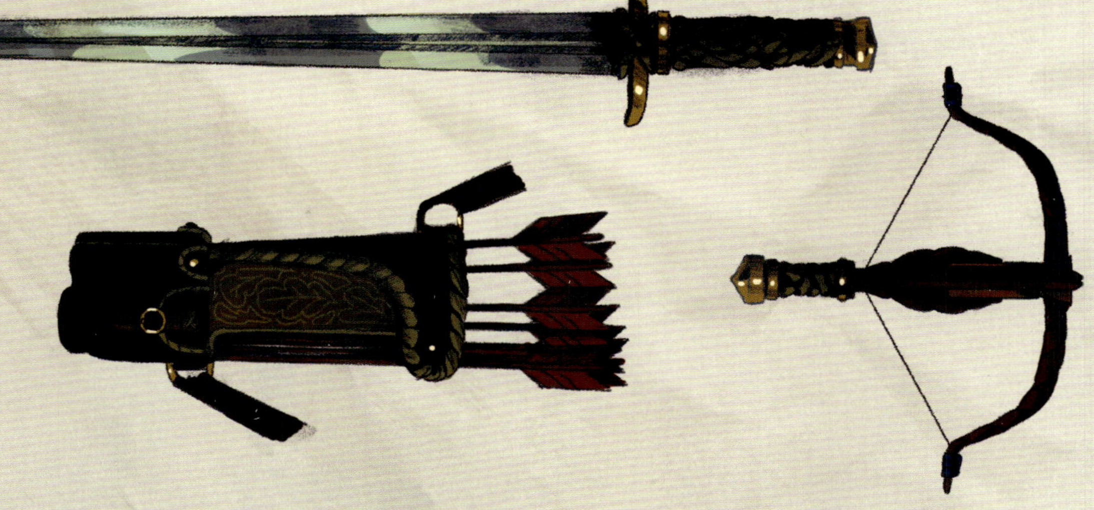

This page (top): A series of patterns and fabrics inspired by research done on the time period

This page (bottom): Robin needs a sword, bolts, and a crossbow

Opposite page: A series of cute colour suggestions for Robin Hood

MORE THAN JUST GREEN

Now it's time to add some colour. This is both one of my favourite parts of the process as well as one of the most daunting. Colours are everything. I wish to avoid the cliched all-green look that is expected of Robin Hood. Green is ironic and important to include, but it's just one part of the visual story I want to tell. Given Robin's noble history, I feel a pull towards using a royal red in his palette. I only want to use a little though, as a subtle nod to his past.

When I approach a character's colour scheme I like to make simplified sketches of the character. This allows me to more easily get a grasp of the mood and feel of each combination without having to colour the whole final illustration. I put together several colour schemes to test out which works best for my vision and find myself drawn towards the greens and yellows of my third design. These below will allow me to add a hint of blue in the lines and details as a beautiful contrast.

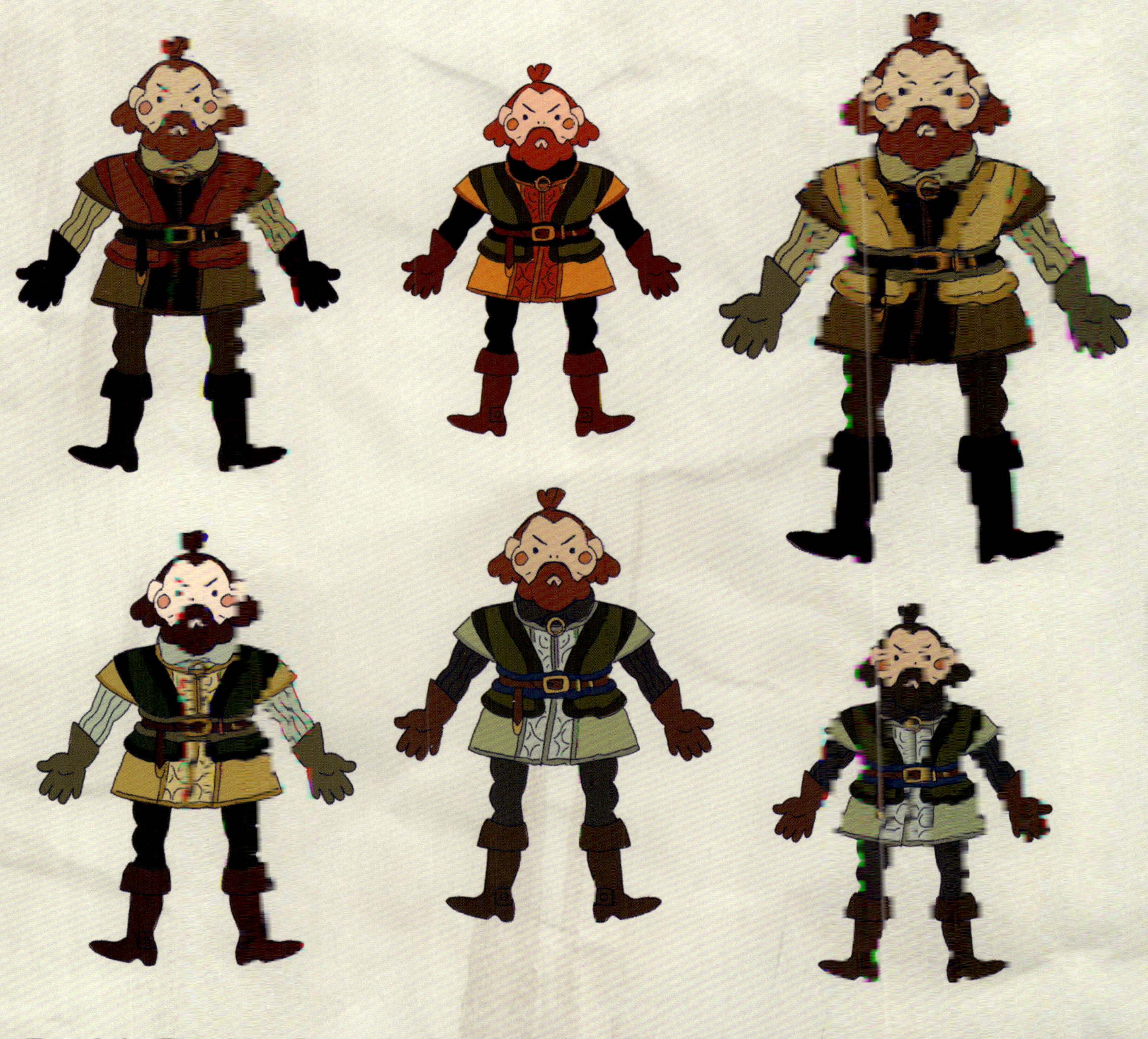

THE FINAL TEST

As I get closer to finishing up this characterization, it's time to pause and ask myself: does this portrayal truly embody Robin Hood's complete identity? The current version blends the iconic greens of history with the nobility of the blue, symbolizing his noble roots. The fabric choices, patterns, and design elements create a balance between his previous societal standing and his life in the forest as an outlaw. I'm happy that this mix of ideas embodies my original vision and captures the feel of my short-story prompt perfectly. If I didn't think this was the case, then I would have gone straight back to the drawing board. I always prioritize story and emotion in a design.

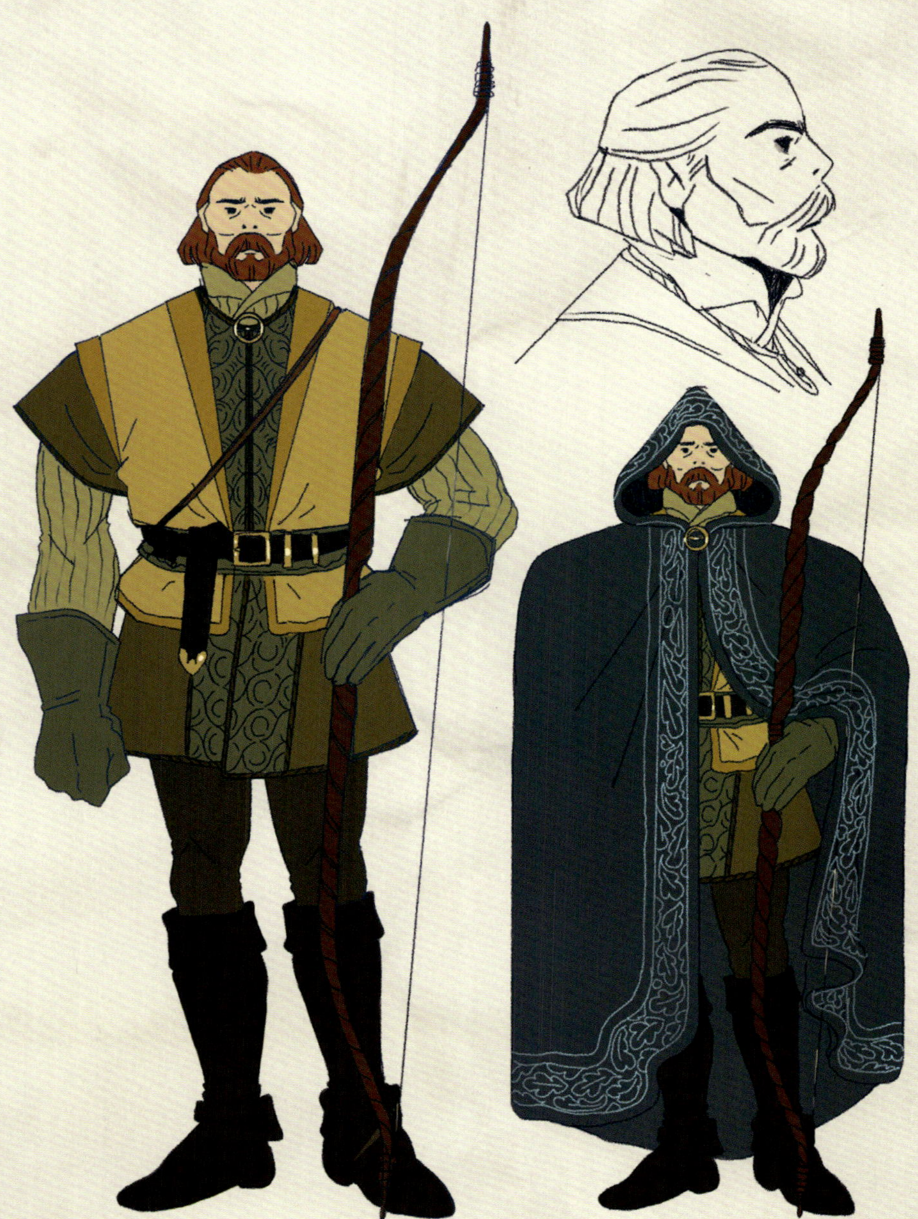

This page: Getting close to the finished look of Robin Hood

Opposite page: Adding shadows to the design brings out Robin Hood's true character

'IT'S NOT ONLY ABOUT FINISHING, BUT MAKING SURE EACH DETAIL AND EVERY STROKE COMPLEMENTS THE ESSENCE OF THE CHARACTER'

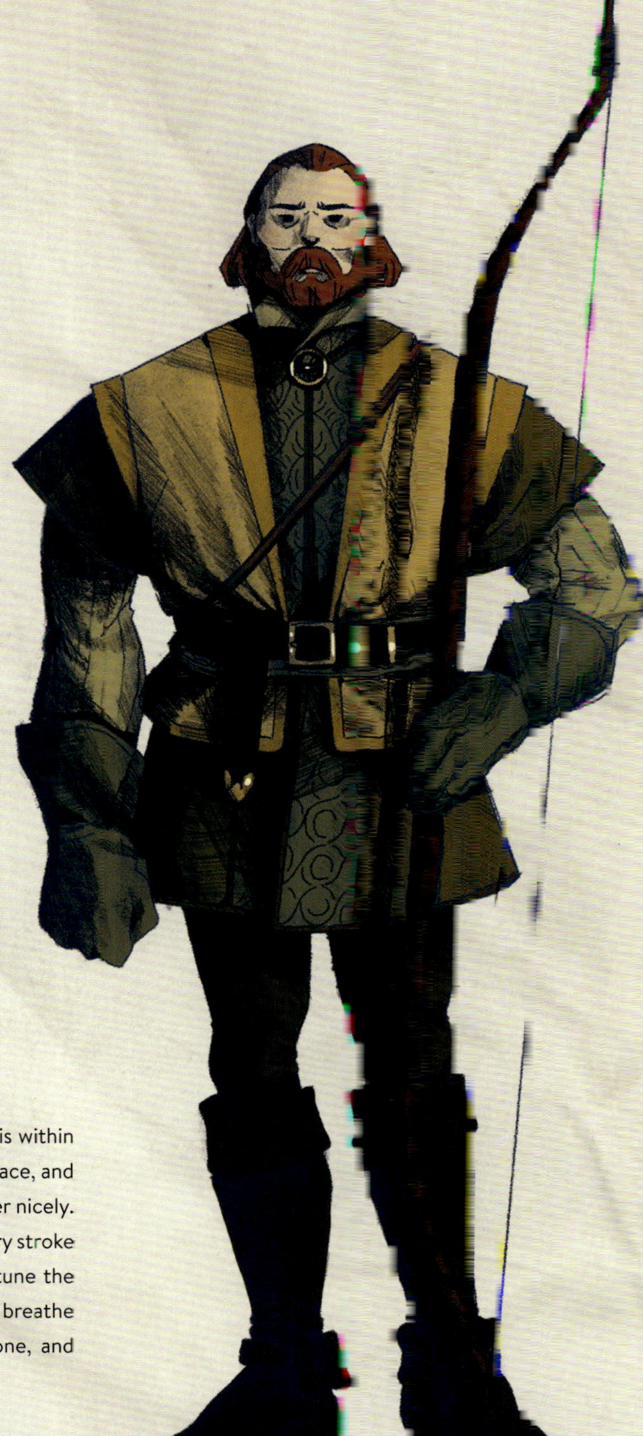

POLISHING UP

As we delve into this phase, the end of our journey with Robin is within reach. Every design choice has been made, every nuance is in place, and every colour decision is finalized – everything is coming together nicely. It's not only about finishing but making sure each detail and every stroke complements the essence of the character. Now I can I fine tune the design, identify contrasts, and add shadow. I believe shadows breathe life into any character, creating shapes where there were none, and knitting all the previous steps of the design together.

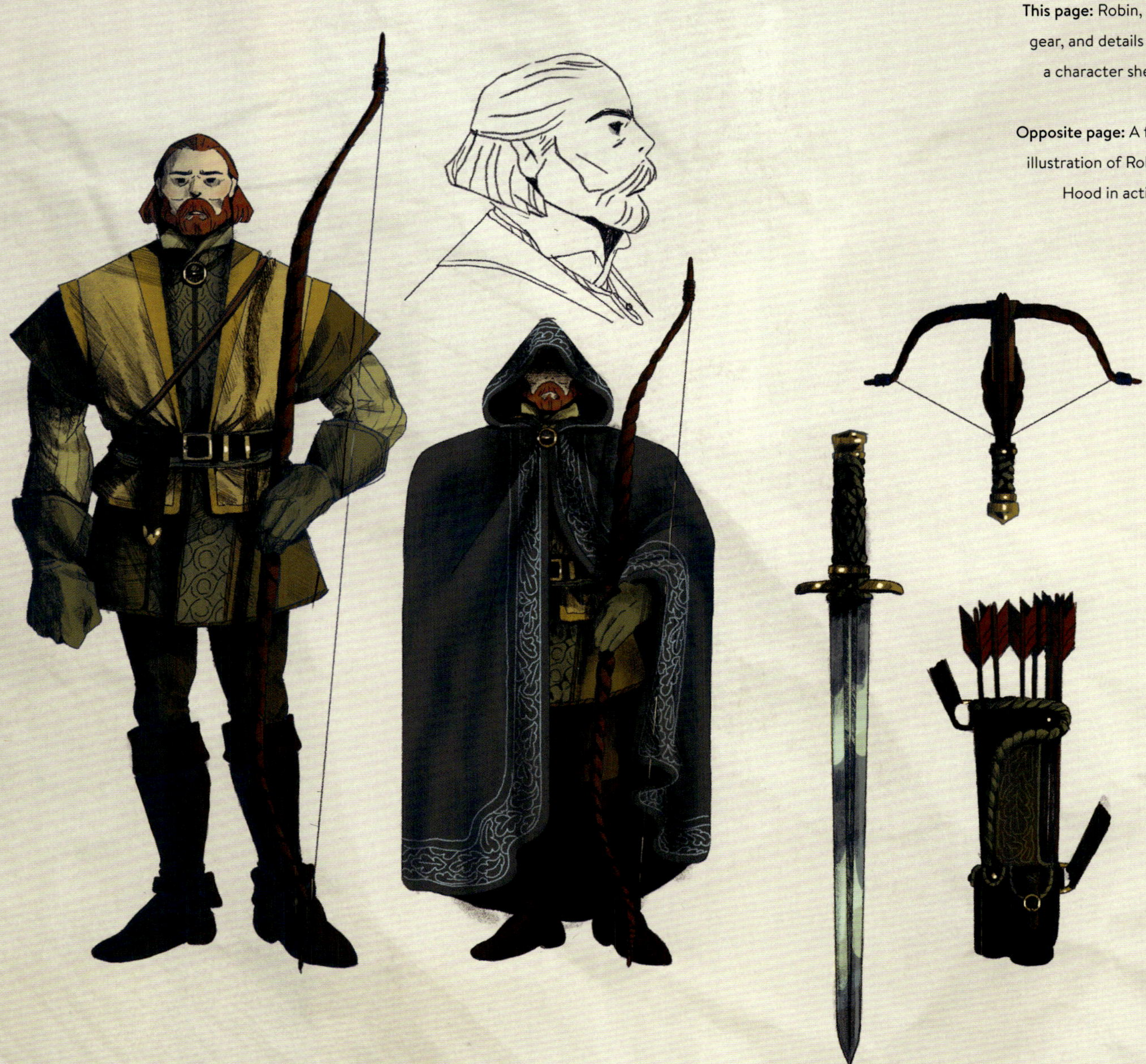

ROBIN RETURNS

At the end of visualizing the character of Robin Hood, it is clear to me that the journey is about more than just illustration – it's about immersing yourself in your character's world and telling their story. In every stage we've been through, from the initial concept to intricate details, we see the importance and purpose of each element of the design. Each nuance, colour, and posture add to the narrative. The payoff from considering how each detail contributes to the whole is evident as I put it all together in a final illustration and see that the character works. Robin Hood is alive, conveying the heart and soul I hoped he would.

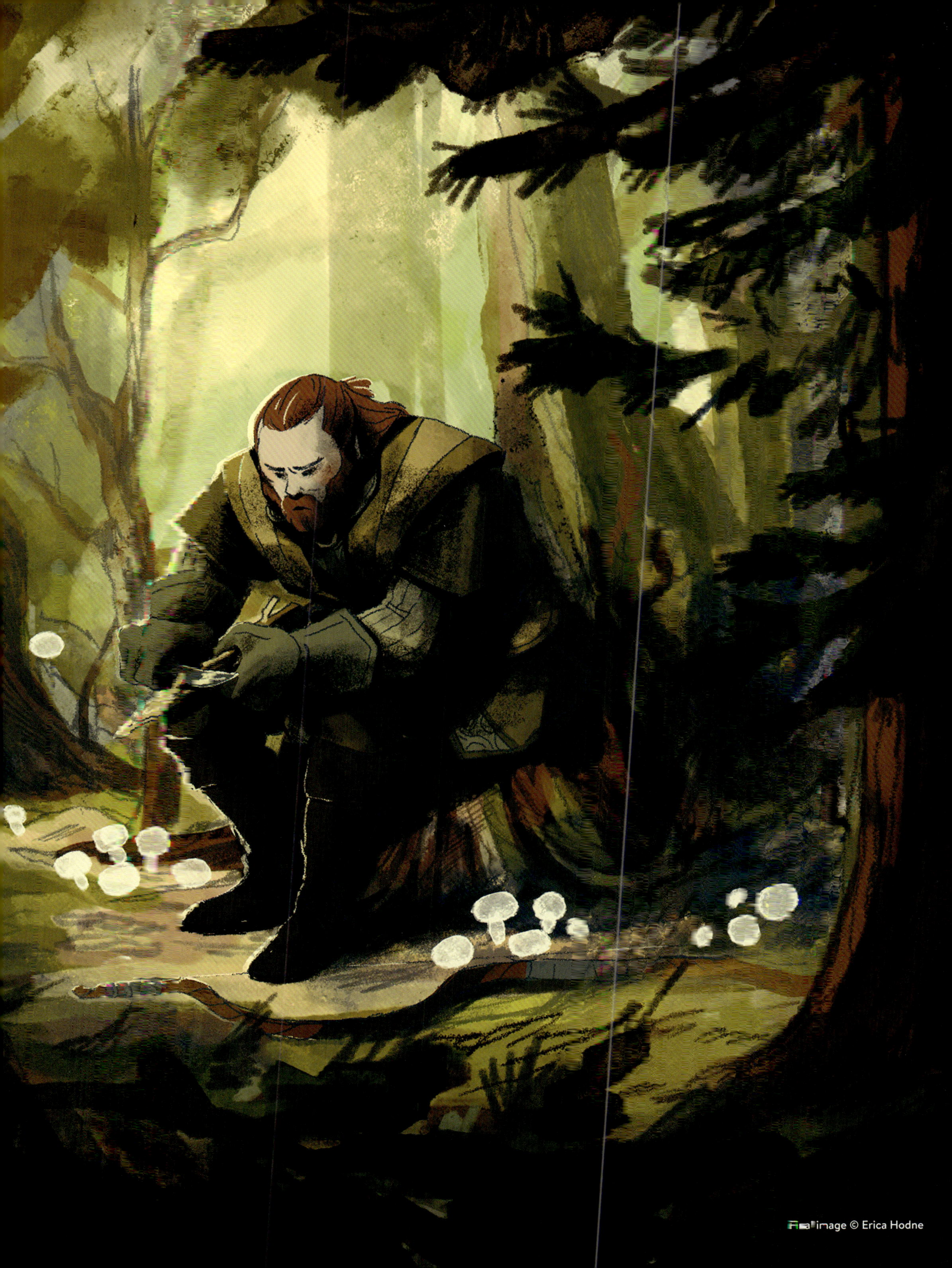
Final image © Erica Hodne

CONTRIBUTORS

LAURA DUMITRIU

Illustrator

laura-dumitriu.com

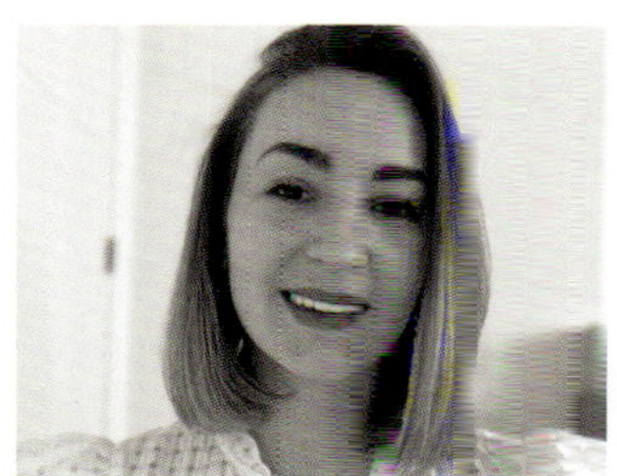

Laura is an illustrator currently based in Barcelona. She worked as a graphic designer until 2019 and now focuses solely on illustration.

BEN EBLEN

Illustrator & Character Designer

beneblen.com

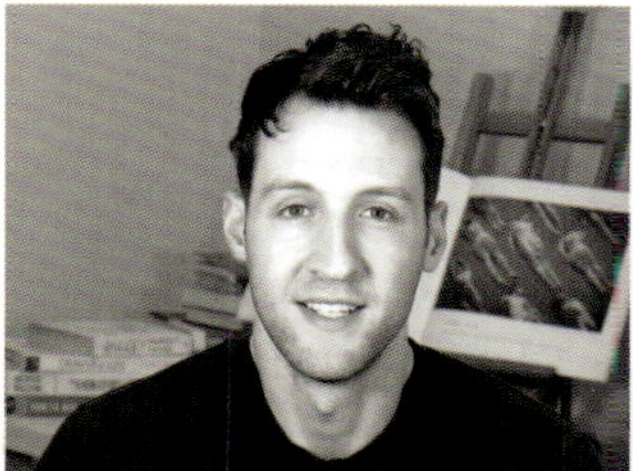

Ben is an Australian illustrator, developer, podcast host, chaser of 'aha' moments, and loves sharing his process and findings online.

SARAH-LISA HLEB

Freelance Illustrator

sarahlisahleb.com

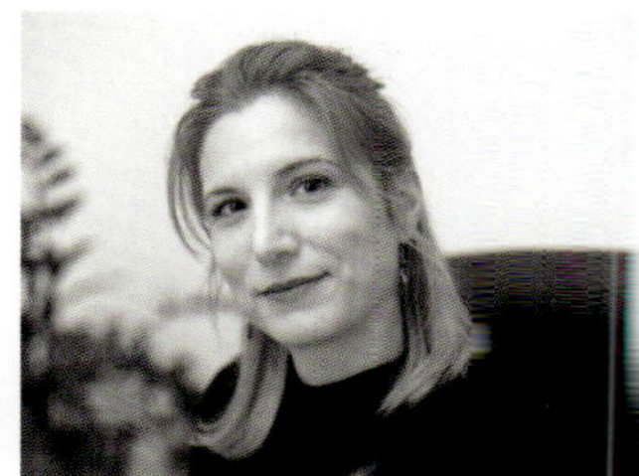

Sarah-Lisa is a freelance illustrator located in Austria. She specializes in character design and digital illustration for a variety of fields.

ERICA HOHE

Motion designer at Eltek

ericahohe.com

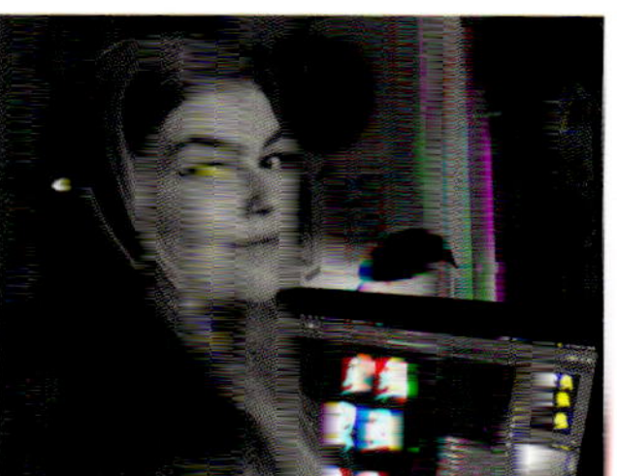

Erica is an animator and illustrator from Norway. She studied animation in London and loves the chance to explore emotions through her work.

KAJA KAJFEŽ (IZ PTICA)

Freelance illustrator

izptica.com

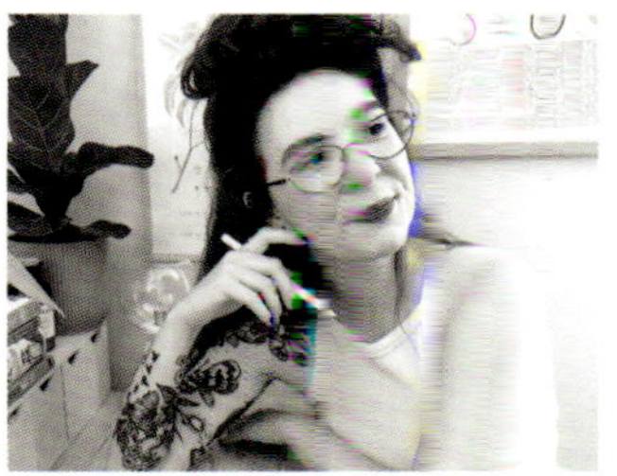

Kaja is the creator behind the name Iz Ptica, who loves to tell stories through her art. Her professional work focuses mainly on children's books.

JOHN LOREN

Freelance Artist

johnloren.com

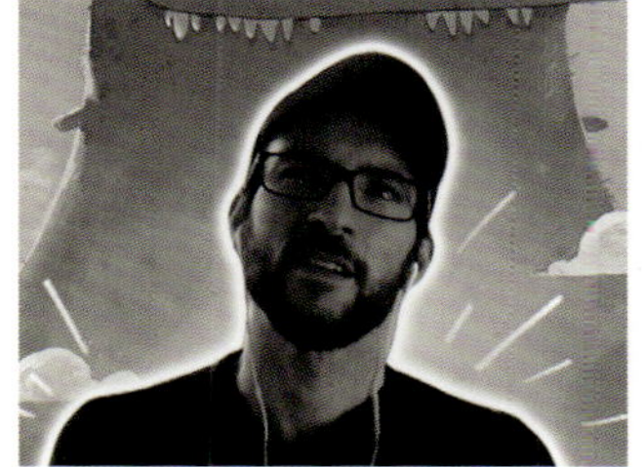

John is an artist from New England. Recent projects he has worked on include *Spyro Reignited*, *Crash Bandicoot 4*, *Hearthstone*, and *Lorcana*.

CORAH LOUISE

Illustrator and Character Designer

corahlouise.com

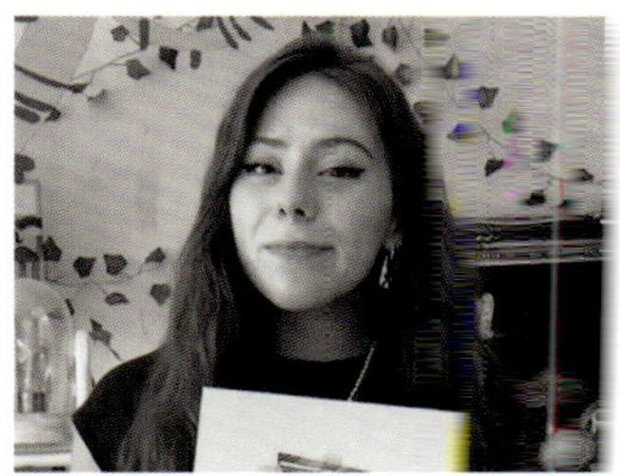

Corah Louise is a freelance illustrator and character designer from the UK, creating magically mundane illustrations of the everyday.

ANDY NA

Freelance Character Designer

instagram.com/andy_n_art

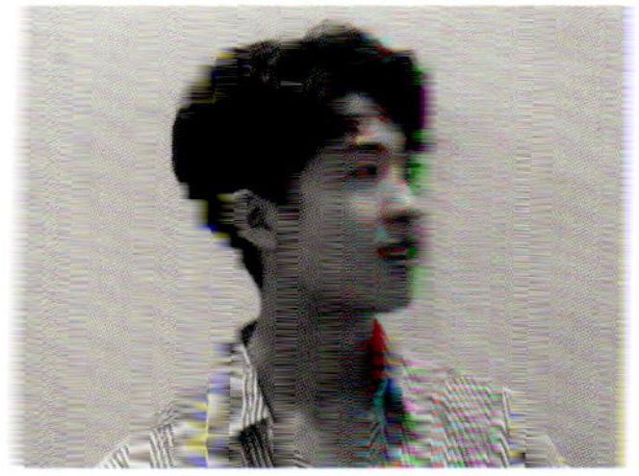

Andy is a visual development and character design artist for TV and feature animation, based in South Korea.

PAUL JOSEPH NICHOLSON

Freelance Character Designer

pauljaynicholson.com

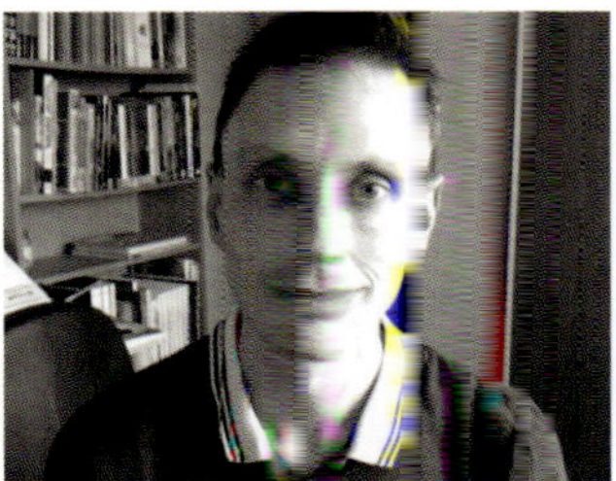

Paul is a UK-based freelance character designer who has worked in the animation industry for the past six years.

KATE PELLERIN (POOPIKAT)

Freelance Illustrator

poopikat.com

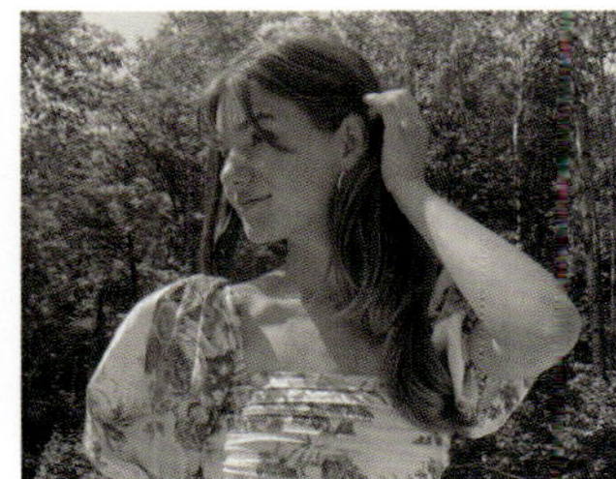

Kate is a Canadian illustrator who focuses on children's illustrations. She loves to create whimsical worlds, characters and creatures.

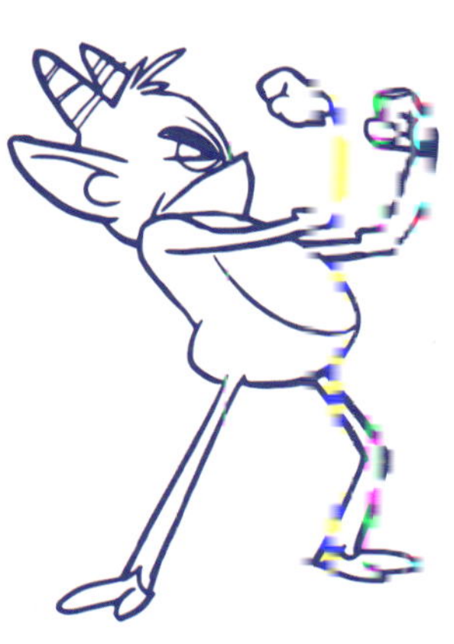

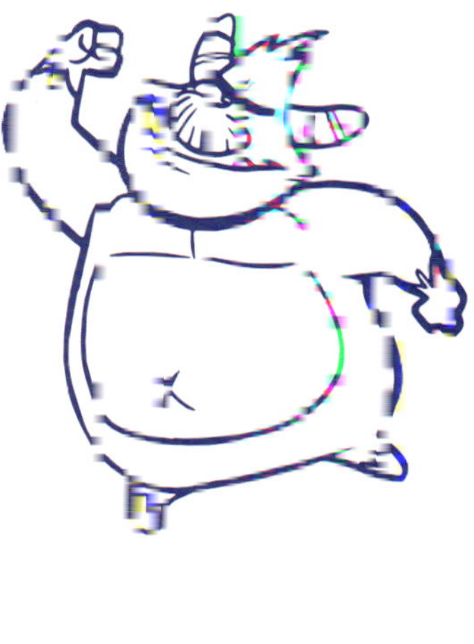

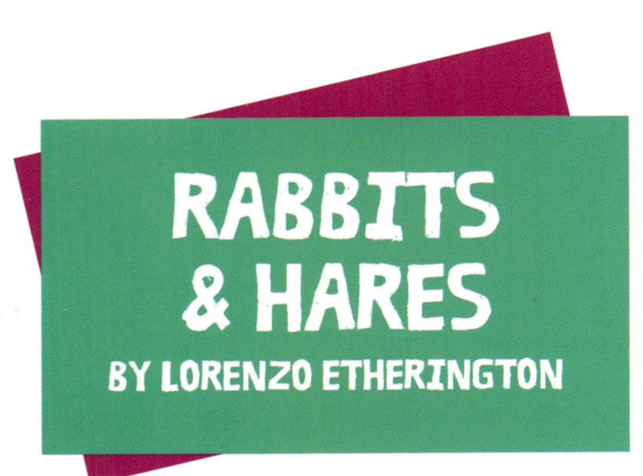

RABBITS & HARES
BY LORENZO ETHERINGTON

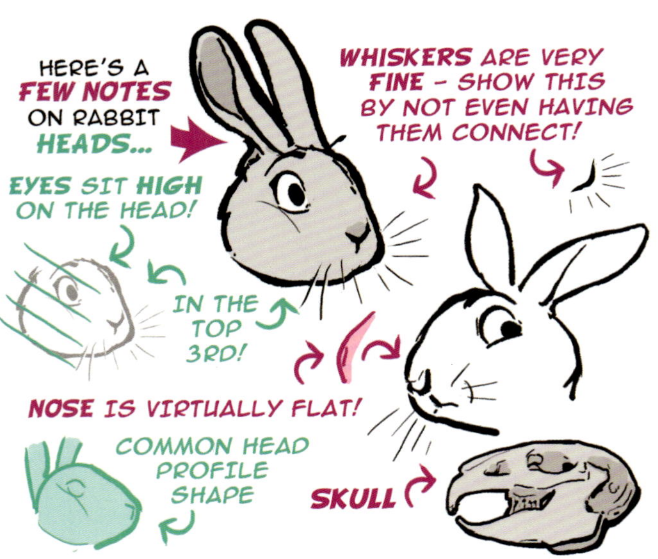

HERE'S A FEW NOTES ON RABBIT HEADS...
EYES SIT HIGH ON THE HEAD!
IN THE TOP 3RD!
NOSE IS VIRTUALLY FLAT!
COMMON HEAD PROFILE SHAPE
WHISKERS ARE VERY FINE - SHOW THIS BY NOT EVEN HAVING THEM CONNECT!
SKULL

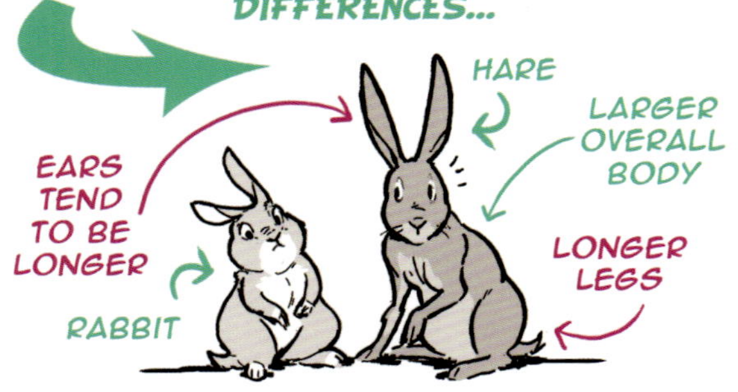

ALTHOUGH HARES ARE SIMILAR TO RABBITS IN MANY WAYS, THERE ARE SOME IMPORTANT DIFFERENCES...
EARS TEND TO BE LONGER
RABBIT
HARE
LARGER OVERALL BODY
LONGER LEGS

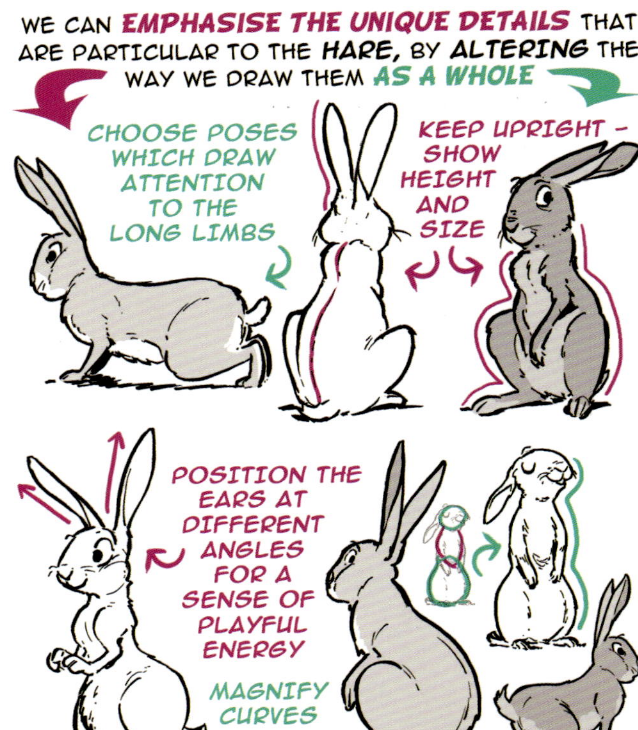

WE CAN EMPHASISE THE UNIQUE DETAILS THAT ARE PARTICULAR TO THE HARE, BY ALTERING THE WAY WE DRAW THEM AS A WHOLE
CHOOSE POSES WHICH DRAW ATTENTION TO THE LONG LIMBS
KEEP UPRIGHT - SHOW HEIGHT AND SIZE
POSITION THE EARS AT DIFFERENT ANGLES FOR A SENSE OF PLAYFUL ENERGY
MAGNIFY CURVES

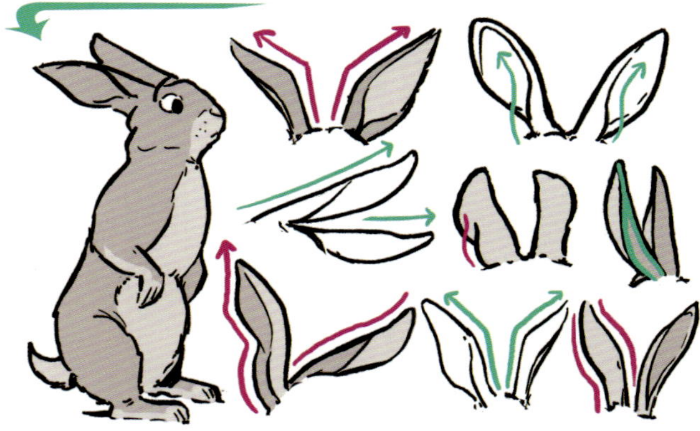

NOT ALL EARS ARE THE SAME! HERE'S SOME SHAPE AND ANGLE VARIATIONS FOR REFERENCE.